THE
Boylan Years

One Man
One Team
Twenty Years

Edited by Liam Hayes

Interviews by
Philip Lanigan,
Paul Keane
and Gordon Manning

Published in Ireland by
Carr and Hayes
An imprint of Sports Business and Entertainment Ltd
Lucan
Co. Dublin

© Carr and Hayes 2002

Cover photograph: Sportsfile
Inside photographs: Sportsfile

Printed By Colorprint Ltd, Dublin
Book Design: Paul McElheron

For Sean Boylan and his boys,

who made 20 years fly by, and the Meath football fans

who never, ever lost the faith

Contents

The Glory

The Misery

The Genius

Acknowledgements

A special thanks to all the Meath footballers who were happy to reflect on The Glory and The Misery of the last 20 years, and remember The Genius of Sean Boylan. And sincere apologies to all the Meath footballers whose memories are not included on these pages.

Foreword

Who can say they know Sean Boylan, except perhaps family and a few close friends. I have opposed him both as a player and a manager for fourteen of the last 20 years, longer than any other individual I am told and, therefore, I now attempt to speak on behalf of the opposition!

At the outset, I must say that I like Sean Boylan as a person, and admire him as a manager, not just for what he has done in football, but for who he is and what he represents. However, I have not always been his biggest fan. When I started playing football for Dublin in 1985, I had a very narrow perspective of the football world and thought that all other counties, especially those 'besieging' our borders, spent 24 hours a day designing cunning plans to dethrone the Dubs as Leinster kingpins. Meath's ascendancy in 1986 heralded three dark years for Dublin football, in which we lost three consecutive Leinster titles.

During that period of time, I can recall meeting Sean Boylan at various sporting functions, and noticed how he made a particular effort to be 'friendly' to Dublin football players – being nice to them, working that old cliché of 'keeping your friends close, and your enemies closer'. It annoyed me, as I believed that many Dublin players' attitudes towards Meath, their greatest rivals, were softened as a result – not me though! I kept things very formal. I would not be taken in by that 'sound fella' stuff.

After each of these Leinster finals, he would come to the Dublin changing room and placate us with the good old GAA rabble rousing chorus of, 'You are a great team and you will be back next year', and I thought, 'Isn't it easy for him to be gracious. They've just beaten us again.'

But he kept coming into the Dublin dressing room over the next ten years or so – win, lose or draw. In 1991, following the four game saga, I started to think that maybe this guy was genuine – it was probably one of his most difficult visits to a Dublin changing room scene. He appeared to have difficulty finding the appropriate words to match the moment, and seemed anxious to leave as quickly as possible. This to me revealed the depth and honesty of his feelings on that occasion, as a man who had been on the side which ended a great adventure between two old pals. Having been victorious, he was still capable of entering into our hell, and empathising and understanding for those few minutes.

Through all those years, Sean Boylan treated victory and defeat with honour, pride and integrity. In 1995, Dublin beat Meath by 11 points in a Leinster final. Now, surely, the time had come for him to go! It had never been that bad for a Meath team against Dublin. They hadn't won a Leinster title since 1991. Let's be honest. There was doubt, even among the 'loyal royals'.

While the football world was speculating his future, Sean Boylan never uttered a word, and the following year produced a new team which won the All-Ireland, and away he went again.

I have been asked by various people was it an intimidating experience to be sharing the sideline with a manager of Sean Boylan's legendary status, as happened in the 1999 and 2001 Leinster finals. As any manager will tell you, Naomi Campbell herself could strut along the same sideline, and it would make no difference whatever – and it shouldn't, as no manager can afford to be distracted by what's going on around him.

In 1999, Meath beat us comprehensively, and I made some mistakes on the sideline. At the time, Des Cahill's 'Sportscall' programme was aired on Monday evenings on RTE radio. Some of the callers were very critical and personally derogatory in the views they expressed and, while hurtful, it goes with the territory! Of course, everybody has kind words in victory, but it's the people who make contact in defeat who you remember, and one of those calls came from Sean Boylan, who had listened to the comments with disgust, sympathised with my situation, and encouraged me to ignore this and continue to do what I loved and believed in. He did the same during my very public 'sacking' last year as Dublin football manager.

I have long since learned that you get to trust people, not by what they say but by their actions. And now I know that Sean Boylan's actions over the last 20 years have been honest and genuine. Of course, he is also cute and smart and ruthless where football is concerned, and he would have to be all these things to have achieved what he has; but there are other very powerful forces at play.

I have just finished reading a book on Muhammad Ali, which is a collection of interviews of people who knew him throughout his career, and the characteristics which shine through are his ability to make a connection with everybody, and his genuine feeling for mankind. He sees good in everybody, and holds no grudges, even against those who have done him wrong. But when he stepped into the ring, he was cuter and more ruthless than most of his opponents. Sean Boylan is not too dissimilar. He picks teams with character. I have seen him sit down, with ten minutes to go in games, with a look of resignation. But he is not resigned to defeat – he is resigned to the fact that he has the work done and he can do no more, except hope that his judgement of character has been correct. More often than not, this is so. The defining characteristic of his Meath teams has been their refusal to accept defeat right up to the final whistle.

Because of his involvement, Meath is now known as a proud and successful football county and, as a result, he has enriched the lives of the people of Meath and provided them with a powerful sense of identity.

Is he the best manager of his time? I am not surprised at the length of time he has been involved in the top flight of football, but what is remarkable is his continuing hunger for the game and for success, and his ability to keep producing different successful teams from the same county. Now, that is something the great Kevin Heffernan and Mick O'Dwyer also did – for a time. But neither great man stayed on the same sideline for 20 years!

Tom Carr
Former Dublin captain and manager
September 2002

THE

Boylan Years

The Glory

Chapter One:

1982

There was no Sean Boylan. He was close to 40 years of age and outside his own village, outside the family business in Dunboyne, he had the face of a stranger.

The same man was definitely a hurler, and he was into some funny sort of home-concocted business helping people who had health problems, and selling them bottles of God-only-knows-what! What he was actually doing was continuing into a fifth generation the expertise of prescribing, and manufacturing, medicine from plants. Still, his life was a secret which a great many people had to search out. Sean was a good son, kind, full of life, full of energy. There was a great, big, giant battery installed between his shoulder blades. An only boy in a kitchen full of sisters. As a younger man he had nursed his aged father until he died, and now he might spend most nights at the foot of his mother's bed. She too was elderly and poor in health. Now and again he would close his eyes for a few minutes but, at this time in his life sleep had become a meek and quite timid adversary.

One man versus the need for sleep – it was no longer much of a fight and, with that clinging, overpowering opponent so easily polished off, there was nothing much left for Sean Boylan to fear in his smallish life. However, his neighbours didn't know that; nor did anybody else living in County Meath.

JIMMY FAY: *I remember playing against Dublin in Parnell Park in the early 1980s. It was before Sean became manager. Anyway, there was a hole beside one of the posts and I stepped into it and twisted my ankle. I fell to the ground and was in a lot of pain, and all I could hear were the Dublin fans shouting and roaring abuse out at me from behind the goal. Next thing I know, Sean is beside me rubbing sponges on my ankle and* *the boys behind the goal are still hurling abuse at me. Suddenly, Sean stands up and roars back at them, 'Hey lads, this man is not joking. When a player hurts himself he hurts himself.' I didn't even know this man who had come out onto the field to help me, and yet he stood up and gave out to the crowd behind the goal on my behalf. I mean, he is not a big man and there he was roaring at a big crowd of Dubs. For a minute I thought there was going to be murder.*

He was handy to have around the place – no doubt about that. He was helpful, and he was always a happy chap. He'd be smiling away as if he was entered in a competition to see who is the 'best man to smile all day'. He always appeared especially happy to be hanging around any hurling team – or a football team. It's got to be said, however, that there were not very many people in County Meath entered in the same happy, smily contests as Sean Boylan. Twenty years ago, Meath was not the happiest place on the planet.

Footballers could no longer figure out what the game was all about, or why they should make any sort of additional effort. To actually show up for training resulted in praise. Jimmy Fay was now, on and off, playing in goal for the team. Fay had won a Leinster title with Meath as a dashing forward in 1970, but 12 years later he had ended up a couple of stone overweight and he also ended up between the sticks. Padraig Finnerty, known as 'Fionn' from the age of 10 because of his courage and incredible athleticism, had been unanimously greeted as the greatest young footballer in the county four or five years earlier. Liam Hayes was 18 months a Meath senior player, but had already been dropped from the team on three or four occasions by the autumn of 1982.

PADRAIG FINNERTY: *I'll never forget that night in 1982 when Sean came onto the scene and spoke to us underneath the stand in Navan. I recall him giving a speech and then, as we talked later, a lot of the lads said that some of the County Board men didn't want him to take on the job and tried to persuade him not to do it. But Sean took on the challenge. And at the time, that challenge was huge. Nobody really wanted the job – nobody except Sean.*

I recall times going back to the late 1970s, and even 1980 or so, when hardly anybody would turn up for training. I remember going to Navan for training and some nights there might be only six or seven present. It was a waste of time. But when Sean came in he got the players to put in the commitment. His man management skills were top notch and he revolutionised football in the county.

I mean, I remember going to see Meath play in the League final in 1975. I went up with a fella and he put me in between two lads and I was sitting on top of the handbrake going up to the game. I didn't care, I just wanted to see Meath play. But what it shows is that even back then the talent was there, the fans were there, but the final ingredient was missing. That came in 1982 with the emergence of Sean Boylan.

GERRY McENTEE: *My first game with Meath was in 1975. Mick O'Brien was the coach at the time and he was a good coach, but the structures in place then were poor because the rivalry of club football in the county at the time was too intense. The two principal clubs at the time were Summerhill and Walterstown, and they actually held back the county team. It wouldn't have been difficult for Sean to improve the structures when he took the job in 1982, because they were pathetic. The approach to training, the way the players were looked after, and the whole preparation of the team was pathetic. Certainly the week before* club championships in Meath, the two principal clubs in particular would take their players away and that was roughly six or seven from each side. So out of a panel of 23 or 24 you were already losing 12 or 13 players. Sean got the job by default at the time, I think really. Nobody else wanted it because the summer before we were beaten by Longford in Tullamore. I don't remember his first speech to the players that clearly, but I do recall saying that this man has a genuine love for the game and a genuine love for Meath football, and he has pride and passion. I thought he was a nice fella, but that's all we really knew at the time. I didn't notice anything about him on the first night that made me believe he would be successful, but I felt within the first 12 months that he would be. The one thing about him was that he treated players with the utmost respect.

LIAM HAYES: *There were nights when we would go to training, but we wouldn't train. We'd end up talking about how to get more lads to turn up. One night I remember sitting there listening to Bertie Cunningham, a selector, who was a great footballer from the 60s, arguing it out with Phil Smith. Bertie had been centre-back on All-Ireland teams and he was still as strong as a steel door. Phil Smith was also a tough, really tough, defender and he was still a great player even though his Meath teams had been beaten in two Leinster finals by Dublin in 1976 and '77. Both men were made of the same stuff, but they were in this ridiculous argument! Phil was saying that if players were given little presents, like socks or togs, they might turn up, but Bertie was doing his nut at this suggestion.*
And I was sitting there, saying absolutely nothing. I'd just come off a Meath minor team which had been beaten by Kerry in the All-Ireland semi-final. We'd have 30, 40 players training every night, and we'd have

lads killing one another to get on the subs bench! Mattie Kerrigan was our coach, and if Mattie said run ten miles, every night, at midnight, for a month, we'd just do it. I remember walking four miles from a summer job I had one afternoon, and then finally thumbing my way to a training session because my parents were away that day.

PADRAIG LYONS: *I remember my first reaction when I heard the news down home. 'Who got the coaching job in Meath?' I says. 'Sean Boylan,' says Mick. 'Who?' 'Do you remember the little lad who was in rubbing your legs the last few matches, doing masseur. He's the coach now.' I remember saying, 'Well, that's enough!' I didn't know what level he played football at, for he was known as a hurler.*
There would have been no immediate impact that I remember. I'd say it took a couple of years and it only started to take shape when he got rid of the seven selectors and got it down to just two. Now whether that was his own idea or the bigger boys on the team encouraged him to do this, I don't know. I remember a match in '83, and they wanted to make a change and they couldn't, because such and such was on the far side of the field, and one of the other selectors was down behind the goal, and they couldn't even get them all together to make the change! When two selectors and Sean were introduced, that was the start of the thing getting more professional. Before that, you'd go into training and get sandwiches under the stand, and the ends of them would turn up and look at you! We went from that to getting a four course meal out in Bellinter. That was all Sean's doing. When you got hurt, you started getting looked after. It was the small things that changed. All of a sudden you felt important and subconsciously it had an effect then on the way you played. Sean started looking out for the player, which was never the way it was done before that. He started getting player-

orientated.

He obviously had a great way about him, and he'd have a way about him of getting people on his side without people even knowing it. He worked his magic that way. But what he used to do that time, around '84 and '85, he used to listen to the older players a lot. He definitely used to seek opinions from, say, half a dozen of the team – O'Rourke, McEntee, Michael, Joe Cassells – now without making a point of going to see them, but he'd be chatting, saying, 'Should we be doing this or that?' After a few years that all stopped. After a couple of years of listening intently to what they thought, he stopped listening. No disrespect to Sean, but I think he should have stayed listening. It does no harm to listen. The group of lads I mentioned there, you'd hear them saying, 'There's no point talking to him because he won't listen!'

MICKEY DOWNES: *When I came in, Mick O'Brien was in charge of the team. He had managed Meath to win the League in 1975 and had managed Meath teams that were narrowly beaten by Dublin in '76 and '77 in the Leinster finals. He had stepped down, but had then come back in again.*

I had been playing for Clare, my native county, for a few years but football at home was in shock after the 'Miltown Malbay massacre' by Kerry in '79. We lost 9-21 to 1-9! The amazing thing about it is that, even though we were hammered, my main memory of it is having a decent game on Paidi O Se. I scored three points off him. What's incredible as well is that Clare actually recovered from that in the League campaign that followed. We actually beat Meath in Navan, beat Laois, and had some very good results. I was playing my club football for Navan O'Mahonys by then as well.

Meath's stock was low at the time. They were beaten by Wexford and

Longford in successive Leinster Championship matches. In the lead-up to the Longford match, training was poor, and it was seldom that there would have been 15 players present. There was a total lack of interest. All that you associate with Meath football now just wasn't there. Part of the problem was that there were too many chiefs and not enough Indians. There were at least seven people on the selection team – I know the County Board chairman and secretary were part of that – but the set-up was in disarray.

I remember Longford in '82, in particular. It was played in Tullamore and they deservedly won it. After that, Mick O'Brien resigned. Nobody was willing to take on the mantle of the Meath management. As far as I can recall, Gerry McEntee was nominated as manager, but his medical career was just taking off at that stage and he was too busy. That defeat sent shock waves through Meath football. Things were at a very low ebb. Meath people take their football extremely seriously. For something like that to happen was an awful kick in the pants, particularly with the county's tradition. It was embarrassing for everybody involved. But you forget about these things. You get back quickly into club football. I guess what everyone was wondering was, what was going to happen next?

I knew Sean Boylan as a hurler. I had seen him playing for Dunboyne against Navan O'Mahonys in an Intermediate County final around '79 and I thought he was excellent, a beautiful stylist. He must have been in his late 30s at that stage yet he was playing midfield. He was well able to look after himself too. I remember talking about him in the aftermath of the game, asking, 'Who is he?' That was as much as I knew about him.

When Sean came in, Colm O'Rourke said that if he stayed around long enough the Meath players would make a coach out of him. He definitely made an impression from the start. He was articulate, he was forthright. There was no bullshit with him. He spelled it out exactly as it was. It was impressive stuff. I remember him introducing one of his selectors, Mattie Gilsenan. Mattie was a legend in Meath football. I remember him being able to spell out Mattie Gilsenan's record, over 50 years, in its entirety. He certainly made an instant impression on me, but if I was blunt about it, I didn't know where he would take us. I don't know if he could see it himself either. I'm not convinced. He inherited a team that had underachieved, a team that had a number of players that just weren't good enough, just weren't putting in the required effort. But things changed rapidly. The days of barely 15 turning up for training vanished.

It is not entirely accurate to portray Meath as one unhappy county in 1982. There were some people who were ecstatic about the way things were going for them. They lived in the parish of Walterstown. And Walterstown, even though they dressed in black from head to toe on the football field, were the 'Kerry' of Meath football in the late 70's and early 80's. Walterstown had a large armful of county titles, and Walterstown also had the 'Mick O'Dwyer' of Meath football.

His name was Mick O'Brien, and he was a genius, and there were no dissenters in homes and public houses in Meath. O'Brien was the supreme motivator and the supreme tactician, and his team played a style of football which, every Sunday, left opponents and spectators mesmerised. Walterstown were playing in All-Ireland finals too! They were not winning them, but they were cutting a dash in black in Croke Park. Walterstown were magical, and half of the Walterstown team took off the black and tried on the green and gold on a regular basis. Six of them had played on the Meath team which had been beaten, 2-9 to 1-11, by Wexford in the first round of the Leinster Championship in 1980. Trouble was, Walterstown were not making Meath a better team. And, as it turned out, Walterstown players were among the first to be examined and effectively retired as Meath players by Sean Boylan. When Boylan and Meath reached their first Leinster final together in 1984, and lost to Dublin but won a worthwhile slice of glory, there was not one Walterstown player left on the field.

What happened to Walterstown's 'Mikey Sheehy'? And what became of their 'Pat Spillane'? In truth, Walterstown really only had one forward who always stood out, and who always seemed to score six, seven, eight points or more, and who filled the combined roles of Sheey, Spillane and Johnny Egan! In 1982, if Meath sent a football team out onto the field without Eamonn Barry, then there was seldom any escape from a long and demoralising afternoon.

But Eamonn Barry retired from the Meath team entirely of his own accord, in a hurry, in his mid-20s, a week or two before the 1984 Leinster final. He never returned.

EAMONN BARRY: *Sean's greatest asset is his fantastic personality and the way he would always get on with the players. He got the utmost respect from them and I'm sure if ever he felt he wasn't getting that he would be off. He's the type of manager that you'd bust a gut to do well for. He gave you the feeling that you were doing it not just for the team, but for him too. His manner was certainly different and it proved successful in the end. He used to say to us – and by all accounts it's the same 20 years later – just before we'd leave the dressing-room, he'd say, 'Right lads, it's time to shit or get off the pot.'*

He took a couple of years to find his feet in the job but, like everything else, management takes time too. Gradually he started to bring lads in and he eventually found the right balance in the team. There were six to eight players who fell by the wayside, me included, as Sean brought lads in and tried different players out. In all, I suppose it took five years to come to fruition but when Meath won the All-Ireland in 1987 it was worth waiting for. I'm not bitter that I wasn't kept on. There were better footballers there than me at the time and that's the way it was. It's a huge regret that I never won a Leinster or All-Ireland medal. The lads who were involved in the team after me won those honours, but you just get on with it. Looking back, those of us who missed out were replaced by better players and they proved that by going on to win everything they did.

I made my debut against Clare in the NFL in Navan in the late 1970s. We won the Centenary Cup under Sean in 1984 and that was a great achievement. Meath had won nothing for years. In those days GAA people were fascinated by the competition because it was run off as an open draw – the first time that had been done in Ireland. I injured ankle ligaments in the semi-final, and missed the final. I was named as captain in the programme, but I didn't play. That was a cruel injury but that's what happens in the game, like it or not. I remember the celebrations well though. The presentation of the trophy and the medals was out in the RDS in Dublin. It was a great night. I was the captain but back in those days there was a policy of letting the county champions choose the captain. It was only because my club, Walterstown, were Meath champions that I got to be captain. I was fortunate.

All club players go out there and each week they hope they've done enough to get the county manager's attention. I don't believe that any manager closes the book on any one player. I always believed the chance *was there for me to get back into the team after I left. I didn't, but I never gave up hope.*

Eamonn Barry, while not part of Boylan's plans for the rest of his career, remained within shouting distance of the team and all his old team-mates for the remainder of the decade. A garda siochana working in Dublin's city centre, he regularly ended up on duty within Croke Park. As the first half of Sean Boylan's managerial career came to a close in 1991 – with Meath's amazing ten-game march to the All-Ireland final – Barry was still there inside the wire in Croker! Always watching.

EAMONN BARRY: *I have fantastic memories of the Dublin versus Meath games in 1991. I was working as a garda in Store Street at the time and one of the perks of the job was that I was on crowd control duty on the Canal End for all the games. It was one of those great occasions in the old days. The ground was so full you could hardly turn around. All you could do was watch the games and they were brilliant. The only time the tension broke in any of the games, was at half-time. Everyone in Croke Park was glued to the action. It was bad luck for the small people in the ground because they couldn't see the game. Everyone was on their feet, screaming. They were games that every GAA fan will remember all their life.*
It was brilliant football, hard but fair. There were so many twists and turns. Meath never gave up, and even though they were always coming from behind, you fancied they were always in it at the same time. They'd keep coming and coming. In the end Dublin didn't collapse. It was just that Meath did not want to lose. If Dublin had gotten another minute or two in the final game after David Beggy's winning point then

I'm sure they would have scored themselves. It was all about mental strength and timing. Luckily for Meath they got the timing just right.

In September 1982, Sean Boylan brought his footballers to Edgeworthstown in County Longford in his second week as team boss, and there managed a Meath team for the first time. Meath won. It lashed out of the heavens all afternoon. When the team sat down for a snack in the Park House Hotel afterwards there was no acknowledgement that at least one of the maddening defeats of the last couple of years – losing to Longford in the first round of the Leinster Championship five months earlier – had been exorcised. Such a dramatic claim definitely would have been pushing it! In February 1983, in a challenge game in Kells, Meath gave Longford a sound beating by 5-17 to 1-4, and the following May, Mickey Downes was the first of Sean Boylan's many captains to get his hands on a trophy. Meath beat Longford, again, in the O'Byrne Cup final in Longford's Pearse Park, by two points, and were mightily relieved to see Eamonn McCormack's fisted effort in the last minute strike the crossbar. There was a little bit more luck now headed on a frequent basis in the team's direction but, more importantly, eight months into his reign Boylan still had the players listening to him and believing more than one or two things he was saying. And eight months of earnest training and serious talking had been a brilliant, though short enough lifetime for every last footballer in Sean Boylan's company.

Chapter Two:

1983
1984
1985

Something was starting to work, and people were beginning to ask, 'What's Boylan's secret?' Hundreds of journalists have sought out that answer over the last 20 years, but in 1983 Sean Boylan was not playing hard to get and after Meath engaged Dublin in the first round of the Leinster Championship in Croke Park and kicked 17 wides, and were somehow denied a remarkable victory by a Ciaran Duff point 20 seconds from the final whistle, he trotted out to one journalist his deepest belief about the making of a great football team. Donal Carroll, the GAA correspondent of the *Irish Independent* was told, in 51 words, pretty much the entire Boylan plan. 'Some people say you should play to get fit. I believe you should get fit to play.' He explained himself. 'Fit, mentally and physically, to accept the many pressures of inter-county competition. It is important, too, that you strive to find a settled side and from that the pattern of play will evolve.' The replay date was set for 3 July, and Boylan said, 'No, thank you' to the Leinster Council's offer to stage the game in Navan's Pairc Tailteann. The attendance at the first game was short of 25,000. Meath's home ground was capable of housing that number of supporters, but Boylan was making it known to his players that they should never ever turn down the opportunity of running out onto the greatest GAA stage in the country. In truth, the Meath footballers were only dying to get back to Croker where they were quietly confident of finishing off the job against the team which would, soon enough, be crowned 1983 All-Ireland football champions. The Meath manager, however, had a rather bigger battle on his hands. He had 'round two' with Heffo awaiting him. Kevin Heffernan was then the second most brilliant, and the second most feared, football coach in the country. There was Mick O'Dwyer number one, Heffernan two, and Eugene McGee three. Sean Boylan was a long, long way back, even if he had a quite brilliant football philosophy and was quickly putting it to work.

In those hectic opening months, the Meath footballers had belief in their new team boss simply because they were winning games, for a change – and winning almost every game they played. In Boylan's first 11 games there were ten victories. Only the Galway team, which was to lose to Dublin in the 1983 All-Ireland final, got in the way of this running start to a new era when they scrambled a draw in Division Two of the NFL in Navan. The first team to beat Boylan's Meath was Kildare, and that 'surprise' left only one county blocking the door to Division One of the NFL and a place in the semi-finals. As they trained during the fortnight preceding the big game the players had one eye on the scaffolding RTE had erected for their cameras – big game, cameras, Sunday night TV, big time, and big names on the Roscommon team which was arriving into town. Roscommon should have beaten Kerry in the All-Ireland final two years earlier. Gay Sheerin, Harry Keegan, Pat Lindsay and Danny Murray were great names and great players, and they were only Roscommon defenders! Roscommon had great forwards too, even though, thankfully, Tony McManus was injured and could not play. But, on his own, Eamonn Barry scored as much as the visiting team. Meath won 0-13 to 0-5, easy as pie, and half the prize was a place in the NFL semi-finals against Armagh on 10 April.

Armagh were a team with a hot label attached to them, but Croker was an icy place that afternoon with showers of hailstones throughout the afternoon.

COLM O'ROURKE: *It was a really wet, cold and miserable day around Easter time. I remember my goal that day also. At the time we were playing against a really strong wind and I scored into the Railway End early in the second half. I took a shot and it just dipped down over the goalkeeper and went into the net. Armagh had quite a good team at the time and it was a big thing for us. Looking back at it now, people might say, 'A League semi-final on a mucky day in Croke Park, so what?' But at the time it was a big thing for us. We got close to them and although we lost we still viewed it as an achievement.*

LIAM HAYES: *Armagh had been beating everyone up and down the country all winter long, but that was the coldest day I've ever played a game of football. It was just a matter of survival out there for both teams, and that helped us. Looking at them nearly freezing to death and falling on their backsides in the mud as often as us, that helped get rid of* *any notion that they were some sort of 'Supermen'. I was marking Fran McMahon and going into the game I knew that he was one of the best midfielders in the country. But Fran looked like a guy who didn't really feel like playing football that day. We set the pace of the game, and we were laying down most of the rules. Mick and Padraig Lyons made one or two tackles that day which could have got a man jail! Although he had a reputation as a bit of a demon, Mick was easily the most disciplined player I ever played with. He knew the boundaries, knew how to go one inch towards being reckless, but he always stopped himself. He was always brilliantly controlled. In that regard he was the supreme example to the rest of the team. But against Armagh in '83 Mick drove an articulated truck through one or two of those boundaries.*

Eamonn Barry kicked the opening point from 40 yards out, 14 seconds into the game. Barry kicked another, and Colm O'Rourke also had two, before Armagh got on the scoreboard. There were 16 minutes gone. Goals from John Corvan and Mickey McDonald had Armagh level, 2-1 to 0-7 at half-time, and despite a spectacular pile-driver from O'Rourke in the 36th minute, which hit the top corner of the net, Meath were beaten 1-7 to 2-8. Although Armagh scored seven times and kicked 12 wides in the second half, while Meath had one score and one wide in the same 30 minutes, Boylan and his boys felt they were robbed! Very quickly, the team which Boylan was building had learned that victory and bitter defeat can be very close neighbours indeed. In May, Meath defeated Longford by two points in the O'Byrne Cup final. The seven men choosing the team had decided to experiment by placing young Martin O'Connell at centre-back. However, O'Connell was switched from the position after 23 minutes and was substituted before half-time, thereby beginning an angst-ridden three years relationship between a player who would later be chosen on the half-back line on the Gaelic football 'Team of the Century' and one of the greatest managers the game has ever known. The teenage O'Connell just couldn't see what Sean was at! Meanwhile, Boylan forever appeared to be subjecting Marty to trials and all sorts of tribulations which would lead to him temporarily walking away from the squad 20 months later.

Longford undoubtedly felt that they should have helped themselves to Meath's scalp for the second time in 12 months. John McCormack scored five points for the home team in the first half and a lucky goal from Mickey Downes, when his long-range shot fooled Longford keeper John Martin and dipped under the crossbar, gave Meath a 1-5 to 0-7 interval lead. Midway through the second half, Pat Mullooly put Kevin O'Rourke through, thanks to some sloppy defending, and he sent a rasping shot past a helpless Greg Twomey in the Meath goal. Longford were a point up! Twomey was deputising for the injured Sean Briody. Meath were also without captain Joe Cassells and Eamonn Barry up front, and it took points from Colm O'Rourke, Finian Murtagh and, unusually, Neil O'Sullivan to steady the visitors and earn the first piece of silverware in Sean Boylan's Meath cupboard. Brothers Neil and Frank O'Sullivan, from Walterstown, had started the game in opposite corners of the Meath attack. Neither would be on the team by the time Meath ended a 16 years' drought by lifting the Leinster title three years later. Both were in their mid-20s and had played with Meath for five or six years, Neil nearly always in defence, Frank usually at the opposite end of the field. In June of 1983 however, when Meath faced Dublin, Neil wore the No.11

jersey and Frank wore No.15.

MICKEY DOWNES: *I was fortunate in that there had been a major blow-up between Walterstown and ourselves, Navan O'Mahonys, in the Feis Cup final (the previous October). The Meath County Board, after carrying out an investigation, decided to suspend players when it best suited the county team – in other words, when the big matches weren't on. Joe Cassells – who was the Meath captain and my own clubmate – got suspended and missed the O'Byrne Cup final. I was lucky enough to captain the team in his place. I think we played three or four matches in the O'Byrne Cup but I actually only captained them in the final!*

The O'Byrne Cup was the first trophy which arrived in 'The Boylan Years', but an O'Byrne Cup medal was the only official reminder Downes would have of his time as a Meath footballer.

MICKEY DOWNES: *I think the kids discovered it recently. I think it was a case of 'Daddy, Daddy, what's this?' I remember it being a tough game against Longford, down in Longford. The team had become a lot more confident after the League run. There was a good effort made to win it – it wasn't just disregarded, as it would be now by Meath. Sure, some of the guys wouldn't even bother turning up for it nowadays. It was important for Meath to win it, and it was even more important that we weren't beaten by Longford again. As far as I remember, Joe was out for another four or five matches, but when the Championship came around, he was back in as captain.*
Around the corner, we had Dublin in the first round of the Leinster championship. Dublin had hammered Meath in Navan in 1980, really

hammered them, and this was the first time we had played them since. We were pretty confident going into the game. Dublin were going through something of a transition stage, so there was a certain amount of confidence, an air of expectation, that we could do something.

NEIL O'SULLIVAN: *I started that game against Dublin at centre-forward and I didn't really know much about the lad that was marking me. I think Frank McGrath was his name – and he was pretty new to the scene. But sure the game was not long on when Padraig Finnerty got injured and he was marking Ciaran Duff at half-back. So Padraig had to go off and I was handed the job of marking Duff. I might not have known my initial marker, but Duff – everybody knew Duff because he had a bit of a reputation at the time as an aggressive player. I think that I had quite a good game that day. I was determined not to let Duff score from play. To be fair, I didn't fear Duff's reputation and he never attempted anything dirty in that game.*

I remember Sean had brought in this thing of getting all the lads to rub oil on themselves before going out to play and I couldn't understand it at all. I certainly never played well anytime I put it on, so I gave up doing it soon after. There you'd be in the dressing room ready to go out and play the old enemy Dublin, and 20 or so Meath players would be rubbing oil all over themselves like it was suntan lotion! It was extraordinary.

MICKEY DOWNES: *What I remember most is that I was playing on Tommy Drumm, who was a super footballer. And I remember the second day, the replay, was blisteringly hot. Just after half-time, Ben Tansey was taken down in the square. I had been taking penalties for Meath – I think I had taken four up to that – and it was the first one I missed. I struck it well, struck it the same as all the other ones, but John*

O'Leary saved it. The memory I have of the game is that, in the first half, I got two breaks inside the Dublin defence. Both times the ball ran kindly for me and the first time I remember passing the ball to O'Rourke, who very narrowly missed a goal. On the second occasion, I passed it to Frank O'Sullivan and again he missed a goal. In the dressing room afterwards, I remember Sean being a bit annoyed that I hadn't taken two points instead of going for goals.

We came back to level it just at the death. I won the ball from a free-kick, passed it to J.J. McCormack and he kicked it over the bar. It was nip and tuck all the way to the end.

There was definite disappointment in the Meath camp at the end of it all. It was felt that it was an opportunity lost. At the time, nobody thought that Dublin would go on and win the All-Ireland. Offaly were the defending champions and looked very, very strong. I think the general consensus was that Offaly would beat Dublin. Obviously, it didn't work out like that.

But, it certainly raised Meath's hopes that we couldn't be that much off the pace. In particular, Sean himself realised that he was doing something right, that if a couple of more players came on the scene, he wouldn't be too far away. That day, Robbie O'Malley and Bernard Flynn played for the Meath minors at Croke Park and both had given outstanding performances. I think they were beaten but I'd say both were marked down as ones to watch.

NEIL O'SULLIVAN: *Padraig (Finnerty) was out for the replay and I started that game at wing-back. We lost and that was that. It was almost like a psychological barrier that we couldn't beat Dublin. We knew that if we beat them once, we could do it again – it was just getting that first win and making the breakthrough that was the problem. It* *would have to wait until next year, or so we hoped. There were a lot of headstrong people on the panel and they believed that the Meath team should be winning All-Ireland titles. Lyons, McEntee and all these boys had set their sights high and were a driving force – to finish second was to finish last for those boys.*

Heffo was the 'master' in Sean Boylan's first summer's day in Croke Park. Kevin Heffernan was attempting to put a Dublin team on the field which might, at best, serve as a passing resemblance to the mighty Dubs who had won three All-Irelands in four attempts in the mid-70s. Some of those players from that truly great team were still present, like Tommy Drumm, Brian Mullins and Anton O'Toole. However the future for his team lay in the hands of younger men, like John O'Leary, Barney Rock, Ciaran Duff, Tommy Conroy and Joe McNally. This new Dublin team would be good enough to appear in three All-Ireland finals on the trot, but defeats to Kerry in 1984 and '85 meant that this fine and talented squad of players were stamped 'second class' by the end of the '80s. Kerry would see to that in two All-Irelands and, amazingly, in the Leinster finals of 1986, '87 and '88, Dublin would find Meath to be smarter, stronger and, most of all, far more ambitious.

A little earlier, in 1983, Heffo had no reason to lose any sleep. Sean Boylan was a nice, genuine man, who had a lot to learn about life on the football field.

MICKEY DOWNES: *I remember in 1983, prior to the Dublin game, it looked as if Barney Rock was going to miss out because of a hand injury. I remember Boylan saying in the dressing room – and he was taken to task over it by some of the players – that it would be a terrible pity if*

Barney missed the game due to injury. He wanted to beat Dublin with a full team and he felt that a player of Rock's calibre, of his stature in the game, should be there. As it transpired, Rock came out and scored a couple of goals. I think it would have been much better if the injury had kept him out! But that would be pure Sean. He never preached cynicism, he never preached any sort of dirty football, but he expected players to stand up and play with the passion that you associate with Meath football.

When Dublin and Meath drew, 2-8 each, in early June it was not Barney Rock who deprived Meath of a memorable breakthrough, even though he finished Dublin's top scorer with a goal and a point to his name. No, it was the Dublin full-back, an unknown from Rock's own Ballymun Kickhams club, who proved the undoing of Boylan and Meath. Heffo's hidden weapon was Gerry Hargan, one of the nicest, most decent and quietly spoken individuals any Meath player had ever come across. But Hargan was obviously under orders to stop Colm O'Rourke at all costs, and that's what he did, fouling the Meath full-forward pretty much every time he got within touching distance. It was an exercise in cynicism which was not lost on an aspiring Meath group of players, or their growing army of supporters who made up the 25,069 attendance in Croke Park. Meath knew in their hearts that, at the first attempt, they were good enough to have secured a Leinster semi-final meeting with Louth and that Ciaran Duff's equalising point with 20 seconds remaining on the clock was a merciless blow.

The day was also the first great performance of Mick Lyon's football career. 'Great Royal County full-backs of the past such as Matt O'Toole, Paddy O'Brien and Jack Quinn must have been pleased to

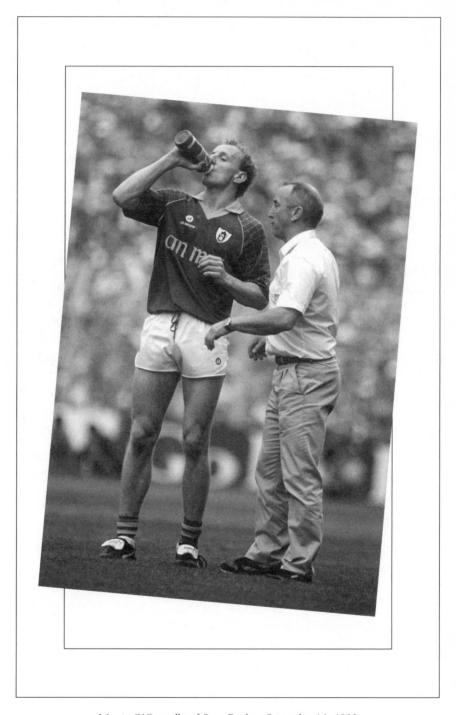

Martin O'Connell and Sean Boylan, September 16, 1990

Paidi O Se and Sean Boylan, September 23 2001

realise that one has come after them who could be as great as they. If Lyons can maintain this form he deservedly will join this distinguished band of immortals', stated Tom Mooney in the *Meath Chronicle*. Lyons and O'Rourke earned Meath the chance to finish off Dublin at the second time of asking. O'Rourke had still managed to score 1-4, despite carrying the extra weight of the Dublin full-back, while Finian Murtagh got two points and Eamonn Barry and Mickey Downes also scored. Meath led 0-5 to 0-3 at half-time. Rock's long-range effort from 40 yards out was misjudged by Meath 'keeper Greg Twomey five minutes into the second half. O'Rourke replied with a goal. Another goal from substitute Ben Tansey with ten minutes remaining left Meath clear, briefly, before a second mix-up in defence resulted in Phil Smith knocking the ball into his own net as he attempted to gather the ball into his chest.

On 3 July, it was a whole different ball game. Meath went out to finish off Dublin and win themselves the position as the second-best team in Leinster after Offaly. Instead, Boylan and Meath spent the afternoon chasing Heffo and Dublin!

Amazingly, the official attendance was smaller than the drawn game, with only 24, 383 people turning up according to Croke Park figures. Gerry Hargan showed up and played No. 3 for Dublin once again. He was cautioned by Offaly referee Jody Gunning after eight minutes for sticking too close to O'Rourke, and four minutes later he was booked for a second offence. The fouling continued, but Gunning never spoke to the Ballymun Kickhams player for the remainder of the game. It was a good day for Meath in defence, and in the middle of the field Gerry McEntee and Liam Hayes had the honour of watching their opposite numbers, Brian Mullins and

John Kearns being replaced by the end of the game. But up front it took ages for Boylan's boys to put their kicking boots to good effect, apart from Finian Murtagh, who kicked eight points for the afternoon and enjoyed probably his greatest performance on the greatest stage of all.

The Meath defence, however, was picking the ball out of its own net as early as the fourth minute. An innocuous looking lob from Brian Jordan was misjudged by Sean Briody, who had won back the No. 1 spot from Greg Twomey after the drawn game, and the ball bounced into an empty net. Three points from Murtagh had Meath trailing by 0-3 to 1-1 after 13 minutes, but then the Dubs played their best 15 minutes' football of the entire summer. They led by eight points at half-time (2-6 to 0-4), with Rock finishing off a magnificent move involving Tommy Drumm, O'Toole, Duff and Kearns, by blasting home to the top left-hand corner of the Meath net. Briody was given no chance whatsoever. Within 27 seconds of the resumption, Meath were awarded a penalty. A lob from McEntee was beaten out to Tansey, but his shot was blocked and O'Rourke gathered and crashed his pile-driver against the crossbar. Murtagh collected the rebound, but his shot was also blocked. However, in the commotion the referee adjudged that Mick Holden had fouled the ball in the square. Downes raced up to take the penalty, and by the time he struck the ball O'Leary was three yards off his line. The save looked easy.

The comeback was indeed heroic, with Murtagh and O'Rourke especially courageous in taking their scores, and J.J. McCormack levelled the match with the last kick of the game in normal time. Dublin looked dead, Meath had the burial shovel in their possession. Another Rock goal was to ruin the entire summer for

Boylan, his players and their small enough band of supporters. Midway through extra time, Briody had proven himself to be one of the team's heroes and the keeper saved what seemed a certain Dublin goal in the 12th minute. However, his block on O'Toole's shot rebounded high into the air and Rock fisted the ball to the empty net. Meath would score 16 times on the day. Dublin would get only 12 scores. The mantra inside the Meath camp – which would last for the next 19 years – was beginning to be heard by the evening of 3 July, 1983. It was a simple reminder, really: 'Stop Dublin scoring goals.' That was it, 'Stop Dublin scoring goals, and the doorway to Leinster and All-Ireland titles would finally be opened.'

COLM O'ROURKE: *Dublin went on to win the All-Ireland that year in '83. We certainly should have won the first game against them. I made a stupid mistake in the last minute. I had my kick blocked down when I was trying to decide whether I would go for a goal or a point. We were a point up at the time. We were kicking into the Canal goal and I should have kicked a point, an easy point, but instead I took too long, had my kick blocked and Dublin went down and got the equaliser. We had been the better team in the replay for most of the game, I think, also but gave away a couple of stupid goals. When Dublin went on and won the All-Ireland we all starting thinking we could have something going here because we could have, and probably should have beaten them.*
Going into the Leinster final in 1984 we had won the Centenary Cup. There is no doubt about it, that the Centenary was a bit of craic, but it was still a big win for us. I mean, we had lost the League semi-final in '84 after a replay to Galway in Croke Park, and we shouldn't have lost it. We had a great lead but ended up losing it by a point. That was a

big disappointment because we were the better team that day and then went to the Leinster final and played very badly. John Caffrey was sent off for Dublin in the first half and we still didn't punish them. They got a couple of goals early on and we never really recovered.

FINIAN MURTAGH: *I was only 21 in '83, only a gasun then. It didn't worry me where we were playing or who we were playing. I had no fear. I just went out to play football. There was no fear of playing Dublin at all. This was only the first round of the Championship now, not the Leinster final. It was the first game, so you probably weren't expected to win. You just went out with a devil-may-care attitude. Whatever happened, happened. After that, when we won the Centenary Cup, people were expecting us to win the big games, but there's a huge difference.*

TREVOR GILES: *I remember 1983. Meath and Dublin played two or three matches in Croke Park, and there was a replay and extra time. Just from early recollections, I think Meath had two or three goalies brought in – one lad got injured, another was dropped and they had to bring in a third fella. That was my first time going to Croke Park. Colm O'Rourke and Liam Hayes would have been with the club and I would have been the team mascot. Colm was the captain in '81 when Skryne got to their first Meath Senior final in ages, and I was the mascot on that day in Navan. I was only 6 at the time.*

Meath and Dublin would meet once more in 1983, in the opening round of the National Football League in Navan, and the 1983 All-Ireland champions were welcomed onto the field by Meath players lined either side of the dug-out. While the entire panel applauded the champs, one of Boylan's men was caught by one photographer from a local newspaper giving the Dubs the two fingers! Sean Boylan did not approve, but he had little reason to be hard on his players by the end of the afternoon after watching them earn a draw, 1-6 each. A crowd of 15,000 had packed into Pairc Tailteann on a grey, wet afternoon, and they watched their home team fail to score for the last 19 minutes of the game. Meath still led by two points with time almost up, but Dublin scrambled the draw for the second time inside six months, and Meath players were left to wonder when they would ever beat Dublin, and how!

Boylan had brought a new goalkeeper into the squad by the autumn, Darren Fay's Dad. Jimmy Fay was a lively, happy-go-lucky character, who turned up for training in Mick Lyon's car and immediately made his presence felt on and off the field. The team needed to put a stop to all the easy goals. It was good to have Jimmy Fay around the place, but he had a vitally important job to do as well.

JIMMY FAY: *I remember one of the first dealings I had with Sean was in 1983 after Meath drew with Dublin in the first round of the Leinster Championship. Before the replay he came to see me at work. I was working in a chemist's shop at the time, and Sean came into the shop and asked me to go back on the panel. Of course I said yes. I mean, here I was at work and the Meath football manager was standing in front of me asking me to play for my county. I was delighted.*

There was this game against Monaghan in Ballybay. That was the first time I actually played a game under Sean. Anyway, after the game we all went to a hotel in Ballybay and, at the time, my car was giving a bit of trouble. The radiator was playing up so I needed a bottle of water to bring home with me to keep filling her up along the road. So we were all sitting around the table and one of the lads told me to get an empty bottle of gin and fill it with water, and let on that it was alcohol. And sure I was always up for a bit of craic, so I said I would and proceeded to do so. I got a few bottles from behind the bar, filled them with water and put them in my car. But a Gordon's Gin bottle I brought back to the table and put it down in front of me. It was full to the brim with water and the cap was screwed tightly on the top. So we were all sitting around chatting for a while. Sean was a bit further down the table, but I could see him make a few quick glances up to see what was going on with the gin. Anyway, I unscrewed the top of the bottle and started drinking the water and I looked down towards Sean. You should have seen the face on him! He was astonished that I had the audacity to take a bottle of gin out in front of him and start drinking. His face was price-less, his jaw just dropped. But he was able to take it as a joke. He has a great sense of humour.

Meath drew with Cork in their second game in Division One of the NFL at Pairc Ui Chaoimh, but in the 26th minute a mix-up between Fay and corner-back Phil Smith resulted in the Meath No. 2 putting the ball past the Meath No. 1. Goals from O'Rourke after 19 minutes and Murtagh five minutes after half-time gave Meath another hard-earned point, but in reality the Royal Express was already gathering considerable pace against the top teams in the country. There was a home victory over Kildare thanks to first-half goals from Liam Smith in the 18th and 23rd minutes, and two weeks later, in the small parish of Killeavy, Meath became the first team to record a victory on Armagh soil in nine years. Padraig Finnerty was Meath's 'Man of the Match', but a magnificent save by Fay from Mickey McDonald early in the second period put paid to an Armagh charge being led by Joe Kernan and really put the visitors on the road to a memorable 0-12 to 0-6 victory. Kerry made the long haul to Navan for the final divisional game before the Christmas break, and when Meath corner-back Padraig Lyons lashed a hotly disputed penalty past Charlie Nelligan, it looked as though another impressive draw had been chalked up. However, Mikey Sheehy swung over a 48 yards free 30 seconds from the final whistle to give O'Dwyer, Paidi, Kennelly, Jacko and the Bomber a victory which they heartily celebrated. The happiness being displayed by the greatest team of all time did strike the Meath players as a little bit surprising. The year could hardly have ended with a greater compliment.

The next 12 months would be brilliant and bitterly disappointing, as 1984 saw Meath once again progress to the NFL semi-finals before losing to Galway after a replay. The reigning Connacht champs were a team to be reckoned with, and if they had managed to keep their heads they would have defeated Dublin in the All-Ireland final a few months earlier. Boylan's boys led Brian Talty and Co. by 0-7 to 0-0 after 17 minutes of the drawn game, and that lead could have been stretched to ten points, for when Finian Murtagh was expertly put through on goal by Colm O'Rourke he somehow managed to blast the ball wide. A 45 from Stephen Joyce was misjudged by the entire Meath defence, including goalkeeper Jimmy Fay, and ended up in the back of the net – once more wreck-ing the good work of the hard-working team. It was 0-13 to 1-10 at the finish, but in the replay Galway won through by one point (0-10 to 0-9) to meet Kerry in the final in Limerick, despite a gutsy scoring spree from little Liam Smith who kicked four points over the hour.

There was the glory of winning the Centenary Cup by the end of the spring, with a vengeful 13 points' polishing of Galway in the quarter-final (2-18 to 0-11) in Tullamore, another 13 points victory over Cavan in the semi-final (3-12 to 0-8) in Croke Park when Liam Smith, Bernie Flynn and Colm Coyle grabbed a goal apiece and finally a two points win over Monaghan in the decider. Eugene 'Nudie' Hughes scored half of the Monaghan total (0-8 to 0-10) but in a patchy performance the Meath team just about held its nerve. Once again, Liam Smith was close to perfection, sharing the top scorer position with Hughes. Smith would score another goal and four points when Meath slipped by Louth in a fairly bad-tempered exchange in the quarter-final of the Leinster Championship in Navan. Laois in the semi-final was a bigger hurdle which the team bundled its way in a manner that was far from pretty – the O'Moore men led by 2-6 to 1-7 at the break, having scored two goals in 90 seconds from Colm Browne. Jimmy Fay had made no attempt to stop the second, when he still appeared to be injured from a knock 10 minutes earlier. Brendan Melia replaced Fay at half-time, Laois scored another quick goal three minutes into the second period and they still led by one point with 12 minutes left on the clock when their keeper Martin Conroy drove his kick-out straight at Colm O'Rourke for the third time in the afternoon, and the Skryneman marked the occasion by immediately lashing the ball back into the net. It was 3-15 to 3-10 at the finish. The team was lucky. The defence was in a bit of a mess, having won through with a new face in goal, with Bob O'Malley in the forwards and with Padraig Lyons and Fay being replaced because of injuries. Finian Murtagh, thankfully, had helped out with yet another magnificent eight points' haul, and with himself, Smith, O'Rourke and the young Flynn, there was confidence that Meath had the shooting boots to win a Leinster title – though Flynn would not win himself a starting place for that provincial final in 1984.

It was midsummer and Meath were still alive and looking to finally deal with the major problem of Dublin.

In order to do so, Meath would need to be stronger, smarter, better all round than the year before. Jimmy Fay, despite his trouble against Laois, was now looking rock solid between the sticks, and in front of him the same team which had made so much ground in just over 12 months was still intact, just about! Boylan was already bringing in new players, older lads from poor senior clubs, and smaller intermediate and junior clubs, and also young kids like O'Malley and Flynn. Boylan's ambition was definitely showing through, and it was telling his players something about him and, more importantly, about themsleves. The manager wanted to go places, and every player needed to be wide awake and stay on his toes. The winter of 1983-84 was also the first time that Meath players were asked to engage in training routines and schedules which, to a man, they had never experienced in their lives before.

JIMMY FAY: *The two semi-finals of the Centenary Cup took place on the same day in Croke Park. We played Cavan, while Monaghan took on Derry. The Monaghan game was first up but it went to extra time, which meant we were left sitting in the dressing room for ages. We were ready to go out, and then we had to go back and wait. Obviously, the lads were a bit anxious and just wanted to get out on the field. Anyway, we were all sitting around the dressing room when Sean walked in with boxes of Cadbury's Finger Snacks and gave chocolate to everybody. We* *then went out and hammered them. In the final against Monaghan Sean gave a speech at half-time that made me just look up at him and think to myself that Meath were lucky to have somebody very special in charge. He was and still is a great man manager. If Sean Boylan talked to you for five minutes, you would walk through a wall for him. He has a personality which is unique.*

I remember we all attended a dinner in the RDS after winning the Centenary Cup. All the Meath team and their families were there. Cork had won the hurling and so both sets of teams and families were at this big function, and Darren was with us scooting all around the place getting autographs off all the Cork players and the Meath players. He spent the whole night collecting as many autographs as he could. I'm sure he got Sean's signature as well. My wife was pregnant at the time, and Sean came over later that night and said to me. 'Right Jimmy, it is time for you to go home. Your wife is pregnant and she should not be out here late.' We were playing a Championship game the following weekend, but Sean would not have come over and said that because of the game, but rather because he looks after families. That's the way he is. He looks after everybody.

When we played Laois in the Leinster semi-final in '84, I got injured in the middle of the first half. I went for a ball with a Laois forward and Padraig Lyons ran in as well, and we all collided with each other and ended up in a bit of a heap. I landed awkwardly on my back and I went into the dressing room at half-time in a lot of pain, but I still played on for a while. We were two goals down at that stage and they got another one after the break, but we hung on and won. I had won a Leinster medal in 1970 and I found it hard to believe that in 1984 I was involved in another provincial final. I mean, 14 years is a lifetime in football, but Sean brought Meath back from the brink that day. We didn't win any silverware, but there was a feeling that it would not be long coming. I remember Padraig Lyons missing a penalty in the opening minutes. He was playing corner-back. Then, all I can recall is Joe McNally taking a shot and I blocked it, but Barney Rock got the rebound and scored a goal. Something similar happened for the second goal when Ciaran Duff pounced on my block and scored.

PADRAIG LYONS: *Boylan asked me to take penalties for that match against Dublin, and I was practising them in training the week before it. It wasn't long on when a penalty unfortunately arrived. O'Rourke was going to take it, but I took the ball off him and said, 'I was told to take the penalties.' I'd be that way. I would have sooner given it to him. I didn't want to take the penalty for my own glory because there are too many pitfalls in taking penalties, but if I was told to do something, that's what I'd do. If Boylan said to go up there and knock out the goalie with a box, and then take the penalty, I'd go up and do that too. So when Sean says, 'You're to take any penalty', I says 'Fine.' I went up and O'Rourke was standing over it, placing it, and I said, 'Colm, I'm taking that.' He didn't say much. I duly kicked it wide. It wasn't that far away. There are those here locally who would tell you that I knocked over some wheelchairs – you know the handicapped section along behind the goal – but it wasn't that far away. It just flew by the butt of the post.*

GERRY McENTEE: *Losing the 1984 Leinster final was a major setback because it looked like we were back where we had started. In 1983 we played well against Dublin and we knew going into '84 we had a great chance of beating them. Mick Lyons was not playing because he had a broken thumb. The week before the game Mick went up to the Mater Hospital to see the orthopaedic surgeon, Mr Martin Walsh, who took the*

37

plaster off. But when he pressed over where he had the fracture, Mick jumped with the pain and that was the end of that.

However, despite the loss of Mick Lyons we still could have won that game. We kicked a huge number of wides and owned the ball, but Dublin got the scores, like they had been doing to us for years, and won. The defeat to Laois in 1985 changed the team a lot because between then and 1986 we got six new players. There was Mickey McQuillan, Terry Ferguson, Kevin Foley, David Beggy, P.J. Gillic and Brian Stafford.

MICKEY DOWNES: *The players had huge respect for Boylan and realised what he could do for them, particularly after Meath's run in the League and the Championship in '83. The training in Bettystown with all the running along the sand-dunes was pretty tough, but the running around the Hill of Tara was just savage. Something like that had never been done before in Meath. It would have been known that Offaly had trained very hard. Guys like Gerry McEntee and Colm O'Rourke knew Eugene McGee from UCD and would have been pretty familiar with what Offaly were doing. I had some friends on the Offaly team too and I was very familiar with what they were doing because I often heard them complaining about the hill outside Rhode. If Offaly had this hill in Croghan, Meath had the Hill of Tara! So Boylan was going one better. It was certainly more significant, more historical. Definitely, a thought went through your mind, 'What was all this for?' But the results were getting better all the time, the team was improving, so he was obviously doing something right. In terms of fitness, Meath teams certainly weren't at the levels of Dublin or Kerry, particularly in the late 70s and 80s, and I'd say that Sean saw a need for that.*

NEIL O'SULLIVAN: *I remember John Caffrey being sent off for Dublin* *that day in the Leinster final (1984). I was sitting on the bench and I was itching to get out because I thought myself that I had been playing well up until then, and it was one game I really wanted to play in. When their man was sent off we didn't use the extra man well enough. I honestly thought that if I was brought on I could have contributed to the advantage gained by the sending off, but it didn't happen and it was frustrating because I was really mad to get out on the field. But we looked like winners – we just let in a couple of slack goals. But, definitely, we should have won the Leinster that year.*

In fairness to Sean, it wasn't until he got rid of the likes of me and a few others after the game, and in the months and years that followed, that things started to happen. I remember we had the opening of our pitch in Walterstown in '86 and Meath were pencilled in to play Monaghan. I had expected to play simply because it was my club, and the whole sentimental aspect of it. I was the only Walterstown man on the panel at the time. However, I didn't start but a lad by the name of David Beggy played and I had never heard or seen anything of him before, and here he was playing for Meath on my club pitch. Obviously I was a bit annoyed but look what Beggy went on to achieve. Boylan had a knack of finding players in the strangest places and Beggy was probably his best find of all. From Sean's point of view, he wanted to try these new guys out before the Championship and he was right to do so. He was looking at the overall picture and you can understand why he wanted to give the young lads a run.

I hated the training, running up and down sand-dunes and then into the bloody water. I suppose I thought it was a bit crazy at the time but you had fellas like Gerry McEntee and the like who didn't ask any questions. They just got on with it and that was that. And if they were doing it you just had to follow them.

Dublin led the Leinster final of 1984 from start to finish, and the nearest they came to losing was between the 12th and 15th minutes when a Ben Tansey goal had left just a single point between the teams. This time around 56,051 wanted to be in Croke Park to see if Boylan could push his team up to a higher level of confidence and performance, and when the Dubs had their 'third' midfielder John Caffrey harshly sent to the line ten minutes before half-time it was the moment for Meath to address a whole new future as a truly great football team. It never happened, however. Caffrey's marker Padraig Lyons had followed him relentiously all over the field, but after the corner-forward's dismissal Lyons retreated back into defence for good and O'Malley, still very much serving his apprenticeship as a Meath senior player, was given the role of Meath's extra man. In the ninth minute Lyons had blasted wide from the penalty spot. It was not the most memorable day in the Lyons family history, as brother Mick was watching the game from the sideline. He had fractured his thumb in a club game seven days after the Leinster semi-final, and while Boylan and his selectors had been tempted to but Mick and Padraig's kid brother, Terry into the famous No. 3 jersey, it was agreed that Phil Smith would be a safer bet. Barney Rock and Ciaran Duff each scored first-half goals and ended up with 2-8 between them for their afternoon's work, and while Meath held their opponents scoreless for 17 minutes of the second period it was looking increasingly futile trying to unlock a blue defence in which Mick Holden was king. Dublin won by four points. The final score-line of 2-10 to 1-9 was utterly fair. Writing in the *Evening Press*, however, Con Houlihan was not rushing forth with his pen to congratulate either team on their efforts and felt he had witnessed a game which was played in a wild west town which did not have a sheriff on duty for the afternoon. He was especially displeased with the thought-process behind the losing team's efforts. 'Meath's forwards were like a man who has a fund of stories but often makes a mess of the punch line,' he insisted. 'And once again the management played Colm O'Rourke as an orthodox full-forward. It was about as sensible as acquiring a print of Van Gogh's "Sunflowers" and hanging it in a cubbyhole under the stairs.' Houlihan parted with the opinion that neither O'Rourke nor any other Meath forward could stand up in a public place and claim 'kinship with William Tell'.

Meath footballers and football fans could not complain too loudly at such verdicts. And over the next 12 months neither party had very much to say for themselves. By the summer of 1985 Sean Boylan was fighting for his life as Meath football manager. Somebody else wanted the job, and there was a sizeable number of people on the Meath County Board who felt that Boylan had shown his hand and there were no more cards in his back pocket. The National League campaign of 1984-85 showed limited progress with the team, and after giving Larry Tompkins, Shay Fahy and the rest of the Kildare team a sound six-points thrashing in the first round of the Leinster Championship in Navan, Meath travelled down to Tullamore a few weeks later and walked straight into a ten points defeat by Laois. By the end of 1985, Boylan, for the first time in 20 years, would have to fight for the job he loved. What's more, he might have lost that job if some of his senior players had not shown up at County Board meetings asking for one more chance – for themselves and Sean Boylan together.

LIAM SMITH: *I was involved with Meath as a player before Sean came in. It was a bit of a mess at that stage because there were seven selectors at the time and the system just never worked. Sean whittled that down to three fairly quickly. It was only when himself, Tony Brennan and Pat Reynolds started working as a trio that things really started to happen for Meath.*

At the time in 1982 when Sean came in I have to admit I was wondering who he was. Someone said he played hurling, but I didn't know him. It was more or less the case that no one wanted the job so Sean got it. Don't get me wrong. He was a good trainer and has been a great manager, but he did get the job because there wasn't much competition.

We didn't know whether he would last even two or three years in the job. The Centenary Cup win in 1984 was the first real win of note for Meath under Sean Boylan. It wasn't an All-Ireland or anything like that. It was something on a level with a Leinster title, but it meant a huge amount to Meath players. I remembered playing against Wexford at Croke Park previously when we were beaten and Meath football was at a very low ebb at that stage. We missed a lot of the good teams in the Centenary Cup and I suppose Meath and Monaghan isn't the pairing everyone had been expecting in the final but it meant a lot to us because our team hadn't any real success before. People started to think we might be able to win a Leinster then.

If 1984 was the first real success I had, then 1985 was a real downer. I got injured about a month before the Laois match. I played in the game when I really shouldn't have. I tore ligaments in my ankle in a challenge match against Derry before the Laois game. Laois gave us a beating and I thought that was the end of it for myself and Meath. But it wasn't. Bernie Flynn, Bob O'Malley, David Beggy and Martin O'Connell were all just starting to appear on the scene, and they took us to another level. Still, at the time, you didn't see it coming.

The Laois game was one of the last times I was involved as a full-time player. I was mostly on the bench after that. I remember the first night David Beggy came in. I knew Bernie and Bob. They had been great club players, but I didn't know David at all. As it turned out he had been on the U-21 team and Sean had great faith in him. Brian Stafford came in too and he was a natural footballer. It was difficult for me after that because all those players were phasing lads like me out.

Of course 1986 was a real breakthrough even if the semi-final against Kerry was a bit of a shambles. I'll never forget the collision of Joe Cassells and Mick Lyons and Mickey McQuillan. It was a right disaster. Yet it was at that stage that the lads realised there was an All-Ireland in Meath. We had run a great Kerry side very close. After that we experienced two glory years. I was just a sub for the two All-Ireland wins in 1987 and '88. Still, even as a sub they were rare occasions up in Croke Park that I'll never forget. The '87 team and the '88 side were probably the best Meath teams ever. It was a bad time for me because I was losing out to lads like Bernie Flynn and Beggy, but I didn't mind when the players were of that quality – you couldn't complain too much. I remember running up around the Hill of Tara in the dark and some of the lads were up there with the flashlamps showing us which way to run. You'd think you knew where you were going but you wouldn't have a clue and we'd be running into each other half the time! It was crazy. Tony Brennan would be there trying to direct us. People laugh at it now but it did us a lot of good. Then we'd go over to Bettystown beach other evenings and on into the Neptune Hotel afterwards for the grub. I remember running up and down the dunes very well. Sean got everyone fit and that's what counted at the end of the day. He was a very honest, fair man. He took everyone into consideration in training. I mean you wouldn't touch Terry Ferguson for fitness when you'd be running around the beach. Terry loved it. But, on the other hand, there were lads like Mick Lyons who wouldn't exactly enjoy it. But Sean knew what buttons to push with certain fellas to get the best out of them.

Martin O'Connell would have been a good friend of mine along with Bernie Flynn and Gerry McEntee. I liked Gerry. He'd call a spade a spade. Liam Hayes was a gentleman too. Himself and Gerry formed one of the best ever midfield partnerships in my opinion. They just complemented each other perfectly. Some said that Liam would be drifting in and out of games, but he was always there working behind the scenes if he wasn't breaking into one of his trademark ventures up the pitch.

After defeats Sean was great. He'd never run down a player. Even after Micky, Joe and Mick had been involved in that clash in '86 that led to Ger Power scoring he wouldn't have given out to them. In fact, Sean was laughing at it in '87 and '88. At the time in '86, I thought for a while that that was our chance gone when Kerry beat us. But over time you'd learn from the experience. A week or two later you realised lads would bounce back stronger.

The highlight of my career would have been the homecoming in 1987, back to Navan after the All-Ireland final win. The reception we got was like Manchester United or Arsenal after winning an FA Cup in England. I remember we were supposed to be back at 8.30 p.m. in Navan, but it was more like midnight. The reception was unreal. It was something like you'd see on TV. You'd never expect to be part of something like that. Coming down on the bus, we were expecting some sort of a crowd all right, but nothing like what we got. There were thousands of people out to cheer us.

There were no hard feelings when I left. I just said to Sean in 88, 'I'm going to move along and I'll let the young lads come in.' At that stage I was only filling in for Bernie or David in the League games, but there was no hope after that as regards the Championship. I just told him he'd be better off having a young lad in as a sub rather than an older lad who had had his chance.

The four in a row of games against Dublin were unreal. Kevin Foley's goal was an absolute cracker. I remember the first night Kevin Foley came in, down in Dalgan at training. We were playing a game and because I was at half-forward that evening I was the first person he had to mark. My first contact with him was when I was half-running out for the ball after a minute or two. I saw him coming in the corner of my eye, but I just presumed it was a training game and he would take it handy enough. He absolutely creamed me – came into me with knees and everything. I just turned around and asked him, 'What was that in aid of?' That was my first experience of Kevin Foley. He was as strong as an ox and a great player. We became good friends in the end and I'd have a lot of time for him. To come along and get the winning goal at that time took some bottle.

FINIAN MURTAGH: *I remember Liam Smith had a great final in the Centenary Cup. He was 'Man of the Match'. He was in a different class, but he was also only a small, little lad. He was just too small. If you couldn't win the ball against a 6'4" fella, you were gone! For the lads who had played for so long, that win was huge. They had trained for ten years for that. But for the likes of me, who was only 20 or 21, it was no big deal. I was just playing football.*

Then 1985 was a real flop. Laois hammered us. I don't know what went wrong that day. Laois were coming good, they had a decent enough team at the time. It was just one of those things, there was no second chance then. You were gone. There were great expectations after winning the Centenary Cup and getting to a Leinster final in '84.

They wanted him (Sean) out. It was only canvassing by O'Rourke and Cassells and McEntee that kept him in. That was it! He was gone otherwise, and things could have been so much different for Meath football.

The first phase of Sean Boylan's career as Meath's football boss was certainly over. And if his tenure had ended in the late summer and early autumn of 1985, then there would have been a longish enough queue at the front door of the Boylan family home in Dunboyne waiting to say thanks. Men like O'Rourke, Cassells, McEntee and Mick Lyons were now being chosen for Leinster every year. So too were a few of the younger lads, like Padraig Lyons and Hayes. What's more, when the Australians arrived in Ireland in the autumn of 1984 for the beginning of the new Compromise Rules series, the Meath representation was on a par with the very best counties in the land. Mick Lyons was knocked unconscious in the first minute of the first Test series in Pairc Ui Chaoimh in October of that year, and in an absolutely vicious and manic encounter which the Aussies won 70-57 O'Rourke and Hayes also saw action alongside the likes of Tom Spillane, the Bomber, Seanie Walsh and Jacko from the Kingdom, P.J. Buckley and Barney Rock from Dublin; and Offaly's Richie and Matt Connor. The Meath crew went drinking with their new Offaly and Dublin colleagues after the game. Whatever notion the Meath team was having about itself, there was absolutely no doubt that individual players in Boylan's dressing room now saw clearly that there were very few

'Supermen' playing Gaelic football. These individuals were no longer shackled by an inferiority complex, and the stories and little anecdotes which they were bringing back to the Meath dressing room were priceless in every respect. If Sean Boylan had been asked to exit there and then at the end of the summer of 1985, his successor would have had a strongly motivated group of men gathered around him. Paul Kenny was being presented as the next Meath manager. He had a good reputation as a coach in Meath and Louth, and he was proving himself with Meath under-age teams. Many people thought Kenny should be the man

The winter of 1984-85 had not been great, though it wasn't that wet or cold, and most Sunday afternoons were pleasant enough for matches. Boylan had successfully argued his case that he should be allowed to choose his own selectors, and therefore would not need the assistance of the County Board chairman and secretary any more when selecting his teams. Bravely and indeed quite unsympathetically he also said 'Good luck' to Paddy Cromwell, Jim Curtis and Mattie Gilsenan, all of them good, honest men who were still highly respected throughout the county. Boylan asked Pat Reynolds and Tony Brennan, one of the strongest defenders and one of the smartest forwards from Meath's 1967 All-Ireland winning team, to be his co-selectors instead. The next 12 months leading up to the débâcle and defeat by Laois in the semi-final of the 1985 Leinster Championship was a lonely time for the three of them.

An experimental team was torn asunder by Galway in the first round of the National League in Ballinasloe, and when Meath beat Cork 1-7 to 0-8 in Navan two weeks later, Neil O'Sullivan was in the middle of the field with Gerry McEntee, while the half-forward line consisted of Colm Coyle, Colm O'Rourke and Liam Hayes. There were newcomers to the squad, brought in to spice things up. Kieran Carr, a buddy of O'Malley's and Flynn's from St Colmcille's was getting his place, as was Meath Hill's Tom Matthews who was centre-field with McEntee in a drawn match with Kildare. Gerry Cooney was in the corner up front which would soon be Bernie Flynn's position for good. Aiden Crickley, a very stylish and lightning-fast half-back was asked to join the squad from Liam Harnan's club, Moynalvey – Harnan would not get the call-up for another 12 months. Tall, rangy, former Meath minor Ray Tully from Trim was being tried out at full-back.

It was trial and error throughout the long winter, which included a two points defeat by Armagh in Navan and an exciting contest with Kerry in Tralee which ended 1-7 apiece after centre-back Tom Spillane sent a pile-driver over the bar from 60 yards out with four and a half minutes remaining on the clock. Gerry McEntee was wearing the Meath No. 6 that afternoon! A victory over Tyrone in the last game in Division One of the National league in Omagh was necessary in order to avoid relegation. Ray Tully was corner-back, Cassells wore the Meath No. 6 with Coyle and Martin O'Connell on either side of him. Hayes and McEntee were asked to play together in the middle of the field for the first time in nine months, Neil O'Sullivan was holding onto the No. 11 jersey thanks to his great positioning and quick thinking rather than his speed or scoring ability, and his Walterstown clubmates J.J. McCormack and Gerry Cooney were helping make up the full-forward line with O'Rourke. That was it. That was the team resulting from the winter's work. Meath won 1-10 to 1-8 in a bad-tempered game which also included plenty of activity in the tunnelled area between the field and the dressing rooms both at half-time and full-time.

LIAM HAYES: *Gerry got sent off late in the game, for a second personal foul. It was not that dirty a match, but Tyrone were giving us a lot of lip, with a lot of Irish history thrown in for good measure. And while I never, ever spoke to opponents during games, for fear of getting completely and totally distracted from the game, Gerry always loved a good chat from start to finish. Himself and their centre-back Noel McGinn never stopped! It was crazy some of the stuff that was being said during the game and, naturally, that sort of slagging continues at half-time and full-time. That was the problem. It was a bit vicious between the field and the dressing room. Kevin McCabe, who was an Allstar half-back, played for them that day and a few months later he became a clubmate of mine in Skryne. He was a great footballer and a really nice bloke. Liam Smith was brilliant that day and scored four points, all of them from play, I think. I remember Gerry Cooney and myself had been trying out a few moves in training the day before, and one of them had Gerry taking a '45'. I would run by him with my marker as if I was heading for the goalmouth and then I would do a quick about-turn and do a one-two. In the opening minutes of the game we tried it, and it worked a peach, and Gerry stroked the ball over the bar from his hands. Unfortunately, you only get to try that sort of move once in any match.*

GERRY COONEY: *I had two brief flirtations with the Meath panel without ever really establishing myself on it. I was involved in 1984 and '85 with Meath. I was captain of Walterstown at the age of 25 in 1984. We had just won the County championship again. We had also done* well in the All-Ireland club championship and I got on the panel on the strength of that. I had played minor and U-21, but didn't really make the step up. At that stage, up to around '85, there wasn't a lot happening at county level with Meath. But straightaway when Sean started putting his mark on the team, you could see that there was a buzz about the place. My earliest memory is the league and going down on the train to play Kerry in Tralee in 1984. Mattie McCabe had cried off with injury so I got in. We drew the match.

It was an important game because Kerry put out a fairly strong side at the time. I'll never forget we got a penalty and because I would have taken a lot of the frees, I stood up to take it. I stubbed my foot on the ground and hardly connected with the ball, but I sent Charlie Nelligan the wrong way all the same and scored! I played against Paidi O Se that day. It was very clear as regards Sean that even back then he meant business. That was a year or two before Meath had won their first Leinster under Sean. I remember coming back from another League match against Tyrone in that campaign. We had to beat them to stay up in Division One and we did beat them. All the senior lads were chatting on the way home about what we were going to do at the time as regards the county's future. They were great lads who didn't mind putting in the graft to make the breakthrough. I was not honestly at their level. Lads like Bernie Flynn, Staff and Bobby O'Malley came along then and they really made the breakthrough. I had a year on the panel at that point, but without ever breaking into the Championship sides. Ultimately, my first stint ended in disappointment against Laois in Tullamore. I remember that year coming to training after watching a Bruce Springsteen concert down in Slane. I only went in for half an hour and then went to training. They were the sacrifices you'd make, but you never minded.

Martin O'Connell, Mikey Sheehy and Mickey McQuillan, August 24, 1986

Mick Galwey and Terry Ferguson, August 24, 1986

After that I went back and played with the club and soldiered on. I was based in Dublin and travelled back to club games. Having won the All-Ireland in '87 and gone to the games in between, I got a call in around June of '88 to make up the panel. It was a first 15 against the rest of the panel in Dalgan Park before the Leinster final that year and I wasn't even going to bother going down. But I did in the end and played the game. I did OK and thankfully I was asked to appear for training the following Tuesday. I was shocked and delighted. Meath won a second All-Ireland in '88 and I got a run of three or four months. I never really looked like making the Championship squad. I hoped to get a chance in the League later that year, but there were four or five of us dropped, me included.

It was a bit of a jump from club to county. There was even rowing on the Royal Canal for county training, but I missed that. You didn't know what would come next. Some of the nights in Bettystown were tough. I didn't know what on earth we were doing some of the time. In more recent years I got to know Sean a lot better. I was training and coaching in Dunboyne. He didn't interfere and didn't get in the way, but he was always there to help. I would have sent several lads down to see him with injuries and he never turned any of them away. We went to the Canaries in '98 with St Peter's, Dunboyne, and he came with us. It was a great week. I hadn't been away with the Meath teams on holiday, so this was something special for me. Sean was incredible too. He just knew everybody. He was a remarkable man for names and memories and the stories he'd have too! He's very knowledgeable about the history of the GAA and Meath football. I wouldn't be into history so much as he would, but even for people who know their stuff, he would beat them hands down. When you're with him and he meets people, it's astonishing. People who come down to training or after a match, he would remember all of them.

With the Meath team, a lot of people felt that maybe you should throw all the Walterstown lads in because they were having success at club level back then. It didn't really work like that. None of us established ourselves as was expected. Walterstown were having great success at the time, but it was at a time when the club scene didn't get the same profile as it does now.

My first game was a League tie against Galway in Ballinasloe. I'll never forget my real inter-county introduction! I was taking the frees at the time and my first effort came from a '50'. I totally screwed the ball way off to one side and it was so bad that the crowd jeered at me. The volume was shocking and I couldn't believe it. I realised I was at inter-county level then!

Myself and Neil Sullivan were good friends at the time and we'd play a lot of golf together. We came up through minors and U-21s together. Neil had been playing with Meath a bit longer than me, but in '85 I had been captain of Walterstown the year before. We knew that it was time for the captaincy of the county to come up. Myself and Neil were going down to a game and we were ribbing each other about who was going to get the armband. In the end we agreed that whichever of us was thrown it we would just accept it and get on with it. There'd be no slagging or anything like that. At the last minute Sean gave it to J.J. McCormack instead. We had a laugh at our own expense. In truth, it kind of summed up my time with Meath. There weren't really too many highlights.

I would have been closest to Frank Foley. Frank used to be our token singer after the All-Ireland wins. Donal Smith was a good guy and a good friend of mine as well. In recent years I would be closer to Liam Harnan. We have an annual golf get-together in October with the Meath footballers. It's very competitive. They're an unreal bunch of lads *because they put everything into their golf now, like the football years ago. Seven or eight of the lads would be off single figure handicaps now. They're still very dogged and very determined.*

The four Dublin games in '91 were incredible. After the fourth game I came out from the old Cusack Stand and walked around to the Hogan to meet the lads. I'll never forget coming around the back of the Hill. There was a very nasty kind of atmosphere. It wouldn't have taken much to start a row. It was a bit intimidating and you wouldn't be too quick to show your colours. Those games meant so much to a lot of people.

Meath were caught in the '91 final. Bernie Flynn scored six points from play and still ended up on the losing side. When I was brought in, Bernie was slightly injured and I thought there was a bit of a chance I could get in. We would have been competing for the same spot if you like but in truth, it wasn't even close.

Back in '88 there was always pressure to cut the panel down, there was always going to be only a limited number of lads allowed on the bench. Sean would always insist on the maximum number of players so as to treat everyone the same in the team.

I have another memory of going to the final in '88. It's a ridiculous memory but it sticks in my mind. All 28 panellists were allowed onto the pitch, but once you weren't on the first 24, or the first21, you weren't going to be considered for the bench. I had a dodgy ankle at the time and I wondered would I wear my ankle strap out on the pre-match run-around out on the pitch. It was ridiculous being allowed out for the warm-up and thinking about that sort of stuff, and then going back in to get changed and sit in the stands!

Martin O'Connell did not make the Meath starting line-up for the first round of the 1985 Leinster Championship against Kildare in Navan. An attendance of 11,000 came into town for the game. Kildare also had a team for the future, including big men and natural leaders like Paddy O'Donoghue, Tompkins and Fahy, and there was every reason to worry about them. There was genuine respect and some fear in the Meath camp in the weeks leading into the game, more respect and greater fear than Boylan's players had for the likes of Laois, who were waiting to play the winner in the Leinster semi-final. Thanks to a stiff wind at their backs Meath led by 0-9 to 0-1 at the interval in Navan. A few weeks later in Tullamore, Meath would trail Laois 0-3 to 0-6 at the same stage. Clearly, somewhere between the two games, the notion that Laois would be merely a sizeable stepping-stone to another Leinster final had taken hold.

Kildare scored five points between the 4th and 11th minutes of the second half, but were allowed only one more score, a Tompkins' free, in the last 24 minutes of the game. Liam Smith had outscored Colm O'Rourke once again by the end of the afternoon, by four points (and only one free) to O'Rourke's three points. It was the same as it had been all through 1984 when Smith played 18 times for the county, one less than O'Rourke, and still outscored him by three points for the year. Smith had three goals and 40 points, O'Rourke's total came to five goals and 31 points and, small as he was, not much more than half the size of O'Rourke, Liam Smith was absolutely vital to Meath's growing ambition. He was not fully fit to play against Laois, but was played anyway. Nobody wanted to see Meath on the field without him, and yet inside 12 months Sean Boylan had removed Smith to the sideline, virtually for good. It was tough on players like him, who were running out of time in their football careers and who had to watch Boylan experiment at their expense. In competitive games, Boylan had tried out a total of 32 players in 1984 and after all that effort only one brand new face was on the team in the summer of 1985, and that was Aiden Crickley.

LIAM HAYES: *We were in a bar in Drogheda one night, very late, a few days after we had beaten Derry in the 1987 All-Ireland semi-final. Most of the lads had a fair bit on them. I didn't drink at the time, and I have this memory of Liam Smith grabbing me by the arm at the end of the night up at the bar. I hadn't played very well in the semi-final, and Liam told me how badly I had played. He had not been given a serious look-in by Sean for about two years. The door had been closed on him really. He grabbed me and, serious as hell, with several expletives thrown in, said, 'You better go and play well in the All-Ireland final, Hayes. I want that All-Ireland medal.' He made it plain that his destiny was in the hands of lads like myself, and he didn't want us to mess up the guts of ten years of hard work on his behalf. It was a great message to receive, a good kick up the back-side.*

AIDEN CRICKLEY: *I was in the Canal End when Meath lost to Dublin in the Leinster final in '84 and my eternal memory of that game was Ciaran Duff's drop-kick goal. He just got it and seemed to have loads of time to let it down to his foot and drop it into the net. I think it was the final nail in the coffin for Meath that day. Dublin appeared arrogant and at times seemed to toy with Meath. Sean Boylan made me feel very welcome from the first day I walked into the Meath dressing room. I mean, there were all these star players I was reading about in there and I hadn't met any of them before as such. But Sean introduced me, telling* *them all who I was and who I played with, so I was made feel very relaxed.*

Before the Kildare game in the Championship, I remember Sean calling Martin O'Connell and myself into a room after training one night. It was the night the team was to be announced. Martin was having a bit of a slump in form at that time and he was in and out of games and getting substituted a lot. So, before telling everybody the team, Sean called the two of us into this room and he said: 'It was a hard decision boys, but only one of you can get on the team as a half-back, and I'm starting Aiden on Sunday.' Martin was obviously very disappointed, but I was speechless to be getting the chance to play in the Championship. Although Martin missed out that day we all know he went on to achieve bigger and better things, so I guess getting the nod that night is my claim to fame.

Sean came over to me before the match and said, 'Right Aiden, you are going into the white heat of the Leinster Championship. I hope you are ready for it because this is the big-time. It is not a League match or a challenge match. This is championship.' He grabbed me by the jersey and asked, 'Are you ready for it?' It was his way of trying to get us going and prepare us for the game.

I played left half-back against Kildare in Navan. They actually flew home Larry Tompkins from the US for the game. He was one of the star names in Gaelic games at the time, because he was so young and so gifted. He played centre-forward and Joe Cassells was marking him. I was one side and Colm Coyle was the other. I remember looking across that line a number of times during the match and every Meath player appeared so focused. I was marking a fella called Donovan. It was the June Bank Holiday weekend and it was really warm. The sun was splitting the stones. I remember being very nervous before the game and just wanting to get my first touch because that usually makes you feel more comfortable. So I got the ball early on actually and I was playing underneath the stand side of Pairc Tailteann. We were playing towards the hospital end in the first half and, anyway, I took the ball cleanly in my hands, had a solo or two and saw Bernie Flynn coming out from the corner. I played a nice long ball down to him and he turned and put it over the bar. That passage of play settled me down and got me in on the game. Sean was full of praise for us after the match, but told us that it was only the start.

I remember being a minor celebrity in Moynalvey for a short while. As it was such a small parish everybody knew everybody and when I walked into the pub the place would nearly go quiet. It was a very proud occasion for Moynalvey to have one of their own playing for Meath – my grandfather founded the club, and so the entire family was very proud that day.

Around the same time my club played against Summerhill in the Meath club championship. It was a hot day and Boylan had come to the game to check out our form. Summerhill won by two points in a very low-scoring match. I was playing midfield and marking Mick Lyons, and he was climbing up on my back and giving me the odd auld sly dig. Anyway, Meath were due to play Derry in a challenge in Navan that evening and Sean came into the Moynalvey dressing room after the game wanting to know if I had any way of getting to Navan for the game. I had no way so Sean said he would bring me along with Mick and Padraig Lyons. So we were all in Sean's car anyhow and he turned around to us and said, 'Did you get any tea fellas?' We said we hadn't, and Sean decided to bring us to his house in Dunboyne for tea. I remember having a chicken salad in his house and we had a grand feed. Sean was so easygoing. Here we were less than an hour before the game having tea in the manager's house. I was actually kind of worried and kept reminding him of the time. But he was taking it in his stride and telling us to have our tea first and then worry about the game. We beat Derry and as a couple of us had played club games that day, we told Sean not to expect an awesome performance before we left the dressing room. 'Ah, not to worry, just do your best. It's only a run-out to keep us ticking over', he said.

Sean Boylan is the epitome of Meath. He represents all that is good in Meath football, honest, fair and hard when he has to be. He makes everybody feel like part of the Meath family when they are involved and he can encompass all that, and get them all into a winning team. He is an excellent manager and says all the right things at the right times – but he'd also give you a scalding if you deserved it.

During my time with the Meath team I actually played hurling against Sean in Kilmessan. He was playing for Dunboyne and I was playing for Kiltale and, low and behold, he ended up marking me. I was half-forward and he was half-back. And I remember he was giving me sly digs all through the game. He was a good hurler but Dunboyne weren't great. He was as fit as a fiddle and chased me everywhere, and any-where I was, he was up my arse. He thought it was great craic chasing me and giving me sly digs. In fairness, I couldn't really turn around and hit him back. Obviously I was still trying to impress him on the football scene so I didn't want to jeopardise that. But it was funny to be playing against your manager.

I played left half-back against Laois in Tullamore. I think we might have been a little bit complacent and we just let them play football and they got two goals. I was at fault for one of them in the second half. I was marking Pascal Doran. I remember he went out and got the ball way ahead of me, turned and just waltzed past me, leaving me for dead, and

*he blasted it into the net. There was just a stunned silence in the
dressing room afterwards. We went from hero the zero. Nobody played
well that day. I attended the 1985 Leinster final between Laois and
Dublin and I remember thinking that I could have been and should have
been out there. I scanned through the programme and looked out on the
pitch, and I knew in my heart that Meath should have been contesting
that final. I broke three bones in my hand in September 1985 and was
out injured for a few months. Then when the '86 panel was announced,
I was not on the sheet. Sean dispensed with my services and brought in
some new faces.*

Laois had won the National League title in '85. They had talent.
Laois, also, had a team which really enjoyed the sort of physical
contest which developed on the day. They had skill in abundance
in the form of Colm and Gerry Browne, and they also had muscle,
and could afford to bring John Costelloe and Michael Dempsey,
both mountains of men, into the game when ball-winning became
particularly aggressive. Three points down at half time, Meath had
lost team captain J.J. McCormack, one of the better performing
players, just before the change of ends, and with Boylan urging for
a big finish from his players, Laois cracked home goals in the 51st
and 52nd minutes from Pascal Doran and Willie Brennan. Brian
Nerney had bottled Colm O'Rourke up completely at the other end
of the field and allowed him only one point, and with Liam Smith
all at sea because of his injury, and finally replaced in the 47th
minute, there was no chance of a Meath flourish. Meath managed
only seven points over the 70 minutes, and by the 60th minute the
Meath supporters were making their way to the exit gates. They'd
seen enough. Aiden Crickley had enjoyed a fine first half on Sean

Dempsey, but on such a landmark day for Meath football for all the wrong reasons it was doubtful if he would ever be forgiven for losing his marker for Laois's first goal. It was a great goal from Doran. Only Meath people blamed Crickley, who was brought up to the front in the closing minutes and showed good composure to slot over a point with his left foot. In 1986, when Meath were back in the Leinster final against Dublin, Crickley was among the Meath supporters back on the terrace. The magnificence of playing in a Leinster final was as far away from him in '86 as it had been in '85 and '84. Crickley had been in the wrong place in the wrong year for Meath football. If he had been introduced to the team in '84 or '86 he would probably have been around the place, getting in and out of the team, for two or three years at the very worst. His heart was heavy in '86, but his clubmate from Moynalvey, Liam Harnan was always able to bring a smile to the nearest face and had quite a time explaining to people how his shoulder charge on Barney Rock in the first half of the 1986 Leinster final had smashed the collarbone of Dublin's most dangerous forward.

AIDEN CRICKLEY: *I remember Liam Harnan's shoulder on Barney Rock that day in '86. Rock had to go off with a broken collarbone. After that, if you asked Liam about Barney Rock, he would reply by saying, 'Who? Barney Rubble you mean?' There were obviously huge regrets, sadness that I was not involved, but these things happen. I knew I had the ability and that I was good enough to be still involved, even if it was as a sub.*
I remember going to McDonald's pub in Clonee after the game and it was a favourite haunt of some of the Meath players at the time. Anyway, I was sitting there and in walks Gerry McEntee, Joe Cassells and Liam

Harnan. McEntee came up to me and put his arms around me and said, 'Jaysus Aiden, you could be still involved. I feel for you that you are not involved.' I thought it was very nice of him to come over and say that. It was a measure of the man that he didn't forget me and that in his own moment of triumph he took time out to come over and have a chat with me. Joe came over as well and we all chatted for a bit.

I was going with a girl up in Dublin when we won the All-Ireland the next year and we got two Hill 16 tickets, and we were just crushed for the entire game. We were like sardines in a tin up there. Mick Lyons's block from Jimmy Kerrigan was superb that day. Mick went right down to his toe to block. Kerrigan could have scored a goal and I think if he had, the match would have been over. The game was about 20 minutes on and Cork were four points in front. Kerrigan broke through and I just caught a glimpse of Lyons. He was outnumbered. There was a Cork forward standing to his right and Lyons briefly glanced over to him. Meanwhile, Kerrigan got closer and closer to the square, with no Meath backs to be seen anywhere. Lyons suddenly burst out and blocked the shot. He threw his entire body in the way. The ball broke and Meath went away up the field with it. I still firmly believe that Lyons' block was the inspiration behind that All-Ireland win.

I had attended the first three games between Meath and Dublin in '91 but I was at a wedding in Cavan for the fourth match. But I remember everybody at the wedding watched the game on TV in Sharkey's Hotel in Virginia. The bride and groom and all watched the game. It was a great atmosphere. Most of the people were shouting for Meath, but being in Cavan there were a few Dublin fans also. Anybody but Meath! Anyway, I remember looking at the screen as the move for Foley's goal began. It was just awesome and when he scored the place erupted. Wedding? What wedding? For a few moments the game was all that *mattered. It made the day extra special and we all had a good few drinks that night up in Cavan.*

Sean Boylan survived the push against him which gathered strength in the second half of the summer of 1985. He kept Reynolds and Brennan as his selectors and, together, in the 'Last Chance saloon', they created the game plan which would land Meath their first Leinster Championship in 16 years. In 1986 Meath's starting 15 would look quite different. Boylan had always been fearless in scouting the county's intermediate and junior clubs for players and, once more, he refused to look in the usual places for new blood. When Meath opened the National League Division One campaign against Kildare in Navan in October of '85 there was a completely new half-back line in the form of Des Lane, Liam Harnan and Terry Ferguson, with Martin O'Connell still in Siberia! Marty wore the No. 13 jersey that afternoon in the absence of Colm O'Rourke and, indeed, he still had a troubled 12 months ahead of him trying to convince Sean that he could become one of the greatest half-backs in the history of Gaelic football. Stan Gibney from Ratoath played full-forward. It would be another month before Brian Stafford from Kilmainhamwood made his debut, and another six months before the 18-year old P.J. Gillic from Carnaross would get his big chance on the senior team. John McEnroe and Declan Mullen from Oldcastle were also invited onto the squad. Boylan loved the element of surprise. He loved surprising young lads around the county by inviting them into the Meath dressing room, and he got a great kick out of seeing the faces of those present in that same dressing room when a strange face appeared in the door. Therefore, one afternoon, when a tall, slim, blond kid stepped out of Boylan's own car for a training session on Bettystown beach, Gerry McEntee had no reason to disbelieve that this was some new midfielder the boss had come across. That's what team masseur and Boylan's trusty lieutenant Martin 'Mochie' Regan told McEntee. From 50 yards away, at the opposite end of the car park in the Neptune Hotel, the new kid was getting the McEntee stare! 'He's a midfielder!' stated Mochie, matter of factly, as he walked past McEntee to the changing rooms.

There were always midfielders coming onto the squad. Tony Gleeson from Ratoath, for instance, had replaced Joe Cassells in the 1-16 to 0-3 victory over Kildare which marked the start of the new 1985-86 League campaign. Gleeson was a big block of a man, who was strong under the ball, though not the best mover around the field. Now, this blond kid was with the Meath squad on the strand at Bettystown and when Boylan told everybody to run, just run, and keep running, Gerry was out in front – not Gerry McEntee – but the new boy who had been introduced to everyone as Gerry who was already miles out in front of almost everybody.

FINIAN MURTAGH: *Oh God! Bettystown. Gerry Reilly! He's from Dunboyne. He went to Villanova, and ran for Ireland in the 1,500 metres in the Olympics. I remember Sean bringing him to Bettystown one day to train us, and sure, Jaysus Christ, this fella would run four million miles and here we were trying to keep up with him. He had us running up the beach. It's grand until you meet the soft sand, then, oh Jaysus, he had us up around the dunes!*

That's one thing about Sean. He might have seemed off the wall at the time but he was very original. There was no such thing as following other county teams. I always got the impression that he would never have any-

thing prepared coming to a training session. The first thing that came into his head, we would go and do it, but everybody would go and do it! There wouldn't be a question asked. There wouldn't be guys going, 'Jaysus Sean, what the f*** are you at here?' Privately maybe, but not to him.

MATTIE McCABE: *Gerry Reilly from Dunboyne, the runner, also came over to train us a few nights. Most of us would stay with him for a while but then he'd take off. Liam Smith was a decent runner and he'd be about the only one that would keep up with Gerry. Training was good because Sean would regularly vary where we'd go. Some evenings we'd be down at the Hill of Tara. Some evenings over in Bettystown where you'd have to go out into the water. One time it was in the middle of October and it was freezing, but Sean told us all to go out into the water. If he told you to do it, you would have to do it. You'd rarely disagree. I often think a lot of managers nowadays lack that same authority and the same respect that Sean had. It was vital and I think it stopped a lot of players on the borderline from falling away or getting an attitude.*

Gerry McEntee, still, was not amused when he was informed that Gerry O'Reilly had the Olympic Games in his sights, and not the Meath No. 8 or No. 9 jerseys. There was so much activity in the squad that everyone was on their toes. Everyone was edgy. And everyone was hurting as training sessions took on a fiercesome quality. By the end of 1985 Meath were heading for the National League quarter-finals thanks to a series of impressive results, but on the training field Sean Boylan had his players engaged in the greatest contest of their lives.

LIAM HAYES: *It was like someone flicked a switch. There was always a fair amount of silly stuff in Sean's training sessions up until the end of '85 – things he would be trying out, off the wall stuff which might look a lot more difficult than it actually was but we started doing sessions all of a sudden which were shocking in their intensity. We were in Gormanston College for a period, and they had four or five playing fields on an open piece of parkland. He had us sprinting the length of two or three fields at a time and literally doing two or three times the amount of work we had ever done up to that in training.*

I'm a firm believer that faces and arses tell you everything you need to know about someone's fitness, one or the other, take your pick. If you look at photos of the Meath team before '86 you will see jolly, normal faces. But from '86 on, it's a whole different look. The team pictures have guys with sunken eyes and hollow cheeks. Look at those pics and you'd think you were looking at a bunch of athletes, a group of milers rather than a load of footballers.

Chapter Three:

1986

If Finian Murtagh was able to find it within himself to forgive Sean Boylan, then how on earth could any other Meath player over the last 20 years stand up in public and quibble? God knows there were times when different men wished Boylan a speedy exit in his life as Meath boss. Others, like O'Malley and Flynn, might behave like teenage kids from time to time, and spend weeks nursing the great wound of being misunderstood. Hayes and Boylan were very close, but Hayes seemed to turn up right on time, every single year, for one mighty, sell-out row with the Meath football manager. Boylan would annoy the hell out of several other players too. McEntee loved him, but occasionally resembled a man who wanted to box him. O'Rourke? Well, theirs perhaps was the simplest, but also the most interesting relationship of all. O'Rourke and Boylan seemed to content themselves early on that they would always have the height of respect for one another without ever quite falling into each other's arms for very long periods.

Great managers cannot make great friends of every footballer they send onto the field, though Boylan tried hard, tried his damndest in the early years. He never gave up trying, in truth, but quickly enough he found a way of distributing the harsh medicine without ruining too many relationships. Ask Donal Smith! Meath's first-choice goalkeeper arrived for training for the 1994 Leinster final, togged out, ready to boot-up, and was told it was all over for him, there and then, before he even got out of his car.

For the guts of two hundred years Boylan offered Jody Devine a teaspoonful of the yukky stuff and Jody never lost faith in either Boylan or the glory of being a Meath footballer. At the height of his career Jody Devine ran onto the field to help out a Meath team which was dying on its feet and six points down against Kildare, late in the 1997 Leinster Championship. Jody scored four of the sweetest points ever witnessed down at the Canal End and single-handedly saved the day for the County, and got another big spoonful of the dark, awful stuff for his efforts. The flying wing forward was at the peak of his footballing life, but Boylan by then in the late '90s, was arguably the greatest Gaelic football manager of modern times, right up there at the same table as Kevin Heffernan and Mick O'Dwyer, and what could a footballer say?

When 1986 dawned, however, Sean Boylan knew that his career as Meath manager might have only months remaining. Unless Meath won something, he was kaput. That something was going to have to be a Leinster title. The county was ready. Boylan had three summers under his belt already. He had been forgiven for '85. And in the early weeks and months of 1986, he was utterly unforgiving when he got out onto the training fields. Finian Murtagh, same as the rest, ran himself into the ground evening after evening after evening. Fino had been on the Meath Under-14 team which won a Leinster title in 1976. He had soldiered with Liam Hayes, J.J. McCormack and Frank Foley. The same foursome were on the Meath minor team which won a Leinster title in 1980, when John McEnroe and Colm Coyle were also on board. In 1986 Fino was entering his sixth year as a Meath senior footballer and in '86, same as ever before, Murtagh did everything which was asked of him, starring in two of the three biggest games Meath would have to play that year.

Those two games were against Dublin, against the one team which always appeared on the end of year report card of every Meath footballer. In the first game, in the National League quarter-final in March, Finian Murtagh kicked three points (two of them from free-kicks). In the second game, in the Leinster final in July, Finian Murtagh again kicked three points (one of them from a free-kick). In the third big game of '86, this young man scored one point from play. His attendance at training all year was excellent, his manner very good, his sense of humour spot on for a Navanman. Fino's proud mother and father had every reason to be delighted with their son. He was still a man, a footballer for 'the big day'. He still had that gunslinger's nerve which saw him aim and take eight points against Dublin in the Leinster Championship back in 1983. Yep, sure had! And Fino would remain a Meath footballer for another five years. He'd retire in 1992 with a clatter of Leinster medals, five in all, and two All-Ireland winners' medals.

Meath would play in the All-Ireland final in 1987, reappear in the All-Ireland final in '88, come back to Croker for a replay three weeks later, quickly win a way back into the 1990 All-Ireland final, and slog their way to the 1991 All-Ireland final. Five All-Ireland finals in five years, and Finian 'Fino' Murtagh did not get onto the field for even one minute of one All-Ireland final.

And Fino forgives Sean Boylan – forgives him and thanks him.

FINIAN MURTAGH: *I was in Navan the first night he came in. I remember it well, all of us gathered under the stand in Pairc Tailteann. One of the lads there was a fella called Paul Murray, a very, very good footballer, but he was working long hours driving lorries at the time – an excellent, talented player but he never could find the time to train. And that night he said he couldn't give the commitment, couldn't be there every night because he was away on the lorries. And that was that. He was gone. Straightaway you knew that if you weren't prepared to put it in for Sean, you wouldn't be part of it.*

I remember Paul Murray being brought back onto the panel a couple of years later and he was there for one training session in Bettystown. One of the greatest memories I have is of that night. He sat down for the meal after training that night and the craic was good. This fella was a real character and he had us in tears laughing the whole night, telling jokes and stories. And I don't think he was ever seen again after that.

He (Boylan) had a great affinity with the old Meath team. I'd say Mattie (Gilsenan) was a god to Sean when he was younger, because Mattie was a star! Mattie would be down in the dressing room every training session. But Mattie wasn't the kind of fella who wanted attention – 'Look at me, I've won a couple of All-Irelands.' That wasn't him at all. Mattie was a real players' man. He'd have a quiet word with you. He was a lovely man.

Mick O'Brien was over the team before Sean came in. Now, Mick was a genius. He was in charge of Walterstown, who reached two All-Ireland club finals. Mick was very deep. Up here, he was great, a great coach, but he wasn't the best man to get it across to the lads.

71

To be honest with you, a lot of fellas thought Mick was too deep. But he was a genius, an absolute genius. He was way ahead of his time, tactically, the way he trained! With most managers then, you'd go out and run 20 lads off the field and have a kick-around. That wasn't Mick O'Brien. All his training was done in a 40 yard square, and that's exactly what they're doing now.

Playing the angled ball was another thing. Sure you might as well have been talking to the wall as talking to the lads about playing an angled ball. Mick O'Brien would eat a wing forward if he got a ball and played it into the same corner. He had to play the ball into the far corner. That's text book stuff now, but sure years ago that sort of thing just wasn't done.

Sean had great enthusiasm. He'd come in and be real bubbly. He'd be talkin' and laughin' and jokin'. No matter who was there I would have responded, but Sean had a great way about him. No matter what he asked, you'd say, 'Yeah, I'd do it for you Sean.'

Being a sub is never easy. At the time, you're mad with yourself, mad with Sean for not picking you, but when you look back on it, if you're honest with yourself, you know you just weren't good enough. You just hadn't got it, and he was right to leave you sitting on the line. That's how I feel.

LIAM HAYES: *There are some things you remember about your career and football games you played in, but mostly you forget whole chunks of time. Funny, one of my clearest memories of the whole series against Dublin in '91 was Fino Murtagh coming up to me in the dressing room, grabbing my shoulder and whispering into my ear. I was captain, and I wasn't playing well near the end of the four games. I wasn't playing well in training either. My confidence had been shot by a couple of things that had happened, but Fino whispered into my ear, before we went out onto* *the field, before I spoke to the lads in the dressing room. He quoted Ian Botham to me. He said, 'Real class never disappears. If you have class, you have it all your life.' I'd known Fino for 15 years and he knew me, and he knew I was in trouble. It was a great thing to hear, simple but great. I didn't play all that well against Dublin that afternoon either, mind you.*

FINIAN MURTAGH: *When we played Dublin in the four games in '91, I was a sub for the first day but I got injured on the Tuesday night after the game and couldn't play the second game. I wasn't togged out for the second or third game, but I was mad keen to play. A week before the fourth game was my first weekend back training and as things hadn't been going well, they (the selectors) probably thought, 'We'll try something different.'*
I was foolish as it turned out. Sean said tog out and I said, 'Yeah, that's great.' Padraig Lyons got injured then and they put me on, and sure I wasn't near fit. I remember going out for the first ball and Mick Kennedy beating me by ten yards. I thought, 'Oh Jaysus, where am I going here?' I was mad, mad keen to play and Sean was probably mad keen to get me on but sure I knew after ten minutes that I wasn't near fit. I hadn't trained for four weeks. I was taken off again, in the first half.
That was the hardest time I've ever experienced. People going to Meath matches for the last 20 years, they'll always remember that day. But I'll always remember it for completely different reasons. For most people, that was their best day, but not for me. That was my worst day.
Being brought on and being taken off again, it was the pits. I lasted about 10 or 15 minutes. They were right to take me off. I wasn't able to play. I was mad at the time, but when I look back on it, it wasn't mad about being taken off, just mad at not being right. The biggest day for

30 years for Meath football and it was my worst day!

Ask anybody, and they'll always mention that goal, Kevin Foley's goal – and I can't even remember it. I've seen it on television, but at the time I had my head down. I wasn't even watching the game. I was sitting on the line, outside the dug-out, and I wasn't even watching it. There I was, roaring my eyes out in the dressing room after it was all over. Sean and Tony Brennan were very good, but sure what could Sean say? He knew I wasn't right, and I knew I wasn't right. It was just the fact that I hoped I would be right, took a chance. And it all went wrong.

Jinksy more or less took the position I had in '86, left half-forward. P.J. (Gillic) came in then. He was only a young fella in '86.

I'll never forget the All-Ireland semi-final against Derry in '87. We weren't going well in the first half and Jinksy was having a nightmare. I was sitting on the bench delighted, and Sean tells me to warm up. So I'm warming up, warming up. The next thing, Jinxy gets a ball on the halfway line, beats three or four players and kicks it over the bar. I come running down and I looked at Sean, and he smiled, and I said, 'OK, I'll sit back down again.' I got on in the second half but if I was ever going to get in for the final, that was it. That made Jinksy. He was always capable of doing that. He's a bit like Ollie Murphy. Ollie mightn't do anything for half an hour, but then he'd kill you in ten minutes.

If I had played two minutes in an All-Ireland final, I'd have died a happy man. That's the one thing that irks me, in all the five finals I was involved in, '87, two in '88, '90 and '91, I never even got a minute in any of them. That's the one thing that sticks with me

In '87 and '88 I thought I had a chance, '87 especially, but not in '90 and '91. They brought on Coyler in '87, and Coyler had been away (in the United States). It didn't upset me because I was good friends with Coyler but O'Rourke was giving out that he got in in front of me. I guess

Liam Hayes, Ogie Moran, Bernie Flynn and Colm O'Rourke, August 24, 1986

Dave Synnott and Finian Murtagh, July 27, 1986

things were too close, they probably didn't want to risk me. I have the medals but the big regret I have is that I never played in any All-Ireland final.

The biggest thing for me was the '86 Leinster final. That was the start of it. We hadn't won anything up to that. We knew after the '86 league game against Dublin that we were well capable of doing it. That game really sold it to us that we were capable of competing with them.

BERNIE FLYNN: *I was close to Finian and I would have known a lot of what he was going through. Nobody knew what Finian Murtagh had given for the Meath jersey. He was so committed and dedicated. He was a great Meath player for years. His record shows that, but he never got the recognition. He had a rough enough ride. Padraig Lyons the same, and Donal Smyth. Finian at the time would have probably felt that he wasn't being treated fairly, and that would have rubbed off on me a little bit as well.*

P.J. GILLIC: *The day Meath went down very badly in '85 against Laois, I was with the minor team that was playing before them against Longford. I can remember talking to Gerry McEntee after that game. I had glandular fever earlier in the year – I didn't actually play in that minor game – and I remember having a conversation with him about the illness, and he was very disappointed with their defeat by Laois. He was even talking about packing it in. When the team started back for the League, word came that I was to go into training, and I remember Gerry McEntee advising me at the time to take a complete break because of the illness. I didn't go in initially, so it was only the last game or so before Christmas that I joined them. I had met Sean Boylan once before. It could have been maybe earlier that year when the minors were starting,* when I had a problem with my knee. Someone at the time probably knew Sean and I got an appointment to see him. I can remember sitting above in this little waiting room for maybe two hours, and Mockie Regan eventually came in and put two glasses of this brew (Sean's brew) in front of me. 'Drink that,' he said. I remember taking a sip of it and, Jesus, it was rotten. Desperate stuff. You'd probably acquire a taste for it after a year maybe, but I remember thinking, 'I can't drink that.' I'll never forget it. There was one of those plants that your grandmother used to have, Busy Lizzie or something like that, sitting on the table. Well, I just chucked the two glasses down the side of it. I don't know what the idea was, what it was going to do for my knee. Sure I hadn't even told them what was wrong with me! Sean eventually came in and, whatever he did, he sorted out my knee. Later, I would drink the brews. They were some kind of herbal brew. I actually took quite a lot of it after the glandular fever and it did help me.

Shortly after I joined the lads, I broke my collarbone and I missed the next game, which was against Kerry down in Tralee. That was the first trip I was on with the panel. It was a very wet day – I think the fire brigade were pumping water off the field down there. And then, after that, I played the rest of the League campaign. We reached the League quarter-final against Dublin, and there were only two or three points in it at the finish, and I think we gained more from that game than any of the other games before. We felt that we had a good chance of beating them that day and everybody felt that if Meath were ever going to beat Dublin, that was the year.

Brian Stafford was on the field against Dublin in the National League quarter-final that year, but he was not yet wearing the No. 14 jersey, and he was not the team's free-taker. That role fell to Liam Hayes on the left of the field and switched to Finian Murtagh on the right, though Hayes took the kicks in the middle of the field and was also charged with taking the penalty kicks. The midfielder scored from the penalty spot and with one free-kick from 35 yards out that afternoon. Hayes scored five long-range frees against Wicklow in the Leinster semi-final, one free kick in the opening minutes of the Leinster final from 60 yards out, and two more from about 30 yards range in the All-Ireland semi-final against Kerry. Murtagh was chipping in with two or three points per game as well, but the team needed a free-taker, one free-taker. It needed a better return from dead balls.

In the No. 14 jersey which Brian Stafford would also inherit at the end of 1986 was Stan Gibney, from Ratoath, one of Boylan's surprises, a big-shouldered wing-back who had been on the Meath minor team which lost to Dublin in the Leinster final of '79, and hadn't been heard of since. Stan sailed into the dressing room, smile on his face, amusement at being chucked in with the so-called stars of Meath football. He was a farmer, but in the Meath dressing room he was a stand-up, sit-down comic. In the most gruelling year in the life of every other Meath footballer, everyone, every night, liked to see Stan. He didn't score against Dublin in the League quarter-final, but he won lots of possession against Gerry Hargan and gave nearly all of it away to the first Meathman he saw. He was no Colm O'Rourke.

O'Rourke had been away from the team all winter, as was McEntee, and they both watched from the Hogan Stand as Meath typically got stuck into the Dubs, treating themselves to four of the eight bookings made by Antrim referee John Gough. Untypically, Meath played Dublin off the field, and despite being decked by yet another Barney Rock goal after only three minutes and falling five points behind by half-time, there was no great panic. The team kept its head. Incredibly. Even Mick Lyons made his way across the halfway line and tipped over a point in the second half. There was no fear, because a young, experimental team was not going to take it to heart if they lost to Dublin. Great Meath teams had been losing to all kinds of Dublin teams for five thousand years. Another defeat wasn't going to be catastrophic, was hardly going to hurt much, and Boylan made this very clear to the boys before they left the dressing room. The door of the dressing room was perfectly safe, for once. Hayes stroked his penalty past John O'Leary 15 minutes into the second period. That left it a one-point game. Hayes also had the last kick of the game and the ball just went to the left of the post, leaving Dublin with a 2-8 to 1-10 winning scoreline.

Rock and Tom Carr had scored goals for Dublin in the first 15 minutes of the game. So, lesson number one from the game was the oldest lesson of all – stop them scoring goals and you'd never know what might happen! The game also told the Meath team something else, however. There was no Brian Mullins on the field any longer. He was managing the team, and there was a world of difference having 'Big Brian' on the opposite side of the white line. In that second half of the League quarter-final, Meath were in the company of a Dublin team which did not have any natural leader on the field. Gerry Hargan was a great guy to know, but also a quiet guy. Same with centre-back Noel McCaffrey. In the middle of the field, John Kearns had never been awarded the deepest faith of Dublin managers and Jim Bissett was a new boy. Carr wasn't on the team all that long either and was still finding all sorts of jerseys with all sorts of numbers being tossed at him before games. Rock, McNally and Duff were all great forwards, no doubt about it, all of them footballers who would be considered nice guys by the Meath team when relations between the two camps fully thawed in 1991 and '92. That evening, after that one-point defeat, there was greater hope for the Meath football team than ever before.

DONAL SMITH: *It was the most important game as far as we were concerned that year, the League quarter-final. That was the time we figured out we could beat Dublin. John O'Leary made a save from Brian Stafford that was just unbelievable. He flicked it over his head, but somehow O'Leary got back under it again and clawed the ball out before it hit the net. I don't know how he managed it but it was a superb save. Had that gone in we probably would have beaten Dublin, and I believe the save was the difference on the day. But our performance drove us on, and we felt we could now beat Dublin.*

TERRY FERGUSON: *The Leinster final was the one we were all aiming for. For years and years we wanted to win a Leinster and to face Dublin, of course, was an added incentive. We had worked very hard prior to the game. I remember we were training up in Gormanstown and he had us sprinting across three football fields instead of one, corner to corner. The training at that time was pure savage. So fitness was certainly not going to beat us and we kinda knew at the back of our mind that we had played Dublin in a League quarter-final on Easter Sunday and they just beat us by a point or two, fortunate, just barely beat us. And we knew from there on that we were good enough to beat these boys. So we got to the Leinster final and conditions I remember were absolutely terrible. They were brutal, wind and rain, lashing rain.*

Stan Gibney, like many players before him, like Aiden Circkley in 1985, spent one year on the Meath team. But Stan won a Leinster senior football medal. His was a good year. It was an eye-opener, in the big games up in Croke Park and mostly every night of the week at Meath training sessions. Stan saw madness and he saw ambition, an abundance of each quality, all rolled into one great effort. At the end of the 12 months, all Stan wanted to do was go to bed and get some sleep.

STAN GIBNEY: *I came into the panel in October of 1985. That period marked the end for players like Eamon Barry and Frank O'Sullivan and guys like that, and Sean was obviously trying to knock a new tune out of the team. A lot of the old guard had been cleared out at that stage and new lads like myself, Brian Stafford, Terry Ferguson, Liam Harnan and David Beggy were coming in. We were the 'Boylan Babes' I suppose, but within the team there was a certain sense of the 'Where do we go from here?' about us. I remember sitting down with Liam Hayes, Gerry McEntee and Mick Lyons one evening and asking that exact question after the poor Championship Meath had had in 1985. I remember going down to play Kerry in the League and it was mad. We had to get a train down but when we got off there was no bus or anything to bring us to the game so we had to get lifts and cram into cars and all types of stuff. Some guys even had to walk to the ground. The game was delayed because the fire brigade were trying to pump the water off the pitch.*

We lost to Dublin in the League quarter-final but we played decent against them. Then the Championship started and it was a really bad summer that year in terms of weather. That made the training even harder and Sean used to like to run us fairly ragged. It was like nothing

I'd ever been involved in before. It got to a stage where I'd go training and then come home and go to bed for the rest of the day.

Sean had us training over on Bettystown beach. One evening, one local golf club official over there came over giving out to us. We thought he had come over to compliment us, but instead he started bawling at us. We didn't exactly look the part training in front of the golf club, I suppose (the team was actually training on sand dunes in which the golf club had invested a small fortune). We trained three nights in a row in Bettystown and I remember the second of them. It was in May and the wind was howling. It was bloody freezing but Sean says to us, 'Right lads, get the boots off and into the water.' It was so cold, but he kept pushing us and pushing us further. So we were walking out with the water up to our knees. Lads at this stage had to hold their tracksuits up to their hips to keep them dry. We were out there in the freezing cold for a few minutes until Sean said to us, 'OK lads, whose got pains in their legs?' The thing was, none of us would have known if we had pains because we couldn't even feel our legs at that stage!

Another night, we were down in Gormanstown training and, again, he was pushing us very hard. It was like when you're drinking and you hit the wall and you can't go any further! Well, this night in particular, we were all off running one way and Sean shouts at us to take a turn a certain way, but we all just went off in the opposite direction. The brains weren't focussing in at all. We were just wrecked. Sean was just shaking his head looking at us.

It's gas. I watched Eamon Dunphy and Brendan Menton on RTE after the World Cup in 2002 talking about the FAI and how certain things weren't done right in Saipan, like getting proper training facilities and that type of thing. Well, we were a bit like the paupers in 1986 in Meath ourselves, going around looking for somewhere to train. Navan was *being done up at the time. We were playing Carlow in the first round of the Championship and money was so tight that the County Board asked us if we'd mind forfeiting the steak dinner after the match. They wanted to use the money to fly Gerry McEntee home from Newcastle for the game. The lads gave up the grub so that Gerry could play. It was the way things were. But none of us minded, it was all for the cause.*

I kept saying to myself at the time, 'How do Kerry keep going and going and doing this year after year?' Most of us lads had no more than say 15 miles to travel to training but it was still tough. I was just thinking what it must have been like for Kerry after all those years at the top. The furthest any of us had to travel was for the likes of Mochie Regan and a few 'hairies' from Dunboyne. There was one or two 'foreigners' living in Dublin too, but I think of all the counties we were in the ideal position.

I remember in the build-up to the big games in '86 young Paddy Reynolds and a few of the kids tripping up in the long grass. It was funny because they were the ones standing behind the goals catching the balls, but ten years later they were the ones hitting the scores themselves.

The Leinster final against Dublin, it lashed rain! Even the dug-outs were full of water and we got drenched in there. We got the win though and that's what it was all about. I only had the one year with Meath and was pretty much gone in 1987, so being involved in that Leinster final win was the high point for me. Physically, I wasn't able for it. I had a very bad back all along and I just couldn't stick it anymore

Sean brought in young lads who had no fear. That year was the big turning point for Meath football. There was no fear after that and they proved it in 1987 and '88. It was a pity I wasn't involved more, but the body just couldn't take it. Even before one junior game against Cork I had to have an injection in my back. The standard of training was just something else. It was as much as I could do to milk the cows in the morning, go to training and then go back to bed for the evening. Players gave up so much I'm sure the schedule is even tougher now and I really don't know how they do it. I remember talking to Liam Harnan and he was saying he couldn't cut silage one year because of all the training he had to do. The effort and the personal sacrifice that went into playing for the county was something else. As a farmer myself it was very hectic because you'd be doing physical work anyway.

Once I was playing a club game for Ratoath while I was with Meath and I could hardly run. I was expected to be the one having a great game because I was with the county team, but I was wrecked. Sean was in the middle of building us up for a big Meath game in two or three weeks time but in the meantime you were just jaded. It was just like training race horses. You don't put them into a big race two weeks before while they're in the middle of a training programme.

I remember one wet Tuesday evening down in Dalgan and I can still see Bernie Flynn wearing the tracksuit in my mind's eye. Anyway, Sean told us all to go down on our bellies on the end-line and set us the task of racing up the field on our hands and elbows. It was sopping wet and, literally, as soon as we lay down on the grass we were drenched, but Sean didn't care. Bernie Flynn took off and won the race, but by the time he was up the pitch his tracksuit was down around his ankles and he looked right stupid. I was left miles back because while Bernie was a smallish lad I had a fair bit of weight on me and found the going tough. Mick Lyons was a good character and I got on well with him. He said at the time, 'You'll be long enough bent over the railings like an S-hook watching the games, so you might as well try and give it everything while you can.'

Sean was a real players' man though. He'd always train with us.

Another night, Joe Cassells or Mick Lyons ran into him on the pitch by accident. Whichever one of them it was, he was sent flying and we all rolled about the place laughing. We were telling him he was too old to be running around with young lads. It was a big joke, but a few days later he was on crutches and it appeared that he had twisted his knee. We felt a bit bad about laughing so much then!

I didn't spend long with the panel, but I brought great memories away with me. Terry Ferguson, for instance, was only a young lad, but it used to amaze me how long it took him to put on a bandage on his knee or wherever. He was like an auld woman! Then there was Brian Stafford. It was a great laugh when he came in because one evening we were training and we were all doing press-ups. We all just stopped because we saw Sean standing over Brian and we were wondering what was going on. As it happened, Brian just wasn't able to do a press-up. I don't know why. He had a long slopey back on him, so maybe that was the reason. There was some turn-around though. This was the same player who'd end up tapping points over the bar from 50 metres out not too long after.

At the time none of us was looking too far forward. The team was living from day to day. Winning the Leinster in 1986 was just awesome and capped it all off for many players. I remember one time I was in Phibsboro with Liam Hayes and I asked him who was going to mark Jack O'Shea against Kerry in the All-Ireland semi-final. Gerry McEntee tipped me on the shoulder and said, 'Actually Jack O'Shea's going to be marking me!' That's the way it turned out as well because Gerry was catching balls up in the clouds that day. It was the start of something special.

Led by their friendly giant Tommy Dwyer, Carlow put up a great fight in the first round of the Leinster Championship. With seconds remaining, and Carlow attacking, only three points separated the teams and Meath were out on their feet. Boylan and his boys trooped out of Dr Cullen Park tired and happy men – though 1-15 to 1-12 was hardly the stuff of future Leinster champions. Dismissing Wicklow by 1-17 to 0-11 in the semi-final was a little more like it, though Martin O'Connell was still parachuting into foreign parts. He joined the game in the second half and took up the No. 13 position. Joe Cassells, after a lifetime at centrefield was switched to right corner-back against Wicklow, and the sight of the elegant, big fielder with No. 2 on his back had Meath's nearest and dearest football fans shouting for an explanation. Boylan was, in fact, preparing for the Leinster final and the fact that he wanted Cassells prepared for the task of following Dublin No. 14 Tom Carr all over the field in the big game just down the road.

It was 16 years since Meath had lifted the Leinster title, and defeats in provincial finals in 1972, '73, '74, '76, '77 and '84 meant that supporters driving in on the Dunshaughlin and Ashbourne roads towards the city were a silent, nervous enough bunch on the morning and early afternoon of the game. It was overcast. Weathermen were promising rain. Enda McManus and Tommy Dowd, who did not know one another from Adam, and who would play on an All-Ireland winning team ten years later, with Dowd as captain, watched from Hill 16. They were deep into enemy territory.

ENDA McMANUS: *I was on Hill 16. There were five of us together on the Hill but it was just great to be there. Colm O'Rourke's point at the* *end was great. It was wet and miserable, but we had won a Leinster title.*

TOMMY DOWD: *Not until then did it all start blooming. I was on Hill 16. That's all I can remember. I remember the team coming back to Navan on the Monday night after it. There were great celebrations. It was all new to Meath because we hadn't won anything in my generation.*

Colm Brady would also win his first All-Ireland medal in '96, coming back from a horrific knee injury and chasing down Mayomen all over the field, but a decade earlier he was in the kitchen in his family home in Simonstown, just outside Navan town.

COLM BRADY: *I wasn't actually at it. I was listening to that game at home in the kitchen, literally hanging on every word. You could sense that it was going to happen, that there was something happening in Meath football around then. Oh, I went berserk when we beat them. I spent the '87 and '88 finals up on the Hill. That was the spot. The colour was one thing I remember. When a county is making a breakthrough, they are the years most colour will be in evidence. You couldn't have seen any more green and gold going to a match. Absolutely incredible. It was just manic. I would have finished secondary school, just starting in college, and the pride – you were mad even to just get out of your own county, and have your colours on. I was studying in Waterford at the time, with loads of Dubs and every other county who hated us – even then! - and I remember going with my flag across Waterford city, running up the streets with another Meath man who was brave enough, and fellas trying to mow us out of it in cars. Just that pride was an* *amazing feeling.*

Frank Foley was a Meath selector in 1996. Ten years earlier he was not Meath's greatest supporter in the whole wide world – he was 3,000 miles away on the day of the '86 Leinster final. The Foleys, Kevin and Frank would both play for Meath in the 1987 Leinster Championship, but on that drenched, historic day on 27 July, 1986, Frank Foley was just a little bit curious as to the result of the Leinster final.

FRANK FOLEY: *Before I came onto the panel late in 1986 obviously I wasn't playing, so I hadn't that much interest in what was going on with the Meath footballers. I wouldn't remember too much of the early days of Sean Boylan in that regard. I suppose it was only in '85 when my brother Kevin was brought onto the panel and started to make a bit of progress that I began to take a big interest in turn.*

It was great satisfaction for me to get on the panel because I had played quite a bit of minor and Under-21 football for Meath, and then disappeared. Thankfully, Sean opted to pull me out of the wilderness and give me a chance. I think in a lot of ways 1986 was a do-or-die year for Sean considering what had happened in '85 when Meath were beaten by Laois in the Championship. It's hard to think now that he was only there for four years at that stage because it seems that Sean has been in charge of Meath forever!

I remember the time just coming up to the 1987 Leinster final and I thought I was getting very close to the first 15. I was thinking to myself that if maybe one or two lads got sick, then I actually stood a good chance of starting. The positions were all but filled that year though and it didn't really happen for me.

The 1986 All-Ireland semi-final against Kerry was the real turning point for the Meath team. Unfortunately, I was away in Canada for that game. I have never seen the full video of the game since, just bits and pieces from tapes, which is something I was always sorry about. I remember being in America for the Leinster final. There was a thing going on at the time that you could ring a number from over there and get the match scores from the GAA games in Ireland, a sort of pre-recorded service. I'll never forget ringing the number and hearing the voice tell me that Meath had beaten Dublin in the Leinster final in '86. I was wondering if the thing was working properly. I missed that game as well, and it was a real pity. Talk about picking a bad year to go away!

Kildare referee Seamus Aldridge had his hands full from the start, but things really became hectic for him when a heavy rain began just before half-time. There were, however, only 48 frees over the 70 minutes, of which 22 came Meath's way. Aldridge let the teams make the best of a field which was completely sodden by the middle of the second half. The all-consuming talking point at the end of the game was Liam Harnan's fair, truck-like shoulder charge on Barney Rock just before half-time. Aldridge refused the Dublin free-taker any time for treatment or sympathy, waving him back up onto his feet. But Rock's collarbone had been shattered unbeknownst to the match official. The entire Dublin team had taken the heaviest blow imaginable.

Nineteen-year-old David Beggy had put Meath into the lead after four minutes. Rock had already missed with two free-kicks. The teams were level at 0-2 each when Jim Bissett fumbled and Colm O'Rourke calmly put Meath back in front. Joe Cassells was chasing Tom Carr all over the field. In front of the Meath goal it was two-on-two with Mick Lyons on Joe McNally, Padraig Lyons on Rock, an arrangement which was entirely satisfactory from Sean Boylan's point of view. Mick Kennedy fouled Bernie Flynn and Finian Murtagh put Meath two up. Twice within three minutes Rock shot over from a '45' and a free-kick to level the game again. Charlie Redmond knocked over a smart point and tapped a free-kick over the bar in Rock's absence. Dublin led 0-6 to 0-4 at half-time. The good news for the losing team was that Dublin did not even hint at a goal in the opening 35 minutes, and Liam Hayes and Gerry McEntee had a definite advantage in the middle of the field, a situation which continued into the second half and was not interrupted until Paul Clarke replaced Jim Bissett midway through the second period. And, best news of all, Rock was gone.

O'Rourke put Meath 0-7 to 0-6 ahead 17 minutes after the restart, and with 12 minutes remaining it was 0-8 to 0-7. Ciaran Duff had equalised with Dublin's sole second-half score, before Murtagh coolly restored the advantage. Dublin were still one point down, but with Meath often getting 10, 11, 12 men behind the ball, and with a goal looking completely and utterly out of the question, the margin between the teams seemed to be growing wider and wider. Ciaran Duff was wide with two free-kicks, McNally was off target with another, and wing-back Pat Canavan curled the ball wide from 25 metres out after ghosting down the middle of the Meath defence. 'I hit the ball as hard as I could because of the wind,' confessed Duff in the Dublin dressing room afterwards, 'but it was like kicking a lump of lead with a boot full of water.' When Mick Kennedy hacked the ball high out of defence in the closing minutes, Hayes fisted it back into the Dublin full-back line for O'Rourke to gather and scoop over the bar – game, set and Leinster

Championship! Gerry McEntee had only an hour to get to the airport for a 6.30 p.m. flight to London and an 8 p.m. connection to Newcastle. The doctor had to get back on his wards.

As McEntee made one final race for a taxi, Vincent Hogan was putting words together for which Meath football fans had waited a lifetime. Great hope had been born for Meath in the '70s, but in the same decade it lived and died penniless. 'This was the day that Meath at last found their footballing soul', wrote Ireland's most gifted sportswriter of modern times, noting: 'The irrational fear of failure – that has haunted their search for dignity over 16 lonely years – finally subsided. For once, they held their nerve. It was not pretty, but few ever expected it to be. All week, the word "physical" cropped up in pre-match speculation. Diplomacy knows no bounds.'

His fellow scribe Con Houlihan felt that not only had Meath advanced on the day, but Dublin had conceded ground which might take years to reclaim. 'Gone since Dublin's last All-Ireland success are Tommy Drumm, Brian Mullins and Anton O'Toole; no matter how much you scan the horizon you can not see their replacements.' What remained to be seen was exactly how much Meath had advanced, and who better to take out a measurement tape and size Meath up than Mick O'Dwyer, the boss of the greatest football team Ireland had ever seen.

GERRY McENTEE: *It was just a slog, a real slog. One of the things I remember from that match was when Tommy Conroy got the ball near the end, and he went to take a shot from about 21 yards out and I was chasing him and there were also a few others chasing him, and I dived full length to block the shot. But, by the time I got down to block him there* were four hands there before me and the ball went out for a fifty. I said to myself, 'I have to get in and make a block.' But when I dived, I can remember two Meath men had stuck their hands in before me.

Dublin actually had a few chances to win the match and it was ironic because in the past they would have won that game. They had done it to us so often before but it was crucial for us that we won. It was fantastic. It probably meant a lot more to me and some of the other players who had been around longer than it did to the new fellas on the panel. The younger players sort of expected it because they were after doing well with the under-21s and minors, but for us it was huge. I had to go straight back to England after the game. I didn't really mind or care that much as long as we won. I knew I was coming home a couple of weeks later anyway because I was finishing up over there. I had some good friends in England, so when I got back we went for a few drinks and had a few laughs. It was a great feeling.

A couple of nights before the Kerry semi-final, I went out for a meal with a friend of mine, who was home from America. We went to a restaurant in Dublin, which should have been better than it was, and I got food poisoning on the Friday night. So I rang Sean on Saturday and told him I was really sick the night before with food poisoning and he said he would be up to me in an hour. So Sean came to my house with a container full of the worst foul-smelling green liquid ever, and said, 'Right, I want you to drink all of this.' He took the lid off it, and Yvonne told us both to get out of the kitchen, so we went out to the back. He told me that it would help re-hydrate me and settle down the tummy. The problem was there was nearly a gallon of it! He told me to take my time with it, but to drink it all. So I went out, plugged my nose, drank about five cups and nearly got sick. A while later I went out again and drank some more and continued like that until I finished it all. I went to *bed for the afternoon and skipped the team session that Saturday evening. I went down for the team meeting but didn't tog out and came home and went to bed early again. I got up on the Sunday morning and was jumping out of my skin, ready for the game.*

Unfortunately, I think we approached that game not believing we could beat Kerry, but we could have beaten them. We let in a bad goal, which always seems to happen to the underdog. But even after that goal we came back and went ahead. But then they got four points in succession just before half-time and we went in two points behind at the break. I think those four points drained fellas a little. But we could have beaten Kerry, and even in the second half we could have come back and won. We had a lot of ball.

I was marking Jack O'Shea that day and played well, but I remember him scoring an absolutely wonderful point from about 40 yards out. Somebody passed the ball to him and I was a good bit away from him. I said to myself that he was never going to try a shot from there, but he did and it sailed about 20 yards over the bar. I also remember dislocating my finger tackling him and he didn't want to put it back into place. I gave him my hand and said to him, 'Here, put it back.' He glanced at my finger but didn't like the look of it and said, 'No, no, get somebody else.' So Anne Bourton came on and put it back.

COLM O'ROURKE: *All modern football in Meath can be traced back to 1986. The success of Meath since that can be put down to that day, as far as I am concerned, because a lot of what happened after wouldn't have happened if we didn't win that game. It set a standard for Meath football and it gave Meath a standing. It also created a tradition of winning which had been absent for 16 years – like no young fella in Meath had ever seen them winning a Leinster Championship until that* *time.*

We had been beaten by Dublin on a lot of occasions in the previous years. From the time I started playing we were beaten in 1976, '77, almost every year up, and Meath could never beat Dublin, so to finally win was a huge result for us. I remember scoring a point in the last minute of that game. The ball went down under Hill 16 and Mick Kennedy got it. We were a point up at the time, 0-8 to 0-7. Anyway, Mick drop-kicked the ball out into the middle of the field and Liam Hayes came running, and I have never seen a man punch a ball further in Croke Park in my life. It was dropping down in the middle of the field, somebody was going to catch it, and he came racing in and hit the ball a punch just as it was dropping and it went right back down into the Dublin half about 21 yards out. It broke down there, I got it and it was an easy job just kicking it over the bar. At that stage it was the first time I ever appreciated a Meath roar in Croke Park, because it was as if every Meath person that was at that match suddenly realised, 'Jaysus, this is one we are actually going to win!' It was a brilliant feeling.

As far as I am concerned, I celebrated that win more than any other ever after for Meath. The All-Ireland wins after didn't even compare. They were almost an anticlimax. The win in 1986 was just brilliant. I wouldn't say it meant more to us who had been playing for years than it did to the newer players. Perhaps we appreciated it more considering we had seen the days of going to play down in Limerick, Tipperary and Clare in dirty miserable auld League matches, and losing in the first round of the Championship to Longford and Wexford, so we certainly appreciated any victories. But we wouldn't have won it had the team not changed so radically between 1985 and '86. A lot of new players came in and they certainly improved things.

We played quite well that day in the semi-final against Kerry, but just a little bit of inexperience caught us out. We just weren't clever enough. A few things went wrong, like the goal before half-time, but we still played fairly well. We all respected Kerry but believed we had a great chance to win. After that there were a few more changes on the team, with Martin O'Connell, who was in the forwards, moving to wing-back. Probably the biggest change of all was Staff starting to take the frees.

FINIAN MURTAGH: *Ger Lynch was marking me in the semi-final. Going into that game, we were thinking this team is absolutely a super team. Looking back, we were well capable of beating them – it was just that we didn't believe. That's the big difference. I said that to Sean after the game, that I felt we weren't good enough to be playing on the same pitch as them. But sure, it was only in our heads.*

Coming into the Leinster final, we were up for it. It was a terrible day, wet and windy. Jinxy got a great score early on, a typical Jinxy run. He went flying through, fell on his arse, got up and stuck it over the bar. Dave Synnott was marking me. I got one ball in the second half – you know, when you're just standing in the right place at the right time. I don't know who played it across, but it hit the post and came straight back out to me. I just put it over. I also knocked a free over and the last point I got was from a pass from O'Rourke. Even though he would always say that he passed to me, he went to kick it into Hill 16. I got it, kicked a 'Hail Mary' over my shoulder, and it went over the bar. It was one of those days that everything ran for me. I remember O'Rourke getting a point after that. I was inside him when he got the ball, praying that he would pass it but, typical O'Rourke, he kicked it over the bar himself!

I was a manufactured free-taker, I wasn't a natural free-taker at all. When I felt confident kicking them, I could put the ball down and put them over the bar all day. But when the pressure was on, it was different.

TERRY FERGUSON: *I remember Colm O'Rourke scoring with his right foot that day which was almost unbelievable. But it really was a great day. That was the platform that we took off from. The one thing I will never forget was at the final whistle when we had won. A fella from Kells, 'Skol' McGovern, was at the match and he ran onto the field at the end. I could see 'Skol' coming from beyond in the corner. He came from the 'Nally'. He had these white trousers on him and a white jacket, and he had a scarf and Meath hat on his head. Underfoot conditions were very bad because of the weather and I could see him running towards me out of the corner of my eye, and he kept coming and kept coming and, next thing, he was just beside me and he let a roar – and the two feet went from under him and slid he right by me in the muck. But he got up, he didn't care less. He was destroyed but couldn't give a damn. That's what it meant to Meath people to win the Leinster. He just got up and threw his arms around me, and he gave me his hat. And to this very day I still have the hat he gave me in 1986.*

That really was the first breakthrough for Meath, for that team and particularly for Sean. In the dressing room afterwards we were all elated. Some of us, like myself and Staff, were only there for a few years and we had won this Championship almost straightaway. But for the likes of Joe Cassells and O'Rourke, Gerry McEntee and Mick Lyons, and boys that had been there for years and years and kept the flag flying, it was a particularly triumphant day for them.

ANDY McENTEE: *I was in America at the time but I do remember listening to the game on the radio. I was with a group of my college friends over in Boston and we heard it live. I spoke to Gerry on the* *telephone afterwards. He was in the airport waiting to fly back to Newcastle. He was working in England at the time and had to return immediately after the game. I'm sure he would have liked to stay around, but he was still delighted. He told me he was about to fly back but, you know, the way he was going on, he mightn't have needed a plane! He was so happy, I'm sure he felt like he could fly all by himself.*

DES LANE: *I came up from the Under-21s and made my debut against Kildare in Navan in 1985. There was myself, Liam Harnan and Terry Ferguson – we were the new half-back line. I was only 19 at the time. Coming into the panel with some of the lads I had played underage football with made it easier. I know some players who were brought in out of the cold and it was very difficult for them because they didn't really know anybody. You'd here stories about someone who plonked himself down in the wrong place being told to get his bag and baggage, and shift! Everybody usually sat in the same place. I would have sat somewhere along the Lyons corner.*

The celebrations after the Leinster final win in 1986 were brilliant but I think there was a bit of realism too. There was a nice mix of players at the time. The young guys were coming along. Flynn and Stafford and myself and O'Malley were mixing with Colm O'Rourke and Gerry McEntee, the 'elder statesmen' if you like. They were waiting a long time in order to win a Leinster, but some of the younger lads like myself were after playing in minor and Under-21 finals, so we were used to competing in big games.

I played against Laois in 1987. I was left corner-back. I was marking a guy called Tom Tynan, who seemingly had come out of minor and was supposed to be shit-hot. We had a team meeting a few days beforehand and they were talking about this fella. When Sean asked me how did I feel and I said I'd take him, and he left it at that! I remember when the first ball came in I won it. I was about ten yards ahead, and I won it and cleared up field. It set the whole tone for the day.

I played against Kildare aswell but don't remember who I was marking. I was booked for an indiscretion during the game. I was playing well though, playing really well. The confidence was booming. I felt I was getting better and better, and then I was dropped for the Leinster final. Sean rang me at work the week before the final, around the Tuesday, I'd say. He told me I wasn't playing. I was gob-smacked after performing so well and then to be dropped suddenly!

He just said, 'You weren't picked.' I never really had it out with him. I tried though, but he wasn't having any of it. Who dropped me? Whether it was Sean or somebody else, I really don't know. It was very difficult to take. Martin O'Connell was playing at half-forward and they brought him back to half-back and it was between myself, Padraig and Terry for the corner spot. Bob O'Malley was in one corner and Foley and Harnan were the half-backs. It was dreadful sitting on the bench looking out at that game. I was wearing No. 17. The way things happened, sure Martin O'Connell went on to be named on the 'Team of the Century' so in some ways you can't argue. I just happened to be the one that was displaced. Because we were so successful it was difficult to get back in the side. The team changed very little over the next two years.

P.J. GILLIC: *I can't remember a whole lot about the homecoming after winning the Leinster title. The very next morning I was on a boat bound for France, so I missed out on the whole aftermath of the victory. Myself and Joanne had one of these inter-railing holidays booked. I wouldn't have even been on the panel when we first booked it and it was supposed to be a month's trip! Sean, I think, was the only one who knew I was* *going away. I probably hadn't the guts or the balls to tell the rest of them. I never said anything when I got on the panel earlier in the year. Reaching a Leinster final was the last thing on my mind. And I kept putting the big decision on the long finger. I finally said it to Sean – it could have been a week or two before the final – and he wasn't too pleased about it at all. He wanted to arrange for me to go to certain places that I could train en route! I actually did quite a bit of training, running and that, when I was away and I think we were only gone for a week and a half in the end. We went to France, Italy, up to Switzerland. It was so rushed, though, I think we spent most of the time on the train. Martin O'Connell had come on as a sub for me in the Leinster final and when Meath played Cavan in a challenge match after the Leinster final, he scored points from all angles. All he had to do was look at the posts and the ball went over. I remember ringing home and my father saying, 'Jesus, you'd better get home quick!' So I kinda knew my place was gone.*

I didn't really enjoy the holiday! It was there in the back of my mind the whole time. I knew I shouldn't have gone, but money had been paid. We had booked it well in advance of me even being on the panel. And even when I was on the panel, the last thing on my mind was thinking I'd be kept on it, or finding myself playing in a Leinster final. But I can remember getting a lot of stick when I came back – from all the players! Joe Cassells never left me alone for about a year after it. I lost my place over it for the All-Ireland semi-final against Kerry, and rightly so. I know what I would do if I was over a team and someone buggered off on holiday! Meath played extremely well for the first 20 minutes against Kerry – we were dominating the game. Liam Hayes, funnily enough, was taking the frees that day and he hit a couple of good long-range frees in the first half. Gerry Mac and Liam were both playing well around the

Tony Nation, Colm O'Rourke and David Beggy, September 20, 1987

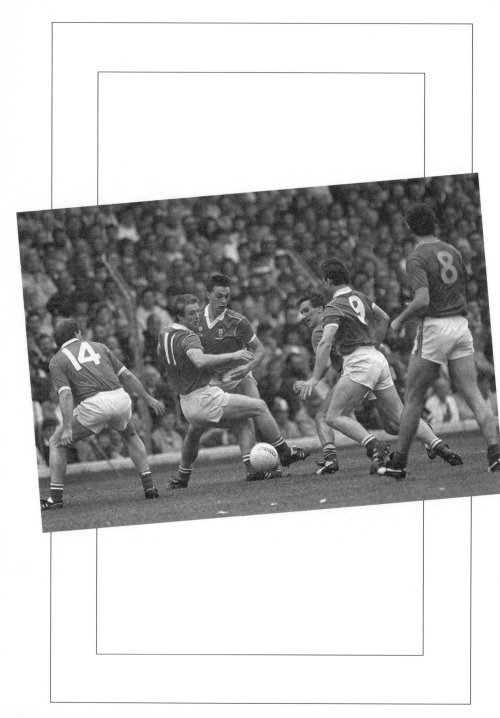

Larry Tompkins, Tony Davis and Mattie McCabe, August 18, 1988

middle. It was cuteness on Kerry's part that got them back into it. I came on for the last quarter. I remember getting the ball a couple of times, but that was it!

The Meath team which was to become one of the dominant forces in Gaelic football for the next five years was edging close to the end of the assembly line. Anybody wanting to make the chosen 15 was running out of time, and the same clock was ticking for those who had to put one final nail on their place on the team. The happy bunch preparing for the All-Ireland semi-final against Kerry had no real idea of the examination which lay directly in front of them. Some players would never be allowed to forget the defeat by Kerry. Padraig Lyons was one of those. Mick's younger brother had spent the guts of three years working himself into the left corner-back spot, but 70 minutes in the company of the ageing but still nimble Kerry full-forward line did him no good whatsoever. Padraig's brilliant nose for the ball had always been his greatest asset, but Mikey Sheehy was more than a corner-forward. Mikey was a magician, and if the ball is not there, how on earth can a corner-back smell it? Sheehy scored four points during the afternoon of the All-Ireland semi-final.

As he galloped down the tunnel after the game, Jack O'Shea yelled to the waiting journalists, 'Now lads, are we too old?' It was a theme which Sean Boylan took up when he entered the Kerry dressing room to congratulate them in person. 'Birth certificates don't count in football,' he agreed. 'If the skill and craft is there then age doesn't count. You had both today and gave us a lesson. We have to admit that.'

The older team, dressed in unfamiliar blue, left Boylan's troops mentally and physically bruised. The losing dressing room resembled a casualty ward after the game. Joe Cassells was in agony on the treatment table in the centre of the room, still trying to recover after a late, robust challenge from 'Bomber' Liston. Mickey McQuillan was receiving treatment for a broken nose. Players either side of the bloodied keeper were white in the face. Gerry McEntee was on the point of collapse. The scoreboard had read 2-13 to 0-12 at the finish, but not very long after half-time the Meath team had stopped checking the numbers behind either goal. The game was over; the season was up. It was so different to the beginning of the game and the opening 17 minutes, by which time Meath led by 0-4 to 0-2. It was a brilliant scoreline, unbelieveable, great to look up at. It should have been 0-7 to 0-2 after 30 minutes, but it wasn't. Kerry had scored a goal in the 18th minute. Denis 'Ogie' Moran centred a ball into the Meath square, and McQuillan, Joe Cassells and Mick Lyons ended up in an undignified, concussed heap on the ground. Each man thought the ball was his! Ger Power ended up with the ball in his hand and an empty goal in front of him and, after 30 minutes, it was actually 0-7 to 1-2. Meath had fought back to regain a two-points advantage, but in time added on due to the earlier, unannounced appearance of the 'Three Stooges' Kerry scored four points in a blinding three and a half minute-spell at the close of the first half. That's how it was at half-time. But 16 minutes into the second period, with Kerry now leading by 1-9 to 0-8 after a third quarter fought at incredibly close quarters, Meath were on the receiving end of another crunching blow. In the flick of a switch Liam Hayes was wide from a 40 metres free-kick on the left-hand side of the field, Pat Spillane shot a monstrous point at the other end, and

Finian Murtagh was off target with a 35 yards free-kick on the right-hand side of the field. Hands on hips, Brian Stafford watched. Kerry were five points in front. Stafford had started the game at centre-forward – Martin O'Connell was at full-forward – but from that day on the No. 14 jersey and the responsibility for taking any free-kick on any side of the field belonged with 'Staff'.

There were going to have to be some additional hurried decisions and changes to the Meath team which had already been four years in the making. Luckily for every last man, woman and child in Meath, these would include Martin O'Connell being selected at left half-back, for good.

O'Connell was finally going to get everything he wished for as a Meath footballer. Others were going to lose virtually everything. Some, like Padraig Lyons and Finian Murtagh, would spend the remainder of their Meath careers waiting for one more opportunity, cherishing the dream of one more day, one more Championship game, when they could prove to Boylan and their team-mates that they were still too good for the substitutes bench! They would train on, and they would contribute as much as anybody to the remarkable spirit in the team, though the likes of Lyons and Murtagh would receive precious little in return.

John McEnroe remained on the bench only for a few months after the 1986 season. Having moved straight up from the Meath minor team and having played for two different managers in 1981 and '82, he had, rightly or wrongly, earned the reputation as one of the toughest and most courageous defenders in the county. McEnroe had his third shot at the senior team in '86, but failed to impress Boylan sufficiently.

MARTIN O'CONNELL: *P.J. Gillic went on holidays after the Leinster final, and he was gone for a couple of weeks. P.J. was very young at the time. You think back now and it was a stupid thing to do, but it happened. We played Cavan in a challenge match before the All-Ireland semi-final . It was to mark the opening of Kilmainhamwood's pitch, and I scored seven points. That was one of my best ever games as a forward. It hasn't happened since or never happened before. So I was picked then at full-forward for the All-Ireland semi-final. P.J. was only back just before the game, and they moved Brian Stafford out to centre-forward.*

We had a final team meeting one of the nights before the game. It was actually down in The Willows, in the restaurant. I remember Sean telling me this, and Pat Reynolds telling me something else, and Tony Brennan saying something else entirely. So in the end I didn't know what to do! I didn't know whether to come out or stay in, go to the left or go to the right. It was that unclear. Sure, how was I going to play? I remember Sean saying, 'How do you feel about the game, Martin?' And I said, 'Sure I feel grand.' That's how naive I was – I couldn't say to Sean, 'I don't know what you want me to do.'

I got one kick of the ball and I scored a point halfway through the first half. I hardly got a kick at all after that. The ball was obviously coming in though because O'Rourke and Flynn were doing very well in the two corners – Flynn and O'Rourke had Paidi O Se and Mick Spillane bet up a stick. I don't think Sean Walsh kicked a ball either. The game just flew by, and that was it. That year, I think a lot of us were just happy to have won a first Leinster title in 17 years and maybe we didn't believe that we could beat Kerry. They got that soft goal and I remember Tommy Doyle getting injured underneath the Cusack Stand and he was down for four or five minutes at a time when we were really putting the pressure on. They were just that bit experienced. They knew when to lie down.

Tommy Doyle did lie down that day. The game was stopped for four or five minutes, and they got the goal and a couple of points then. I think from four points up, we went in at half-time a couple of points down. I'd say we were a bit naive about it. If it was Dublin, I'd say there probably wouldn't even have been a team meeting because everyone would have known what to expect, but Kerry were the All-Ireland champions! Everyone looked up to them, they were going for three in a row, and I'd say we got caught up in that.

JOHN McENROE: *I'll never forget the Kerry goal that day. I should have been playing that year. I have no doubt at all in my mind. I should have been playing, and that goal would never have gone in, and that is for certain. I saw it coming before it ever dropped in.*
I sat on the bench looking on as Mickey McQuillan, Joe and Mick all ended up going for the one ball, and not one of them was left standing. And all the Kerryman had to do was tap it into the empty net. I didn't tell Sean I should've been playing but, sure, you mightn't be bothering anyway. If you were in and he wanted you, he wanted you. And if he didn't, he didn't, and that was it.
You know that is the bottom line. But, then again that's the point about being a manager – you have to make your mind up and Boylan was fit to do that. He didn't want me to be in on the first 15. He had his starting line-up and sure Bob O'Malley was hanging over my spot anyway, and Bob was a very good footballer. I broke my cheekbone in a League match – can't remember exactly where or when – but I got dropped after that and never got back in favour again. I never started a Championship game under Sean.
I was never really told I wouldn't be wanted on the Meath panel and Sean never came up to me and said why he was dropping me from the

squad. The message was, 'Don't call us. We'll call you' – just like that. And that was the end of my days with Meath. But at the end of the day Sean Boylan had to think of the team. He is the manager, bottom line, and there are no nice fellas in football. It's a tough sport.

I continued training with the team right up until March of 1987, and then I was dropped. I remember going to the All-Ireland final that day and looking out at the fellas I had played alongside all year, and I wasn't involved. I had a hell of a job getting a ticket. I gave my Oldcastle club ticket to my wife Patricia and, somehow, I just about got a Hill 16 ticket for the game. I remember standing on the Hill, after training with all the boys for half the year and they couldn't even hear me shouting out at them – that's a bad memory. After me training with them, that was as close as I could get. I was roaring out at them, 'Come on Giller' and so on, but the boys didn't even know I was there. That really hurt. I felt bad that day. Even though we had won the All-Ireland, I felt bad. Of course, I was delighted for the lads, but I would like to have been involved.

Finding it difficult to get a ticket for the All-Ireland in 1987 was particularly tough on me because I had sweated my balls off in Bettystown running after those boys. Bettystown was the pits. I was working very hard at the time and building a house, and I used to go straight from work to Bettystown for training, and the boys would be coasting along the sand, whereas I'd be knackered and have to run after them. For anybody like myself, and say Liam Harnan and Terry Ferguson, who were doing hard physical manual work, I think it was too much. My back packed in for the best years of my life and it was purely because the muscles in my back got tired and couldn't take it any more. But when I quit doing the real serious training, it was no bother. For anybody doing manual work it was probably pushing them too far.

Sean had to rebuild the team after 1992 – it just doesn't come out of nowhere. People were correct to give him a chance between 1992 and 1996, to let him start over and structure another team. I remember when we started off with Sean and we had won a few matches, people noticed us. We played Offaly, who had won the All-Ireland in 1982, in the League, and afterwards Richie Connor got into our bus and said, 'Right, you have a good manager now lads. But it is going to take three years to build a team', and he was spot on. Fair play to him coming onto our bus and telling us that. We started to believe in ourselves more after an All-Ireland winner told us we could achieve something.

Sean is a pure professional at what he does and he has a brilliant way about him. Sign of it all is that he has lasted so long. I mean he was ruthless as a manager, but what manager isn't? All the good managers are ruthless.

I called into Sean one day not so long ago. I had been out in Kepak and there was a good smell of slurry off me, but fair play to him, he didn't say a thing. Boylan wanted a footballer that would cut deep the whole time, but then I was the other side. I cut too deep and he didn't want me either. He had his guys. But you have to hand it to him. I mean, what other manager would have tried out David Beggy, a rugby player who turned into the player teams feared more than any other, especially Dublin?

MATTIE McCABE: *I missed 1986. That year was the real breakthrough and it was a wrench to miss it, but that can't be helped now. At the time I thought I'd never get a chance again. Looking back on my time with Meath I should have five Leinster medals. But I don't, I've only got four, and I should have been there in '86. But even when I missed the whole of '86 the door was never closed on me. You would think that Sean's not watching you and that he's forgotten about you but it was never like that.*

Any lad with a bit of potential is always being watched. Brian Stafford was like that. He was old enough starting with the seniors but was a revelation when he came in. There'd never been a free-taker like him, he was worth seven or eight scores a game to us. They were often the bulk of our scores. After the Kerry match in '86 everyone knew that it was going to be our time soon.

I couldn't believe it when I got my chance again in 1987. We played Dublin in the Leinster final that year and I scored 1-3 against John O'Leary. It was the best moment of my career at the time because John was a legend even at that stage. I still have the cuttings of the game in my scrapbook.

Right at the start of the year I said to my father that I would bring the Leinster trophy down to his house after we won it. I told Sean that early in the year too. It's amazing how he never forgets a thing! I had totally forgotten about what I had said to him, but then after we won the Leinster title Sean reminded me it. I was overawed at the man's memory and I did bring the cup back to my father's house just like I had promised. It was something very special to be bringing home!

Mattie McCabe was on and off the team for the next four years, though, remarkably, he managed a hat-trick of goals against John O'Leary by also scoring in the 1988 and '89 Leinster finals. Nobody ever tired of watching McCabe, even in training, as he was arguably the most naturally talented ball-player Boylan possessed in the first ten years of his managerial career. A series of bad injuries prevented him from claiming a regular place on the team for the remainder of the decade, but he was still around the place in 1991 when he, more than anybody else, played possibly the most important role in one of the greatest goals ever witnessed in Croke

Park.

MATTIE McCABE: *1991 was a great high. I didn't play in the first three matches against Dublin. I remember coming on in the fourth game, the final one, that we won. I made a run during the game when I came on and I called out to Colm O'Rourke that I was going to pass to him. But he didn't hear me and I got done for over-carrying. After that I said to myself, 'That won't happen again.' So the next time I got the ball I had a pop at goal from 30 or 35 yards out and it went over.*

Kevin Foley's goal was something else. It was funny because everyone always goes on about why Kevin Foley was so far up the field. It was very unlike him. But the reason was that, in the build-up to the goal, we had a chat in the middle of the field. He told me to go on up and I said, 'No, you go.' So he did and he scored the goal. When I was walking back to our defence after letting Kevin go forward Mick Deegan said to me, 'What are you coming back for?' You should have seen the expression on his face when Kevin scored the goal. When the game was over Kevin came up to me and hugged me. He just said, 'You knew what you were doing all right.' If I had gone forward one of their backs would have picked me up, but nobody was going to notice Kevin Foley up at the other end.

If you look at the video of the game you can see the two of us talking on the pitch, even when the ball is in motion. For me it was the best ever goal in Croke Park, next to Mikey Sheehy's in 1978 for Kerry against Dublin.

Down in Clem's Pub in Navan afterwards the big question was, 'Who had caught the ball under the Hogan Stand that led to the winning point being scored?' No one knew who caught the ball from O'Leary's kick-out, but it was actually me. I gave it to Willie (Liam Hayes), he gave it to P.J. Gillic, and onto Jinksy who finished it off. Well everyone in the bar thought it was Willie that had caught the ball. There was a fair pot of money riding on it, but I didn't take it. I was there with my wife and we just kind of winked at each other. The banter was great at the time. It was a great year apart from the final, of course. I played against Wicklow after the Dublin game and scored two points. I was kind of mad that I was dropped after that. I didn't even know why I was dropped. Any game I did start we seemed to win.

I came on in the last few minutes against Down in the final. We really could have won that game. We were ten points down when Colm O'Rourke came on and he single-handedly brought us right back into it. We just ran out of time. Down had done their homework on us in fairness. Barry Breen's goal was the real killer. It would have been some year to win the All-Ireland, considering everything we'd been through.

I remember one day Willie (Hayes) and Sean having a bit of a spat at training. I think they were having a bad hair day! Willie was commenting on Sean's training techniques or something like that and Sean just grabbed the bib off himself and said, 'Right Liam, go and referee the bloody game yourself.' It was great.

Joe Cassells was the only one that'd really give Sean a bit of lip. But it would only be having the craic. Joe was a bit of a smart alec and he'd always be making wise cracks at Sean. Depending on what humour Sean was in, he would take it or not. There was absolutely nothing malicious in it.

At half-time in a game I used to always go up to Willie and ask, 'How am I doing?' Every time he'd say the same thing, 'Doing good, Mattie.' And every time Joe Cassells, who sat in our corner, would butt in and say, 'Mattie, you're doing shite!'

One time we were training down in Dalgan Park. Down behind one of the pitches there was a load of long grass just where the beginning of a field was at the back of the goal. One evening Sean had us doing sprints. We had to run away and then when he shouted at us we would come running back to him. This time anyway we ran away and he said: 'Keep jogging on the spot til I shout, then you can turn around.' So he shouted and we turned around but he was gone! We could still hear the shouting from him but we didn't know where he was. We were sprinting in pairs and I was there with Gerry McEntee. He says, 'Where the fuck's he gone now?' Then we spotted him. He was down in the corner of the field hiding in the long grass, and he came out with a big grin on his face.

Joe Cassells, in return, would never stop giving Sean a hard time. We'd be stretching away and Sean would say, 'Lads, can you feel that in the backs of your legs?' Cassells would say, 'No.' Then Sean would ask again the next time and Joe would say, 'No Sean, can't feel that either.' Then Sean would get a bit thick and say. 'Right, well can you feel that one?' shouting it out. Joe would always back down and go, 'Ah OK Seany, I can. I can feel it now all right.'

I have great memories from my days. Back in 1984, when we won the Centenary Cup, I replaced Eamonn Barry in the team because he dropped out with an injury. I wanted the No. 11 jersey to keep as a souvenir but he wouldn't give it to me! I think it was that day, in the final, I was coming out of the toilet and Gerry McEntee dragged me to one side and said if I didn't play well he'd never talk to me again. He was my idol and I bloody listened to him. The two of us got fairly merry that night. I scored a nice few points that day.

Chapter Four:

1987
1988

The Meath team knew exactly what lay in front of them, what had to be done. And, like the general of an armed force, Sean Boylan had to weigh up the strength of his team against football teams all over the country who would be fighting it out to become 1987 All-Ireland football champions. He knew the landscape extremely well. He knew who and what was to be feared. Kerry, the reigning All-Ireland champions from 1986, were not going to be any better than they had been 12 months earlier. Ulster champions Tyrone had lost to Mick O'Dwyer and Co. in that All-Ireland decider, forfeiting a seven-point lead early in the second half. Boylan and his boys were happy enough thinking of Kerry – not confident – just content. Meath had played against Tyrone possibly more than any other team over the preceding four years, so if Meath had to meet Tyrone in the All-Ireland semi-final, and then go head-to-head with Kerry on the third Sunday in September, that would be all right. Boylan had to put a team on the field with the strength and confidence to defeat Tyrone and Kerry. It didn't work out like that, of course. Derry landed the Ulster title, as it turned out, and at the second attempt Billy Morgan's Cork retired the greatest team of all time in the Munster final.

But in the early weeks of 1987 nobody was to know that. Meath knew for sure that they would have to defeat Dublin for a second time in the Leinster final. They also knew that to get to the provincial final they would have to contend with Laois first of all in the first round of the Leinster Championship, and no Meath team ever slept well thinking of Laois. This particular Laois team had beaten Meath in the 1985 Leinster championship and had surprisingly fallen to Wicklow in '86, much to the satisfaction and contentment of a great many Meath players who would much rather forget about Laois altogether than go out onto the field and attempt to extract revenge against them. It wasn't that Laois had a brilliant team in the making. They were just dogged, strong and good footballers to a man – and, worse still, Laois were one of the few football teams in the country which seemed to know the secret of the Meath team. They liked playing Meath for some crazy reason.

Sitting at his kitchen table at his home in Dunboyne, Sean Boylan could see what had to be done. It was hard not to think about Kerry, but in the opening rounds of the 1986-87 National League a younger Kerry team, possibly the Kerry team of the very near future, had driven the whole way up to Kells to receive a 1-12 to 0-4 thrashing. For sure, Kerry were going to be no better in 1987. More likely, on the evidence of the 11-point defeat, Kerry were already going backwards. In Kells Jack O'Shea started at full-forward, while Tom Spillane was tried out at full-back. There was a completely new half-back line, while Dermot Hanafin and Timmy Dowd were sited in the middle of the field. Willie Maher and John Kennedy were either side of Ogie Moran in the half-forward line, and the great Ger Power was still up front, alongside his new buddy Jacko. But Boylan had his very best team on duty on a pitch which was still frozen over when the ball was thrown up into the air by Seamus Aldridge. The win meant that Meath were virtually assured of a place in the National League quarter-finals.

Meath did qualify to play Galway in the quarter-finals, in Portlaoise in March. The same ground would also host Meath and Laois in the first round of the 1987 Leinster Championship in June. Boylan, the little general, had his dates and he had his opponents. Two games in Portlaoise! After that, Meath might be ready to head for an All-Ireland – or Meath might be history as far as 1987 was concerned. Portlaoise, and 140 minutes of football, would decide everything.

The tension was growing in the Meath camp long before Sean Boylan marched into training one night, read the riot act to the players, and resigned.

Boylan sat in the middle of the dressing room on a wooden chair, the players were on seats or sitting on the floor around him in a semi circle. He spoke for 10 minutes before announcing, 'I don't mind people shitting on me now and again, but when they start wiping their arses with me, well, lads!' He made it clear that he didn't want to start a discussion. It was over. He was going. He thanked everybody for their effort over the years and wished the team the best in the future. Next thing, he was gone. 'You're Leinster champions, but you're going to win nothing more. Nothing!' The team talked for almost two hours after his departure.

Three days later Sean was back. A few weeks later, Meath lost to Galway, 1-8 to 0-9, after a clumsy, heavy-legged performance in the League quarter-final. Val Daly split the Meath defence in two with a brilliant pass three minutes into the second half, and Tomas Tierney's half-struck shot spun into the corner of the net. Joe Cassells was brought into the action for his first game since the All-Ireland semi-final the previous August. He went in at full-forward to pull the game out of the fire, and Mick Lyons, who was having an off-day, was sent up to centre-forward to give him a helping hand. Didn't work. Not much was going Boylan's way. Colm Coyle had disappeared in a puff of smoke a month earlier, ending up in Chicago without having told any of his team-mates what he was doing or where he was going, and Martin O'Connell informed the management team a week after the Galway defeat that he was quitting the team for good. He was tired pretending to be a forward. Two of the best half-backs in the country were gone it seemed.

LIAM HAYES: *I never knew what all that was about, to be honest, when Sean resigned that night. We didn't think we were doing anything different, nobody was kidding around and cutting corners, but obviously Sean saw things he didn't like and felt he needed to make a stand. When he walked out the door on us, there was a stunned silence. I'd say half the lads felt like laughing their heads off, because the dramatic nature of his departure was comic in a way. But nobody laughed. We all had too much to lose, and whatever was bothering Sean, whatever more he wanted, was vitally important. Joe Cassells, and Colm O'Rourke I think, were sent to sort things out and get him back.*

P.J. GILLIC: *It was actually embarrassing, because myself and John McEnroe walked in late and we met Sean coming out the door. Whatever mix-up there was that night, myself and Mac thought that the training was on in Seneschalstown, so it was rubbing salt in the wound bumping into him coming out, and us there, 'Jesus, sorry Sean, we got the wrong message and we were up in Seneschalstown.' We were quite taken aback with his reaction, 'Ah, that's all right lads, that's all right. Go on in, there's a meeting on in there.' So we walked into the dressing room and everyone looked down at us. We thought it was our fault. He had said that he was packing it in, for whatever reason. That was a particularly lively meeting between ourselves.*

FINIAN MURTAGH: *That's the one thing about Sean, you could laugh and joke with him, you could pass a comment towards him and, like that, he'd have one straight back at you. He would never say, 'Well, who do you think you are?' Once it wasn't serious! If it got serious, Sean would be serious with you.*
I remember Liam (Hayes) one night in training, when he wouldn't back down. Sean threw the whistle at him and said, 'You do it.'
Another night, Gerry's (McEntee's) brother Andy was on the panel and he had a run-in with Bernie Flynn. Flynn was as fiery! Oh, yeah! Say one word to Flynn and he'd go off – and Andy was the exact same. So the two of them got into a bit of a row and start throwing punches at each other. So Boylan says, 'Lads, what the hell are you at? Will you give it up?' But then they starteded at it again. So Sean jumps in and says, 'OK, go on, go on, I'll have the pair of you...come on, throw a punch at me.' And that ended that. There's no way you'd throw a punch at Sean – he'd kill you. Oh, Sean had muscles. I remember him in training one day, he got up on the bench in the dressing room and Liam

Hayes was standing in front of him. Now Liam Hayes was 15$^1/_2$, 16 stone at the time, and he put his arms under his shoulders and around the back of his neck, and lifted him straight off the ground. Straight off the ground! So there was no messin' with him.

He wouldn't have lost the rag much because fellas were responding to him, but if you didn't do what you were supposed to do, he'd let you know it.

FRANK FOLEY: *At the time, it was very strange when Sean walked out. He only stepped down for a period of two or three days, but for a while none of us really knew what was going on or where we stood. If my memory is right it was Joe Cassells that rang Sean and sorted out whatever was wrong with him. The night Sean came back we trained in St Pat's school gym and there was a kind of a joke made out of the whole thing. Sean gathered us around and thanked us for the effort we had made to bring him back. He said to Joe, 'I believe I owe you ten pence for the phone call.' And Joe said back to him, 'Nah, it's OK, I reversed the charges.' That got a good laugh, and after that it was more or less back to normal.*

LIAM HAYES: *The row between Sean and myself, before the Leinster final in 1987, was over before I even knew it had started, to be honest. Everyone talks about it, even still, but it was just a heat of the moment thing – even though it was lashing out of the heavens that night. Sean had been in bad form for a couple of weeks. We all knew that. I knew it better than most because Sean and myself were close. My brother Gerard died when Sean was in his first year as manager, and tragic events like that can bring people together very quickly. I was living at home with my parents and two younger sisters, and Sean was at the side* *of the entire family for a long time. He was great. I could talk to him about anything and the really remarkable thing about him is that, when you are talking to him, it's like you are the most important person in the whole world. He makes you feel number one.*

The night of the big row, I knew he was in bad, bad form. He was shouting a lot, he was all business, and I was fully aware that this was not the sort of night to mess with him. Even Joe Cassells wasn't saying boo! The problem was, Padraig Lyons said something to me. He was holding a golf umbrella over his head. He was out injured at the time with a very bad leg. Padraig was standing beside me, helping Sean out with the training, and Sean was at the other end of a line of players. We were doing this ball exercise and I heard Sean saying, 'I'm only going to tell you once', but then he said something else. I didn't hear him because Padraig said something to me. 'What was that?' I said to Sean, and he snapped. 'What did I say?' he roared, 'I WANT EVERYTHING DONE FAST. I'M NOT GOING TO REPEAT EVERYTHING TWICE!' And I snapped back, 'I didn't f****** hear what you said.' That was it! Big mistake. Marches over to me, walking in front of the line of players, and throws his whistle at my feet. Then he storms off towards the dressing room. 'Jesus, don't do that,' I shouted after him. 'I didn't hear you!' I could see all of the other lads looking at me, delighted with themselves that it was me who had dug the big hole and that I was the only one down in the bottom of it. At the same time they were all soaked to the skin and fed up. There was nothing else to do but pick up the whistle and run after Sean. I handed it to him and said sorry, and he said nothing, and training continued. The lads gave me hell for the rest of the week. Bob (O'Malley) kept calling me 'Coach' every time I walked by him, and Rourkey was as diplomatic as usual. 'If you weren't so thick and if you'd any sense, you'd have kept the fucking whistle', he told me in front of the whole team. That was all that happened, but the reason it is remembered is that the pair of us were stubborn as hell, and often pretended to be two bulls. He was the manager and he was always going to win any battles with me, but because we were friends I didn't always let him away with things, especially if I thought he was in the wrong.

When I was captain in 1991, for instance, Sean got it into his head one night that I should apologise to the rest of the squad. He told me exactly what he wanted to hear, but I told him and a few other players who were sitting around me, that I wasn't getting up on my feet to apologise to anyone. What happened that time was simple. I was late for training. It was about three weeks before the All-Ireland final and the lads had just started a game of football in Pairc Tailteann when I ran onto the field. I was working for the Sunday Press at the time as a sports journalist and I had to do a piece on the Kilkenny team who were playing in the All-Ireland hurling final. I decided to do a piece on the Hendersons, which meant talking to Pat Henderson and John Henderson over the phone, but travelling down to Johnstown to interview Ger Henderson in person. In a situation like that, a journalist has to work to the other person's schedule and the only day Ger could sit down with me was a Tuesday. So I was with him most of the afternoon and the interview went brilliantly. He was really at ease and talking away, and telling me all sorts of interesting stuff, and I couldn't leave. Raced up from Kilkenny for training then and I was a few minutes late. Ran onto the field and played really well. Felt like a 2-year old, and then Sean tells me I must apologise to the rest of the players for being late! We argued hot and heavy. He wasn't having any of it, and I wasn't having any of it. I told him that everyone, including himself, had been coming late to training for the last ten years. I didn't stand up,

I didn't apologise. And he never mentioned it again to me. But those sort of episodes would crop up between us. I would have a bit of an agenda at times because Gerry (McEntee) would always be getting praise for flying home from London and Newcastle and New York and all sorts of places for games, but Sean seemed to take it completely for granted that I would turn up. I was covering the Five Nations Championship every year for the paper, for example, and I was also making special arrangements to fly home from Paris and London and Edinburgh. I remember spending ten hours making my way from Paris to Belfast for a game, and nobody said, 'Fair dues!' All I got was a Meath supporter telling me to take the lead out of my arse!

In 1992, a few months after the 1991 All-Ireland final, I was covering the World Cross-Country Championships in Boston and I was out there for the week. It was a big story because Catherina McKiernan just missed out on the gold medal. I was supposed to get a flight back to Ireland on the Saturday evening after the race but at the last minute I decided against it. I said work had to come first. My editors had asked me to do some extra stuff on McKiernan the day after the race. That didn't go down too well with Sean. I could see that he was questioning my commitment, that old hunger. Then, a month or so before the first round of the Championship against Laois he organised two games for the one weekend, a Thursday night game against Wexford down in Gorey and a Saturday trip down to Cork. We were all sitting down in the dressing room after training and he wanted to know who was available? He went around the players one by one, asking who could go to Gorey and who could go to Cork. I said, 'Gorey, not Cork.' Sean said nothing.

On the Thursday evening I got out of Dublin that little bit early because I didn't want to be late for the game. As it happened I was the first to arrive in the dressing room in Gorey and I was about an hour waiting around for the room to fill up. I was there so long that I had changed for the game about 40 minutes before the team left the dressing room. I was waiting for my jersey, sitting there with no top on. But there was no jersey handed to me, and I found myself having to search my bag for an old training jersey and a tracksuit top. Again Sean said nothing to me. We won the game. I was put on for the last 15 minutes. It was no great surprise to me when I didn't get picked for the first round of the Championship against Laois. Again I was brought on in the game for John McDermott, when he was knocked out in the first half, but I was sent off in the final minute. We lost and I retired that evening. I didn't tell Sean. He had said so little to me for so long that I didn't feel inclined to let him know of my decision.

It was foolish, childish stuff, and considering everything we had been through together it was a bit of a shame to leave the team in that manner. But that was Sean and me, I suppose. Communication was never the best. Over the last ten years we've only met five or six times, and spoken over the phone half a dozen times.

Driving back down to Portlaoise in June of '87 was one of the longest journeys in the lives of almost all the Meath footballers. There was more than a Leinster crown on the line. The greatest opportunity the team might ever have of winning an All-Ireland title was also up for grabs. Laois also had everything to lose, everything to gain, as they had contested National League and Leinster finals over the previous three years and had worked their way up the ladder to become one of the top 10 teams in the country. It was definitely a winner-takes-all game of football. A Liam Irwin penalty kick left Laois 1-2 to 0-3 ahead after 15 minutes and despite a fierce shouting match among the players in the dressing room at half-time, Meath did somehow regain their composure. The teams were level, 1-7 to 2-4, with 12 minutes remaining. A long kick from Colm Browne had somehow bounced almost on the Meath goal-line, fooling Mickey McQuillan and a clutch of Meath and Laois players, and had ended up in the net. Four points in a seven-minute spell won the game for Meath. Really, Brian Stafford won it for Meath more than anybody else, shooting seven points quite effortlessly. Two weeks later, Meath would beat Kildare in Navan in the Leinster semi-final by six points, 0-15 to 0-9, and Stafford would kick ten points in total, six of them coming from free-kicks. In the Leinster final, in a 1-13 to 0-12 victory over Dublin, Stafford stroked over six more points, five of them from free-kicks. Twenty-three points in three games from the new full-forward gave Meath a look of all business.

The team had definitely entered an impressive stride, and without Larry Tompkins and Shay Fahy, Kildare were killed off very much at Meath's choosing in the last quarter of the game. Much the same was the case in the Leinster final. It was like Meath owned the provincial title, and knew it! It helped that Martin O'Connell was chosen to play left half-back. It was 1-5 to 0-2 to Meath midway through the opening half, Mattie McCabe having glided through a dozen players in the Dublin goal mouth and side-footed the ball past John O'Leary. Dublin kicked six points in the second quarter of the game and held a one point advantage at the interval, but this time there was no shouting, no arguing, no fuss in the Meath dressing room. Almost without realising the change, Meath had become a far more mature group of footballers in the 12 months since winning the 1986 Leinster title. The country's most

Brian Stafford, October 9, 1988

Colm Brady and Brian Murray, August 19, 1990

respected and authoritative GAA writer, Martin Breheny, noted the difference. 'For some time now, Meath's battle to prove that substance comprised more of their character than shadow had been undermined by a tendency to collapse just as the point was about to be made', wrote Breheny, adding, 'Last year, Dublin identified the absence of Barney Rock for much of the second half as a major contributory factor to their defeat. This time they could have no excuse because they really were an inferior side and were ultimately fortunate to escape with just a four points defeat.' Stafford, Mattie McCabe and Finian Murtagh were the Meath heroes, with Murtagh replacing Beggy 17 minutes into the second half and tipping over two ice-cool points to help Meath ease away from their opponents.

The newspapers also went to town identifying villains on the field as, typically, the game had been frenzied and chaotic in the first half. After winning the throw-in, Liam Hayes was flattened as he went to run down the middle, and things took off from there until Kevin Foley and Charlie Redmond were sent off after a free-for-all in the 25th minute. But Dublin had no complaints, and team boss Gerry McCaul admitted, 'But for Gerry Hargan, Mick Kennedy, Dave Carroll and Noel McCaffrey, we would have been deeper in trouble.' The defence had almost saved the day for Dublin, but with no goal coming at the other end, Meath had never looked troubled.

MARTIN O'CONNELL: *I remember some of the lads saying to me in the build-up to the Leinster final, 'You seem to be in better form.' Obviously, because I was on the team in the position I wanted. It was actually the day that Stephen Roche won the Tour de France. That came* out over the speakers in Croke Park just before the game started. The Tour de France was over and this came out over the PA and there was a massive cheer all around the ground. There was a gale force wind and we were playing against it in the first half. The punch-up started in the second half – it was a ball that Mick Lyons went for underneath the Hogan Stand, a kind of a dribbling ball along the ground. Ciaran Duff was coming flying towards him and I remember thinking, 'If Mick goes down on this ball, he's going to be absolutely killed!' But I think Mick actually stepped over the ball and hit Duff fair and square. Duff fell on the ground and the referee came over to book Mick. What happened after that was that someone must have been passing by Kevin Foley and the next minute, there was a bit of a bang. Then Charlie Redmond jumped in and it was hand bag stuff for a bit after that. It did have an impact on the game because we were five or six points ahead and going well enough, and this row broke out and they came back within a point of us. I don't even think Mick got booked at the end of it. I remember him pointing over to what was going on and the ref running to try and sort it out. I don't know whether Dublin knew what they were at but it unsettled us.

DONAL SMITH: Colm Coyle went to the US before the 1987 Championship started. However, he returned after we won the Leinster title and some of the players were not very pleased with him at all, as they believed he was a glory hunter. The first night he was back at training I got the feeling there was going to be a problem. I said it to Colm O'Rourke, and he agreed and said he was waiting to see what would happen. So we were playing a two-on-two game. I was in goal and there were two backs and two forwards. Liam Harnan was the man chosen to meet the forward coming in with the ball and Mick Lyons was to mark *the other forward. Anyway, Colm Coyle was the forward who was carrying the ball and Brian Stafford was the second forward. So Coyle comes in first time and 'Bang!' – straight into Harnan, no side-step or anything. It happened three times! The next time Stafford was told not to move or help Coyle out. This was all done to see if Coyle really wanted to be back. So Coyle came forward again and Harnan stepped sideways and let him through, and he ran straight into Mick Lyons. That was it – he had proved to the lads that he wanted to be back. He had not backed down.*

On All-Ireland final day, it was one of the first times our fans were on Hill 16. We came out of the dressing room and ran towards the Hill. It was just a sea of green and gold. What a sight to emerge to! I felt the hairs standing up on the back of my neck. To this day, I can still feel the shivers when I picture that image.

FRANK FOLEY: *It was great for Kevin and myself to be involved in the team in '87, especially as it was the first All-Ireland win since the great team of 1967. We had a middling enough League campaign, there was nothing earth shattering about it. Going into the first Championship game against Laois, I was expecting to be in the subs, but I thought Kevin would start at wing-back. As it happened we both ended up on the bench and Terry Ferguson got the nod instead of Kevin which surprised me. Terry hadn't a great first half and he came off to be replaced by Kevin. Then Kevin got injured, and I came on. I remember the game well. It was nip and tuck a lot of the way through. Laois got a goal in the second half and we just about held out to win. The next game was all about the rise of Brian Stafford as a big name in football. He got eight or ten points that day in our win over Kildare and I think from then on people really started to sit up and take notice of him. It was his first big* national appearance. I played that game and Kevin was out injured. When it came to the Leinster final he was back in instead of me. Coming into the Leinster final against the Dubs the feeling was that Dublin were going to over run us for the previous year's 'fluke' – but we had decent weather that day, not like the previous year, and it was obvious who the better team was.

LIAM HAYES: *I was down in Killarney the week or so after we won the Leinster in '87, writing a piece on the Munster final. It was the replay game in which Cork really took Kerry apart, and afterwards I was waiting outside the ground to meet up with a couple of other journalists and I bumped into half the Kerry team. They were down in the dumps all right, but they were far from tears. Their run was over and they knew it, and I think some of them were probably relieved. Tom Spillane said something like that to me when I offered my condolences. They could now start the rest of their lives and live like normal people. It was strange seeing Tompkins and Fahy in the red jersey, because I had played against them in white jerseys since I was 16, 17-years old. They were on the Kildare team we beat in the 1980 Leinster final, the day I missed a penalty in the first half, and then kicked another penalty wide in the second half, just to be sure to be sure! They played really well against Kerry, and seemed like they had been on the Cork team all their lives. But after the game, it was Ger Lynch whom I spent longest talking with and he said there had been nothing out on the field that day to worry us in Meath. 'It's yours now. There's nothing to stop you', he assured me. I told him we still had a lot of work to do, but he just shook his head and said, 'You'll win it all right'.*
That year (87) was definitely the great adventure for the team. After that, once you have an All-Ireland under your belt, football becomes

more like hard work. It's like having a great wall in front of you that you've already climbed once and viewed what's on the other side. Climbing the wall a second time, as ultimate proof of your ability becomes absolutely vital, but after a while climbing the wall becomes tiresome. It just becomes like a day's work. And that's the amazing thing about Sean Boylan. He's never lost that innocence, that sense of great wonder. It seems like a million years ago since we all started out in the mini-adventure of winning the Centenary Cup in '84 and trying to beat Dublin in '86. It was a long year in '87, and '88 seemed like it was three or four years long. We've all grown up and grown old. When I see Colm Coyle now as Boylan's trusted lieutenant, I smile, because I was sitting beside Colm the whole way down to Charlestown in Mayo and the whole way back in February or March of '87. We were going down for a League game, which we lost in a right old battle, and Coyler and myself talked about everything on the team bus, but he somehow forgot to tell me that he was going to be leaving the country a couple of days later, and would not be coming back! We had played college football together, on the St Pat's Under-14 team, and we'd played minor and Under-21, and then senior. I was as mad as anyone else with him for going out to Chicago. I actually played football against him when we were 11 and 12 years old, because himself and Mattie McCabe would play for Seneschalstown against Skryne in tournament games back then. I knew the two of them. They were two toughies, two terrible twins. I always felt a strong bond with Coyler and Mattie.

My closest friends on the team early on, however, were John McEnroe and Frank Foley, but they were both only around for a short time. John McEnroe was like his namesake on the tennis court, except John McEnroe from Oldcastle didn't throw tennis racquets – he'd throw an arm, a leg, his entire body at a truck running through the Meath defence if he had to. After he was knocked off the panel early in '87, I knew there was not much I could say to him, but I did phone him the week before the All-Ireland final and asked him how he was for tickets. I had Hill 16 tickets if he wanted them, but he didn't take my hand off! We had been close friends for 10 years or so up to then, but we've hardly spoken once since. The last time we met was when Skryne played Oldcastle in a championship game in 1990 or so, and it was a forgettable day all round.

I had made the mistake of telling John once that if Oldcastle ever became a senior team that Skryne would give them a six points start and beat them by six points! I was pulling his leg, but, unfortunately, when we did meet up John was intent upon making me eat my words. I was centre-forward and he was centre-back, and for the first half he was throwing his weight around and putting the boot in, and I did nothing back. I'd scored a goal and a few points, I didn't have to mix it with him, and as it turned out Skryne did beat Oldcastle by exactly 12 points that Sunday. But in the second half Rourkey was obviously fed up with the carry-on and when John gave him a bit of lip, Rourkey laid him out cold. I remember the referee coming up to send Colm off, and I began to plead with the ref, but Colm grabbed me and told the ref and myself, 'I'm going.' He knew all hell would break loose if he stayed on the field. All hell broke loose after the game anyway.

It's funny, football made my relationship with John McEnroe, but it also broke it! The day my brother Gerard was buried in Skryne in 1983, it was a cold, snowy Sunday morning. The graveyard was full of people and all the lads were there, but at the graveside I would look around every so often and I noticed that John was standing behind me, about two yards directly behind. He had been with me over the few days, but he kept standing there, with no coat on, just in his suit, in the cold. When everybody had offered their sympathy and left, and only the family and a few friends were still standing there, I was still conscious that John had not moved. He had just stood there, for about an hour, right behind me, covering my back – just like a game of football. He was a great friend, but a mad man on the football field.

In '87 I didn't know if he was at the All-Ireland or not. That summer was the busiest of our lives. A lot of lads who had helped us reach the All-Ireland final, by giving their best over the preceding years, were not around, but there was little time to think about that because we talked about nothing but Cork and Cork, and Cork. There was great excitement leading up to the final, but we were all tense and nervous, all wound up, and it showed on the training field. And I was getting a reputation for damaging Meath players before the biggest games of the year. In '88, before the All-Ireland final replay against Cork, I gave Gerry Mc a whack as I challenged him, and nearly put him out of the final. And it was the same in '87. We had a training game on the Saturday of the final week before the All-Ireland and things got a little bit out of control. Liam Harnan was throwing his weight around and I was getting thicker and thicker, and late in the game when he came forward with the ball I threw everything at him. I didn't see him off balance, and he crumbled to the ground. Normally it would take an articulated truck to bother Harnan but suddenly he had Sean and Gerry Mc, and Doc Finn and Anne (Bourton) around him. He had fallen on the point of his shoulder, and he was taken off the field. I felt really bad and luckily Rourkey was on hand to help me out, telling me in front of the entire dressing room, 'Y'know, you're a horse of a man Hayes. Who're you going to kill next week?' Colm O'Rourke was great for breaking the ice at times like that.

The night before the All-Ireland was so calm, for most of the night anyhow! We had our usual kick-around in the early evening, then Mass in Dalgan Park and then back to the Sisters of Sion in the big house in Bellinter for a talk and a bite to eat. Mick Lyons was captain in '87 and he and Sean were in charge of all the organisation. We ran through the big day, and through the Cork team, finished everything, and Mick and Sean gave out sheets detailing the next day hour-by-hour. Someone noticed that wives and girlfriends were being driven back to the team hotel in Malahide after the game in a different coach, and the row started. Mick and Sean, who had been like Mutt and Jeff for weeks, got fairly mad but kept the cool, and Mick finally exclaimed, 'Wait a second. I don't honestly give a fuck where the girls go as long as we win the game.' That was Mick. He always had his priorities right. Mick always cut to the chase. It was Mick who introduced me to my wife Anne back in 1984. Anne and his wife Helen were best mates and flatmates, and Helen wanted Mick to introduce us, which went down brilliantly with Mick! I remember the evening he finally decided enough was enough, and after a game he came into the dining room, told me he wanted me out in the bar in the Beechmount Hotel in Navan, passed me over to Helen for the introductions, and walked back to the bar to finish his drink.

When I was captain in '91, the evening before the All-Ireland final against Down, I was handed a sheet of paper by Liam Creavin, the County Board secretary, which detailed exactly what I had to do the morning of the game and the minutes before the throw-in, what I had to say and how I had to act with President Mary Robinson, and everything! And just as Liam Creavin handed me the piece of paper, Mick grabs it, tears it up into small pieces and says, 'You'll be needing none of that!' I remember laughing but feeling slightly pissed with him, because I did want to know exactly what little chores I had to do before the game started.

My favourite memory of my whole career is actually the All-Ireland final in 1987, but it would be before the game rather than after it. We were in the dressing room, and I was in my usual corner, with Mick Lyons, Liam Harnan and Padraig Lyons on my right, and Colm O'Rourke and Gerry McEntee on my left, and I just remember feeling so happy, so lucky to be there. I was talking to Rourkey, and it was like both of us were in a dream. We were about to play in an All-Ireland final, and while we were all nervous as kittens I'll never forget a great contentment. It was, like, we had made it! We had arrived at the Promised Land. It was never the same for the All-Ireland finals afterwards. Then, we knew too much, we knew how much there was to lose, and that day becomes the worst day of the whole year if you are on the losing team. The more I played in All-Irelands, the more I feared playing badly, losing, just messing up such a great opportunity. But in 1987, I was completely relaxed in comparison. It was the perfect dream. I'd look over at Rourkey and think of Skryne, and all the years we'd played and all the games we'd played, and all that time we never imagined we'd ever play in an All-Ireland final together.

In the All-Ireland semi-final Meath beat Derry by 0-15 to 0-8 in a fairly dour game of football. It was 0-8 to 0-4 at half-time. Dermot McNicholl, the most exciting young talent in Gaelic football had pulled a hamstring a couple of weeks before the game and, as he did so, the plug was also pulled on any chance Derry had of defeating Meath. Derry were inhibited and unimaginative, and with McNicholl hobbling around the field they had a constant reminder of what might have been! McNicholl, actually, had a goal chance despite his problems but was unable to make it count and admitted after the game that he should not have been out there on the field. 'I would have hit that a lot harder if I could,' he explained, 'but the power wasn't there. I knew in the kick-about that things were bad but the team management wanted me to play so I decided to give it a go.' Stafford kicked another four points in a fairly poor performance all round from Boylan's boys. Bernie Flynn scored four as well, and Colm O'Rourke got three points. And with the Meath full-forward line on song, the rest of the team appeared to take the day off!

The 1987 All-Ireland final was the start of a new era for Gaelic football, but would Cork and Meath be able to follow on from where two of the greatest teams in the history of the game had left off? For 13 successive seasons from 1974 to '86 either Dublin or Kerry had been present at Croke Park as one of the contesting counties on All-Ireland final day. On the eve of the 100th All-Ireland football final, Con Houlihan finished his piece in the *Evening Press* with a few special words on Sean Boylan. 'Some people in Cork believe that he is a witch-doctor, and that he should be barred from Croke Park on Sunday', wrote Houlihan. 'Sean, in fact, is a herbalist and, by most accounts, a very special person. He brought Meath out of the pit to win The Centenary Cup, and he cured Moss Keane's long ailing back. A third miracle could lead to canonisation.'

Brian Stafford missed the first free-kick he stepped up to in the 100th All-Ireland football final, but 70 minutes later Stafford was his team's top scorer once more with seven points, four of them from play, and nobody would have argued if he had received the 'Man of the Match' trophy instead of Liam Hayes. Larry Tompkins, in comparison to Stafford, missed five of his last six kicks at goal.

The final score was 1-14 to 0-11, and shortly after the final whistle Meath captain Mick Lyons was being photographed sitting himself down in a spare seat right next to Charlie Haughey and having a little chat with the Taoiseach. In the opening minutes of the game, however, the Meath captain had appeared many miles away from such company as Charlie and Sam! John O'Driscoll and Colm O'Neill were enjoying an amount of freedom, John Cleary won three balls ahead of Bob O'Malley, and Tompkins was seeing very little of Liam Harnan. Jimmy Kerrigan, Cork's renowned defender-turned-attacker was hustling and bustling, and Meath were 0-2 to 0-7 in arrears. With 21 minutes gone, Niall Cahalane surged out of defence to slot over the last Cork score. Incredibly, by half-time Meath led by 1-6 to 0-8. The goal came after a David Beggy run in the 25th minute, when he intercepted a cross-field pass from Tony Davis. O'Rourke passed inside to Bernie Flynn, but his effort was blocked and in the ensuing scramble O'Rourke punched the hopping ball into the net. Another jinking run from Beggy, which brought him around three defenders, levelled the game, and Stafford put Meath in front before the half-time whistle.

P.J. GILLIC: *Funnily enough, the night before, I remember being up in Bellinter where we had our pre-match meal, and I was sitting at the table with Gerry McEntee. A few of the other lads were around and someone was ragging me about not having scored all summer – I think it had been in the papers that I hadn't scored – and Mc said not to worry about it. He hadn't scored either in the whole Championship campaign and I remember him saying, 'Fuck them. The two of us will score tomorrow.' And it turned out that we did. I got the first score of the game, and McEntee also scored in the first half.*

I really enjoyed the build-up to the game. It was taking it to another level for me, to have won a Leinster Championship the year before, and then a second one, and then to be playing in an All-Ireland final – that is exactly what I wanted. It's something that you dream about as a kid and for it to come true was just fantastic. I didn't feel any pressure. I was just happy to be playing. That was one game that I felt absolutely confident we could win.

It actually started off desperately for us. We were down five-one, I think. We had a couple of goal chances – for one of them, I was mad with O'Rourke. I remember Mick Lyons getting a ball off under the Nally Stand, a massive clearance, and I remember catching it. I thought I put a bloody brilliant pass into Colm but he fumbled it in his hands for a minute before kicking it straight up against poor John Kerins, who's since passed away. Colm could have had two goals before he actually fisted the one to the net. I think Staff had a desperate first half – six or seven wides with frees – so I think we were lucky to get back and only be a point or two down at half-time. But we came out and dominated the second half, and won pulling up.

I thought I played well that day. The last 20 minutes were great. I felt confident that we were going to win it as we were dominating right throughout the field. So it was a nice way to win, no mad panic, no pressure at the end. It was an incredible feeling. I remember walking around in the parade before the game and thinking, 'Jesus, this is great!' I was walking down around by the Canal End and I didn't lift my head at all. I was looking right at the ground. I lifted my head then as we were passing by the old dug outs. I remember looking up at Hill 16 – Meath were on the Hill that day - and the colour was just unreal. The noise was incredible, and I let a roar out of me. Tony Brennan was looking at me from the dug-out, and he burst out laughing. Whatever emotion was in me, it came spilling out.

At half-time, Meath knew that they were only starting to play the sort of football they wanted to play on the biggest day of their lives. Cork knew that they had played brilliantly for 25 minutes, but they had lost a five-point lead and in the second period the Munster champions played like a group of men still struggling to forgive themselves. Liam Hayes and Gerry McEntee would go through three Cork pairings in the middle of the field before the final whistle sounded, and McEntee would also have time for a 'quick-step' with Cork manager Billy Morgan when he rushed onto the field to remonstrate with Kevin Foley. Bob O'Malley was racing out the field with every second ball which was directed towards the Meath goalmouth, and he too would have been a worthy recipient of the 'Man of the Match' award. Anything up to a dozen Meath players excelled in the second half, and without Conor Counihan's one-man battle in the Cork defence the game could well have ended in a rout. Cork failed to register a score between the fourth and 32nd minutes of the second half, and Larry Tompkins ended up their top scorer, as everybody expected. Unfortunately, no other Cork player managed more than a single score. It was time for Meath's old boys to celebrate. 'Gerry McEntee and Colm O'Rourke held each other in a long and tight embrace', wrote Donal Keenan in the *Irish Independent* the next morning. 'On the steps of the Hogan Stand, Joe Cassells was mobbed by his younger team-mates. Mick Lyons sat chatting to Charlie. The years of toil and sweat had all been worthwhile.' A Roscommonman who understood the savage hunger of waiting for an All-Ireland, Keenan was writing from the heart. Bernard Flynn raced into the Meath dressing room, saw a short, happy-faced man in the corner of the room and went over to give him a hug. 'We've done it, we've done it,' beamed Bernie. The man was rather surprised. He was a Sligoman, Sean Kilfeather of *The Irish Times* who, since he had never spoken to Bernie Flynn before, felt compelled to give the Meath corner-forward a long look of surprise. 'I've got the wrong man,' admitted Bernie, embarrassed. Kilfeather insisted that Flynn tell him who he had mistaken him for. 'When he told me he thought I was Pat 'The Red' Collier it was my turn to be pleased, for 'The Red' was a central figure in Meath's last All-Ireland win in 1967.'

Meanwhile, Martin Breheny was having a chat with Jack O'Shea behind the Hogan Stand. 'He was full of praise for Meath', wrote Breheny. 'He admitted to being extremely impressed by their recovery powers and remarked with a glint in his eye, "They will take some beating next year." In the end it was Meath's day. More so, it was Gaelic football's day. For in recent weeks one could be forgiven for thinking that there couldn't be a real All-Ireland without either Dublin or Kerry.'

BRIAN STAFFORD: *I went to bed early the night before the All-Ireland final. I wasn't nervous really at all. In fact it was only in my latter years that I started to suffer from nerves. When I was younger I didn't give a damn because I was quite confident in my own ability and knew what job I had to do. Nerves never really came into it at all. Even standing up to take the frees I never felt that there was any huge pressure on me – I knew I was the free-taker and in that sense I was relied upon to kick the frees, but to be honest I never really felt massively nervous. I was practising every evening and had the work done. Any other night we* *weren't training, I was out practising frees.*

I scored seven points that day, but when I look back at the video I missed a good few chances early on and it wasn't down to nerves, just a bit of bad luck. Cork started very well but Rourkey's goal brought us back into it and after that there was only ever going to be one winner. Colman Corrigan was marking me that day and he picked up a bit of a knock when he ran into P.J. Gillic or somebody. I remember my first point from play in particular. I had to bend down and scoop the ball up with my left hand. Then I took off and ran towards the Cork goal and put it over the bar. It gave us the lead for the first time in the game and was probably one of my best scores in Croke Park.

COLM O'ROURKE: *My goal that day was a scrambled affair, to be honest. I had given a brilliant pass forward to Flynn, but he was too slow altogether and he should have scored himself. But as I had to do so often with Bernie, I dug him out of a hole by scoring it myself! No, seriously though, I was falling when I just slapped the ball and it went in.*

After the match was over I remember we went across somewhere for a drink and nobody seemed to pass too much remarks on us at all. My opinion about the All-Ireland final was that it was an anticlimax – I wanted to go home afterwards. I wasn't big into celebrations at that stage of my life. I was 30 years of age, had been married for a few years, and had children and I can't say that the celebrations were better than the Leinster win in '86. I remember coming home on the Monday night with the Sam, and it was great, but that was it for me. I wasn't interested after that. We had been training for so long too, almost a year, constantly, that it was a relief when it was all over. Of course, it was absolutely fantastic to win, but I was just happy to get back to normality.

The next year was the hard year because we had won the League after a replay, and the All-Ireland after a replay. We went back doing a bit of training in October or November of '87 for the League because we had never won a League and were keen on winning it, so it ended up we trained for a year again, constantly. By the time '88 was finished, I was just glad it was over.

I think that this whole idea that Meath were going to do X, Y and Z to Cork in the replay is overdone. At the meeting on the Monday morning after the drawn game, people just more or less said that we had played badly and that it was up to us to get the finger out as such. But there was no such thing as somebody saying they were going to do X, Y and Z!

I had been sick for a good while and got a heavy knock in the drawn match. I got a very bad wallop and I hardly trained at all between both games. I was suffering from headaches a lot. I remember we went off to Cooley and I didn't train up there at all because I was sick. I was suffering badly in the week leading up to the game, but then, when the game started, I was fine.

BOB O'MALLEY: *I would always go out for a couple of drinks the night before a Championship match. I knew I wouldn't sleep otherwise. The night before the All-Ireland final in 1987 was no different, I went out with my own regular group of friends and had two pints of Guinness. It was a great experience to play in an All-Ireland final. I had attended many finals beforehand and wondered what it was like, so it was fantastic to get the chance. It was something you dreamt about as a child. I was marking John Cleary that day and had a dreadful first 15 minutes.*

DARREN FAY: *I remember being on the Hill for the All-Ireland final of*

'87. I was so small that I had to stay on my tippy-toes for the whole lot, but it was worth it, even to get a few glimpses of players like O'Rourke and Lyons, and Larry Tompkins. Tompkins, in fact, came in for an awful lot of abuse back around then from the Meath fans, but it was part and parcel of a Meath versus Cork game at the time. If it wasn't him, it would have been another Cork player, I suppose. 1987 was an amazing time. I remember the All-Ireland winning team travelling around the national schools and then they came into ours. As Meath kids there was no distinction between the senior team coming back from winning an All-Ireland and the Irish team coming back from a World Cup. They were our heroes, even more so considering Meath hadn't won an All-Ireland since 1967.

To win it in 1988 again was a great achievement. I think they got bored after that, and decided to give it to Cork! The one thing I think is that Cork never got the same recognition as Meath did back then. Cork won back-to-back All-Irelands in 1989 and 1990, yet Meath were always talked about as the real legends. Maybe it was Cork's style of play. I don't know. Cork were in four All-Ireland finals in a row and ended up winning two of them, which was a massive achievement. Even though people agree Cork were a great team back then, I don't think they are put in the same league as Meath, right or wrong.

JIMMY FAY: *The defeat by Laois in Tullamore in '85 had been bad, but I will never forget all of us going to the Beechmount Hotel in Navan for dinner the following Friday night. I could feel it then – something was going to happen with this team. Everybody was there, nobody failed to show and that is quite unusual for a dinner, especially after losing by a cricket score the previous weekend. That was how much the players liked and respected Sean Boylan. They all turned up for the dinner.*

I remember sitting in the Hogan Stand two years later on the day of the All-Ireland final. I sat there praying and praying. Cork started brilliantly, we came back. O'Rourke scored a goal and we finished stronger – the praying had worked! All-Ireland champions! All down to God and Sean, but it is easy to mix those two up.

I met Sean after a League match in Navan in early 1996. And, to be honest, even though Darren was involved, I thought that we would be knocked out in the first round of the Leinster Championship. So I was chatting to Sean and I said, 'Jesus Sean, we are not going to do much here this year.' Immediately, he looked me in the eye and replied, 'Jimmy, we will win the All-Ireland.' I said, 'You're joking?' He said he wasn't. Short, sweet and true, but that just shows you the belief he has in his players – because, we were useless at the time.

Almost every year our family go abroad on holidays and we miss a Meath game. As it works out, it is usually a Meath-Dublin game, but the first thing I do every Monday morning is send a postcard back to Sean congratulating him. It has become a habit almost. I get up, have my breakfast and go out into the sun and send a postcard to Sean. If Meath lost I would still send him a postcard.

MARK O'REILLY: I was watching the games at home on the box in those years, but a lot of legends emerged from those football games. I remember the cup coming back in 1987 when Mick Lyons was captain. He was from my club in Summerhill and it was just amazing. Mick, Padraig and Liam Hayes came down to the school in Trim with the cup. Myself and Darren Fay were in school in Trim at the time, and it was brilliant to have the senior lads coming around.

MICKEY McQUILLAN: I never really had a problem with sleeping *before big games because I didn't really have a problem with nerves. The night before the final I was at home with my feet up watching a video. My mind drifted a bit sometimes to the game but on the whole I was not that nervous. Sean didn't do anything different in the dressing room that day. He just walked around with his hands in his pockets, saying, 'Well, fella!' He just told us to compete and do our best. We were all mad looking forward to the game that day.*

TERRY FERGUSON: *The Cork-Meath saga began that day, and it was a great thrill to come out on top. We all had a routine. Sean was always a great believer in never changing your routine. So if you usually went out on Saturday night and had a drink then do so, not to excess of course, but he didn't want us to change our routine. He didn't want us to sit at home and dwell about things or worry about things. 'Do what you normally do', he would say. So I remember going out in the town of Kells that Saturday night before the game, and I went to the Round Tower pub and I met the lads as I always did. I had my few 7Ups like I usually did. I went through the normal Saturday night routine, as if I wasn't playing the biggest game of my life the next day. People were around the pubs selling good luck cards and the like. Of course there were loads of fellas coming up messing, asking me what the hell was I doing there, but it was all good natured and everybody was wishing me the best. The fans were looking forward to it just as much as we were. Sunday morning, myself and Martin O'Connell, like always, had a steak on the morning of a big game because Kepak supplied all of us with meat. We usually met up at Ashbourne House, – myself and P.J. Gillic, Staff, all used to travel together as the same crew, but that day we met in Malahide, got our rooms sorted and went for a walk along the beach. Over the next few years this too would become part of a routine for all* *of us.*

Sean wished us all good luck in the dressing room. We would have had four or five meetings prior to the game and he would not come over and talk to us individually. I was marking Colm O'Neill and I remember for weeks before the game it was drummed into my head that he only had a left foot - his right foot was only for standing on – so I said good enough! When the first ball came in, he got it and I stayed on his left and, suddenly, he turned over onto his right and put it over the black spot. That put our weeks of team meetings out the window. After that, I just had to make sure he didn't get a ball because I didn't know what way he would turn.

Billy (Morgan) came onto the field on one occasion and started giving out and, Gerry being Gerry, pretty much told him he had no business out here on the field. Billy was a very enthusiastic man, just like Sean, and naturally enough he was looking after his own corner. The dressing room was just hectic afterwards and the one vivid memory I have is that after a while, when it all calmed down, I looked up and saw the Sam Maguire perched proudly on the warm-up table in the middle of the dressing room, our dressing room, on our warm-up table, our Sam Maguire. And that image has stuck with me since.

MARTIN O'CONNELL: *It was seven points to two, and Cork were just picking off points to beat the band while we were running all over the place. I remember Jimmy Kerrigan getting onto a breaking ball around the middle of the field and he soloed in – he must have gone about 40 or 50 yards – when Mick Lyons blocked the ball on his foot when he went to shoot. That lifted the whole thing. That was the turning point for me. We got the goal then and went from seven-two to a point ahead. It was O'Rourke's goal, but I started it! I remember John Kerins (Lord have* *mercy on him). He was the best man to kick balls out to the left wing, right wing, or down the centre. He was always able to pick men out. John O'Driscoll at that time was a huge name, and I happened to be on him. He had been in Australia and he was the best thing over there. He had a massive jump to catch a ball. He was like Teddy McCarthy, but he could go even higher. I remember Kerins kicking out the ball to him – it wasn't that high – but he caught it in front of me on his chest. He soloed and hopped it, but I just kept knocking him back and I must have pushed him back about 20 yards when the ball broke out to Jinksy, and Jinksy just pulled on it. It went straight in to Colm O'Rourke. He passed it to Flynn, I think, and when Flynn's shot was blocked, Rourkey ran in and punched it to the net – a scrappy enough goal, but that was the start of it. And then we tagged on a few points. David Beggy scored a few fantastic points.*

When the final whistle goes, it's unbelievable. I was crying out on the pitch – a first All-Ireland – sure this was what I always dreamt about. To get your first one is just fantastic and to do it the way we did it! Add in the fact that it was 20 years since the last. After '87 we sat down and said to ourselves, 'This is not going to go on forever, so we might as well make the best of this.' At that stage it all came back to me, what I had done the previous year. Walking away from the panel brought it all home to me all the more. And I remember thinking, 'What the feck was I at?'

Bernie Flynn and Bob O'Malley had made it. Clubmates and good mates, the pair often struggled to see eye to eye with Sean Boylan, whom they continually claimed liked to climb up on their backs more than any other players in the Meath dressing room. O'Malley had badly regretted missing out on the glory of the first Leinster title in '86, when he tried everything he knew to get into the manager's good books. Boylan, in truth, didn't spend too much time worrying about the older, married or more settled players in his squad. And he knew that the new boys he had brought in over the previous 12 months would not dare 'misbehave' behind his back. O'Malley and Flynn? They were different. Flynn, for starters, was the first Meath footballer to walk into the dressing room on match days with his bag in one hand and his best, after-match clothes over his other shoulder. It did not take Inspector Morse to deduce that Flynn, and O'Malley too, each had a night life.

Bernie Flynn had been full-forward on the Meath team which lost the 1983 Leinster minor final to Kildare. O'Malley was full-back. Flynn and O'Malley had won a Meath junior football title with St. Colmcille's in 1983. In the semi-final of that junior championship, St Colmcille's had played Dunboyne and Flynn found a squat, stocky figure marking him in the second half. He did not need to be told that it was the Meath manager who was trying to chase after him.

BERNIE FLYNN: *I didn't think anything of it at the time, but he was fairly fit. We were well ahead as I recall, and there wasn't that long to go when he came on. I didn't realise I'd spend a good few years after it with him. He was very clean. I'd say there were times afterwards he regretted not giving me a box. Sean is extremely strong*

The likes of Lyons, Cassells, Hayes, O'Rourke, these guys were pretty set in their ways at the time. O'Malley, Martin O'Connell and myself came on the scene at that time, but I was probably a little bit different. Or so I was told afterwards. I dressed a bit differently – their (the older players) dress at that time left a lot to be desired.

Right up until the early '90s, when we were focused and going for the Championship, the training sessions were pretty vicious. It was always played as a match, and there were a good few schemozzles. I remember being involved in a punch-up with Mick Lyons on a particular day. He hit me a few times in a match, and I remember saying to Mick, 'If you do that again, I'm going to hit you back.' So he did it again. And I turned around and I burst him with a box, split his nose. But afterwards in the dressing room, Mick just shook hands and said, 'This is over. Forget about it.'

Probably the most famous incident I was involved in at training was with Gerry McEntee's brother, Andy, who was a panellist at the end of the '80s. Jesus Christ, I'll never forget it. Andy was put in at corner-back and he was hitting pretty hard. That was OK but I remember saying, 'Andy, if you hit me again!' Well, he hit me one more time and I burst him with a box too. The second that happened, Sean got so annoyed! He stopped the training session and made us do laps until the end. He told us to fuck off, basically. 'Fuck off there, and come back when you've manners.' I think they were the words used. Well, we had hardly gone halfway around the top of the field when we started punching the head off each other again. So he stopped the training session and ran the whole way up, and he hit the two of us in the chest. 'You think you're hard men?' That's exactly what he said. 'You think you're hard men? I'll take the fuckin' two of you on', he says. If one of us had have struck him, there would have been a free-for-all. All it would have taken was for us to lift a hand. Sean wouldn't have struck first.

I was close to hitting him. Sure he hit me right into the chest! I remember being so mad and annoyed. I remember storming home after training that night. When Sean lost the head over something, he lost it.

He wouldn't lose his cool too many times, but that was one of them.

I actually don't think I had a short fuse on the football field. But I used to get a good bit of stick in training. Beggy got some awful treatment as well, but Beggy would just take it and keep going. I'd never start anything, I never started a row in my life, but if someone was genuinely acting the bollocks I'd stand up for myself.

I remember a dreadful incident with John McEnroe in training, kamikaze stuff! He literally tried to take the head off me. I had a couple of rows with him.

But the one incident that sticks in my mind more than anything – and it didn't help his career – was with Padraig Lyons. We were going for a ball one night in training, early in 1987, and he went to kill me with his boot. I think it was touch and go whether Padraig was going to be picked for the Championship, so he was trying to make an impact. He just missed me. But it was such a bad kick that if he had got me, he would have definitely killed me. He even says himself, he would have destroyed me and what happened was that he actually damaged his own leg. It was the reason that he was out of the team for a long, long time. He probably puts the incident down as the finish of him being a regular.

PADRAIG LYONS: *I got bad news before that training session. On the Tuesday night before the first round of the Championship against Laois in Portlaoise, I got word I was dropped. So on the Thursday night at training, Bernie was going down for a ball and I was coming across. He went down to pick it up and I pulled for all I was worth, and tore all the ligaments in my knee and missed '87 completely. I was in plaster for six weeks – it would have been better to break a bone. The reason I would have done it was pure frustration. It wasn't his head I was going for. I was going for the ball, in fairness, but on the Thursday night before a big*

The Row, September 29, 1996

Colm Coyle and Liam McHale, September 29 1996

match it would have been a fairly reckless challenge. It was nothing to do with Bernie.

I was there with Meath from '81 to '91, and it was probably the best ten-year period of my life. For the first six years, I was No. 4 – I was corner-back from the time I was first thrown the jersey until that night before the Laois match in '87, and from then on I was jockeying for the position with Terry Ferguson. But, all in all, I wouldn't change a thing. Myself and Michael were working together for nearly all of that time. At the time, we were in plant hire, machinery and that. In the late '80s, when the evenings were getting shorter and Sean wanted to train when it was bright, we were working up in Dublin, and we could be leaving the place at half past four. We had a good few lads working for us at the time, and it was debatable what they were at when we were gone! But the way I looked on it was, 'I could never do this again. When I'm finished football, I can always work – if I want to – for the rest of my life. But I can't go back playing football at 45. So while I'm able, I'll do it.' Work-wise, there would be lads who couldn't understand what we were doing, but Michael was of the same frame of mind as me.

I'd say if I hadn't done myself in that Thursday night, I might have got back. The lad that went in for me was Des Lane. Things didn't go well for Des and he was dropped later on. Now, I know work wasn't helping me and that it wasn't all down to that – I have to take a certain amount of responsibility myself – but I think I would have got back in when things didn't work out for him, and you never know what might have happened after that.

I played ten minutes or less in the '87 final. I think Boylan even togged me out for the Leinster final too, but it was just for show. I was never going to play. At the time he put me on, I was half-reluctant. I said, 'It's OK, Sean.' But I remember on the bus on the way home, I thanked him for that ten minutes. It would have been terrible if you had played for all those years and, let's say we didn't reach another All-Ireland, and I hadn't played in that one. It didn't matter whether I touched the ball or not. Some of my cousins often laugh at me, that I seemed the busiest player on the field. They say that I wanted to pack in the whole match into those ten minutes. It was a help to be on the field when it finished up. Without a doubt it was, but would I have felt the same as the lads who had played all year, in all the matches? I doubt it. I got rid of my sub's jersey, however, and got a Cork jersey at the end. I off-loaded the sub's jersey and got Colm O'Neill's jersey instead.

BERNIE FLYNN: I remember when I went in first in '84, we used to train on the sand-dunes at Bettystown, even when it was dark. Sean had this run made out – up and down the sand-dunes. Well it was so bad, I literally couldn't stick it. I vomited on the ground. I stopped and I waited for the lads to come around again and join up with them. I didn't think Sean had seen me but just as I got up to get back into the line, Sean stopped the whole training session. I never felt as low. He made me feel so small. He absolutely devoured me for not sticking at it. He said, 'If you ever do that again – out!' What he was saying was, you never bottle it, you never stop! You don't give in at any stage. No matter what, you keep going. And I did give in that night, but I never gave in again. I remember training on the Hill of Tara with some fellas and they were getting sick as they were running, and they'd just keep going, do it to one side and keep running. It was crazy stuff.

I would say in the '87 All-Ireland final, O'Rourke and Stafford and myself worked extremely hard. While we didn't score that much together, it was probably one of our best performances collectively. I remember going out in the second half to the midfield and half-forward *line, and the two lads inside getting that bit more space. If things weren't happening, we would always try and create two inside. Colm would go out to the half-forward line quite a lot. But if one of the lads was tired, I often went out to half-forward to try and win a bit of ball, try and leave a bit more space inside. We would actually give the nod to each other, give a signal to change tactics. At that time, the marking was extremely tight, particularly against teams like Dublin and Cork. We met quite regularly at that time and to get a score, by God you had to earn it. At that time you wouldn't score five or six points from play off any defender, something which happens now. I, personally, would love to be playing now. Back then, there was a huge amount of pulling and dragging.*

O'Rourke was able for it. He was a huge man to win a ball. I still think people don't realise how good Colm O'Rourke was. There were times when we played a lot of particularly high ball into Colm, and he was fantastic at winning it. But we could have played more lower ball to him, tried to change things around a bit.

Sean kept it extremely simple, very basic. Tactics as we know nowadays, and tactical moves, they were a virtual no-no! First and foremost, you killed yourself winning the ball, and you tried then to give it to a team-mate. There was no pussy-footing around.

After a while, Sean knew that he was dealing with lads who were shrewd, who knew what forward play was about. But the team meetings went on for ages. And then Joe Cassells would start talking, and that would be it! We christened Joe the 'Salmon of Knowledge'. Just when we were ready to go home, Joe would start the whole thing again. I used to dread that. The team meetings were actually quite good, but we used to get together for training at seven or half-seven and we wouldn't get home until twelve, half-twelve. Every night, practically, we had a meeting.

We had a meal afterwards in Bellinter and then we'd have a chat. Sure it would take an hour to get everyone congregated together. Jesus, it used to drive me crazy! Everyone would have an input. Sean at that time had no real family. When he did start having the family later on, the team meetings were a whole lot shorter!

When you look at the great men we had, leaders now – Cassells, Hayes, Lyons, Harnan, McEntee – we didn't win enough for the quality that was there. That squad could easily have won four All-Irelands. We blew it against Kerry in '86, but that was a learning process. The '89 Leinster final sticks out for me. We should have beaten Dublin. We were in brilliant shape that year. Dublin beat us with a last-minute goal that was deflected in off Martin O'Connell's elbow.

The Dublin games around then took a lot out of the team. Only for us, that Dublin team would have probably won quite a bit. Beating Dublin in a sense though was the be-all and end-all.

It was absolutely incredible. I marked a good few Dublin players, Pat Canavan, P.J. Buckley, Mick Deegan – they were all good, tight players. Deegan in particular was very fast. Even though you would get a lot of ball, he would get a lot of ball too.

BOB O'MALLEY: *Sean came across as a very welcoming person when I first got on the panel. I was only 18 years of age going in there and it was a little bit daunting with some of the experienced players that were around at the time, but Sean made me feel welcome from the very outset. In my first Leinster final in '84 I played all right as the spare man when Dublin were reduced to 14, but I think I had done the damage when playing at corner-back because I slipped twice and was effectively involved in conceding two goals. Rock and Duff scored a goal apiece for Dublin that day.*

I was dropped for the Leinster semi-final in '86. It was tough and difficult. I didn't feel I deserved to be dropped at the time but retrospectively, yes, I probably did because I wasn't playing good enough football. Sean would come over and tell a fella he was being dropped if he didn't feel you were going well enough. That was his way and his was a good way too. I went to the front of the pack in 1987 in training because after being dropped I realised I was going to have to change. Training was wonderful and brutal all at once. It was very tough and demanding.

Winning the All-Ireland in 1987 gave us a bit of confidence and we knew we had a good thing going heading into '88. The attitude going into that Championship was that we had to make the most of it while it lasted. When Gerry McEntee got sent off in the All-Ireland replay in '88, there seemed to be a switch flicked, or a trigger pulled, and all the players realised we were going to have to come out of the traps now and just go at it, and we did. But it is not one of those things that you have the time to make a conscious decision about. You just react.

It took a lucky goal to beat us in the Leinster final in 1989. Vinny Murphy won a ball, turned and was kicking for a point, but it actually struck Martin O'Connell on the elbow and deflected into the net. It was just one of those things, I suppose. There were matches where we got those breaks, but on that day Dublin had the luck. We had to take it on the chin, but it was very disappointing at the time – painful.

The Meath team worked its way through the National league in 1987-88 without a care in the world, and played some outstanding football, culminating in an eight-point victory over their greatest rivals in the NFL final replay in Croke Park. It was the third time Meath had played Dublin over the winter and spring, as the teams had drawn in the opening round of the League in November, and again ended all square in the League final. The November meeting, however, did not go down great with the Meath players. Before they left their dressing room they had laughed and chatted about the Dublin players waiting outside in the cold, ready to clap the reigning All-Ireland champs onto the field. That was always the case in the league games between September and Christmas, the All-Ireland champs receiving an official welcome from their opponents. Kerry would give Meath such a reception a few weeks later, in December, when Boylan proudly brought his troops down to Tralee as High Kings! And, back in '83, the Meath team had given the visiting Dublin team a warm welcome in Navan. Never mind that it was totally insincere, and that Gerry McEntee had said to the players before leaving the dressing room, 'Let's clap them onto the field, and then kick the shite out of them!' The fact was that Meath had grinned and borne it. But when Meath ran out onto the field in November of 1987 the Dublin team were nowhere in sight outside the tunnel, and were instead down at the Hill 16 end of the field kicking the ball around.

In the drawn League final, Dublin had thrown everything at breaking their losing sequence against their neighbours, and they had narrowly failed. Declan Bolger and Jim Bissett, for starters, had outplayed Gerry McEntee and Liam Hayes in the middle of the field and after Mick Galvin punched the ball to the net eight minutes from the end it appeared that Gerry McCaul had received the breakthrough he had worked so hard for as Dublin manager. Meath, however, scrambled four points in the last seven minutes, as the fear of losing to Dublin once again became absolutely overwhelming. With the last kick of the game, Joe McNally equalised. The replay was a different matter entirely. The Meath team had taken off to the United States for the Allstars tour, for two weeks between the two Dublin games, and came back wanting to play some serious football. Liam Hayes came back a week later, two days before the game, after spending his honeymoon down the West Coast of the States also. Meath defeated Dublin 2-13 to 0-12. Stafford got five points, Flynn also scored five, and Hayes scored the 'goal of his life'.

LIAM HAYES: *There was definitely somebody looking down on me that month. Three times in San Francisco I had been uncomfortably close to trouble. I bumped into fruit-cakes all over the place. First, on one of the trams going downhill at 30 miles per hour one afternoon, I happened to glance at this guy who threw a paper bag full of milk onto the street. He patted me on the backside and called me a couple of names and wanted to continue our conversation at the next stop. I had my new wife by my side, and decided it was not time to prove my manliness – I still had the Dubs waiting for me back at home! When I went running around Golden Gate Park on a training spin one afternoon this madman suddenly started shouting at me and running beside me. And then when Anne and I took a train ride out to Oakland to see the local team, the A's, in a baseball game, a row started on the seats right next to us. If that was not bad enough, Anne's father J.P. picked the two of us up at Shannon Airport on the Friday before the League final replay, and half an hour out on the road we took this corner and discovered there was a truck parked in the middle of the road! J.P. jammed on the brakes. I was in the front passenger seat and the truck was on my side, and I ended up with my face about two inches from the rear of the damned thing. Whatever was happening, there was luck coming my way, and on the*

Sunday I scored the goal of my life, the one I had always dreamed of scoring in Croke Park. I saw P.J. Gillic gathering the ball and took a quick pass from him about 70 or 80 yards from the Dublin goal. I was running towards the Canal End and I had a fair bit of steam worked up. Nobody was catching me, and the defenders were backing off, staying with their men, and I just kept looking at John O'Leary and the Dublin goal. And, honest to God, the goal got bigger and bigger! None of the lads has ever believed that I was going for a goal, because I kicked the ball into the top right-hand corner of the net from about 21 yards out, but believe me, I had been running for so long the goal looked 50 yards wide. And the top right-hand corner was like the side of a house! I said to myself, 'I'll put it in there.'

DES LANE: We went to Boston and San Francisco between the League finals against Dublin. That was another great time. It was just all the fellas themselves. I remember meeting up with Dennis Murtagh. He was a guy who used to play for Summerhill and went to America to earn his fortune or whatever in Boston. Anyway, we were having breakfast one morning and there was myself, Murtagh, Padraig Lyons, Bernard Flynn and an Armagh footballer who was in America with the Allstars. Anyway, Murtagh brought us to every Irish pub in Boston and this was about 12 o'clock in the day. At one time we were actually on the second round of the pubs. We went into a bar and were all sitting with a drink when we heard this music and thought, 'Hold on a minute, that sounds familiar.' So we went to the lounge and who's in there sitting on a high stool in the lounge with a guitar, playing to his heart's content, only David Beggy. Honest to God. Anyway, we remained out all night and never came home. We ended up staying in Dennis Murtagh's place. The next morning he gave us a lift back to where we were staying. Beside the *hotel there was one of these twisty multi-storey car parks where you just keep driving round and round. Anyway, the Armagh footballer kept saying all day, 'Jaysus, you Meath boys can't drink at all.' But on the second storey of the car park we had to stop because he had to get out to get sick. Not only that, but he was trying to hide from Fr Sean Hegarty, a little priest who was with the Allstars team at the time. Eventually we arrived back and in the middle of the lobby of the hotel we noticed all the Meath boys standing with their gear on them. I asked, 'What's going on?' They told us that Sean said there was training, but myself and Padraig thought, 'Fuck sake, sure we can't go training.' So we tried to skip off up the stairs but we bumped into Sean on the way. We told him, 'We're just going around here Sean for a minute. We just left our gear in another room and we're just going to get it'. So it ended up that we had to go training that morning. But I think once everyone was on the pitch he abandoned the session. He lost the head completely - we were running around for 15 minutes and he just went mad because he knew we weren't up for it at all.*

Packie Henry wasn't feeling well either on one of the mornings because he had probably been out the night before. Anyway, Sean brought us to some park to train. It wasn't even a pitch, it was something like a public park and it was all bumpy, not flat, and Packie was running for a ball at one stage but stepped into a bump and went head over heels. Sean nearly had a complete mickey-fit! He went mad and made us run around for the next hour. He'd be losing the head over things like that. I was gone off the team in 1989. I finished after '88. After the All-Ireland in '88 I was asking myself did I still have the interest. I mean, when you're not getting back in the team you start thinking, 'Jaysus, what's the story here?'

MICKEY McQUILLAN: *Sean worked us hard over there, especially if most of the lads had a few pints the night before. I remember we were running one day and P.J. Gillic was in front of me and Sean got him by the nicks and actually pulled P.J. along. I couldn't stop laughing. Sean ran all the way around with him like that.*

There was a fair quantity of bad blood on display in the League final replay, with Kevin Foley once again being banished to the sideline after an early altercation involving five Meath defenders and five Dublin forwards. At the end of the off-the-ball scene, three Dublin players were on the ground receiving some attention, and among them was their new hot-shot forward Vinny Murphy. The Meath team had been hearing a lot about young Murphy. And, unbeknownst to him or anyone else in Dublin, there was a secret agreement within the Meath team concerning anybody new who appeared in the Dublin camp – manager or footballer, it didn't matter. Any new Dublin manager, any new Dublin footballer, had to be stopped from making a name for himself. There would be no new heroes in blue! That was the promise within the Meath squad, though Foley happened to be a quite innocent party in the incident which led to his sending off. For once in his life, at least, he was half-innocent! As he was on all-fours on the ground in the 11th minute of the game, he was kicked by one of the Dublin forwards. That started the fireworks, which were completed in double-quick time. In the dressing room afterwards there followed one of the most famous interviews in the history of the Meath football team. As he emerged naked from the showers and stood by his clothes, Kevin Foley was asked by one brave reporter, did he throw a punch? 'I did,' replied Foley.

'Was it the first punch?' asked the reporter.

'The fourth, I think,' replied Foley.

'Who threw the others?'

I don't know.'

'How do you feel?'

'Bad.'

'Was it a good win?' continued the reporter.

'You're standing on my fucking towel!' stated Foley. The reporter withdrew to safety.

As Meath and Dublin sized each other up before the 1988 Leinster final, there was a sniff of unfinished business about the game. Dublin were also desperate to prevent Meath recording a historic three-in-a-row of provincial final victories. Meath were just desperate to beat Dublin, for no other reason than that Dublin had been beating them for about 800 years. On the night before the game, Brian Stafford failed a fitness test and, while there was no panic, everyone on the team felt shaken. With Staff missing, Meath would have to win a low-scoring game. Next day, Staff never took the field, and O'Rourke and Flynn also failed to score, and Meath only managed seven scores over the 70 minutes. And, somehow, Meath retained the Leinster trophy, 2-5 to 0-9, incredibly. Charlie Redmond kicked a penalty over the bar in the final moments of the contest, after Vinny Murphy bit the dust in the Meath goalmouth. Mick Kennedy, Dublin's No. 1 penalty-taker was limping down the other end of the field with a foot injury, and Barney Rock had been rank out of form all afternoon, so the horrendous chore fell to Redmond. Dublin deserved the draw. They had lost Dave Synnott through a sending-off 12 minutes into the second half, and even in his absence they continued to fight back courageously from the double-whammy of conceding two goals to Meath in the opening 15 minutes of the game. Early goals! How times between Meath and Dublin had changed! P.J. Gillic and McCabe had scored the goals, and the pair also scored four points between them, while Liam Hayes was also on target. Three players scored – not Staff, not Rourkey, and not Flynn – and Meath, amazingly, had held onto their Leinster crown. In the Dublin dressing room Sean Boylan poured his heart out in sympathy after the match. 'You gave us a lesson,' he began, 'We were very lucky. It's not nice, lads, I'm telling you. It's not nice coming back into your dressing room. It looks like rubbing salt in the wounds. Please don't think I'm doing that. I'm not doing that.' As the Meath manager continued to speak, Dublin full-back Gerry Hargan turned to a reporter and remarked, ' You'd think he had lost it!' The Dublin manager Gerry McCaul, like so many Meath team bosses down through the years before him, explained exactly how Dublin had been defeated. 'It was the two goals,' he stressed. 'That's how we lost it, and it's as simple as that.'

BERNIE FLYNN: *Dave Synott and myself, we played in two Leinster finals on each other. I was actually working with him with Tennents at the time - there were eight of us on the same sales team. In '88, I remember being with him all week before the game, chatting and doing a bit of promotional work for the business, a bit of PR work for the company through the newspapers. Now Dave was marking me on the Sunday. Dave's wife and my wife Madeline were above in the stand together for the match. He had been taken off me the match before that, so I knew it was going to be fairly tense. Yet our company had us doing promotional work in Meagher's of Ballybough together after the match –*

we had a tent and everything laid on! It was wrong – it was a bit of naivety on our part. If you lose at a Dublin-Meath match, you don't want to see anybody. But we had agreed to this promotional work together, and the girls were to meet us afterwards.

We agreed that no matter what happened in the match, we'd meet each other afterwards. Little did we know what was to follow!

Dave was on me and, for some reason he became very aggressive, which wasn't his style. He was thumping and kicking, and thumping a good bit. I said Dave, 'If you keep this up, I'm going to burst you' – that's exactly what I said. And with that, he hit me a box right to the side of the jaw. The referee copped him but, well, the next thing that happened – and I don't know how I got away with it – I hit him with the butt of my elbow as hard as I could, and broke his nose. The referee comes over, Dave's pumping blood and I'm on the ground, and whatever the linesman said to him, he sent Dave off and left me on the field! I didn't get caught, which was dreadful. So the two women are sitting in the stand, and I'm left on the field, and we win the Leinster final.

I remember meeting Madeline and Dave's wife Maria. She was crying and I put my arm around her and apologised. I went down to Meagher's then and the girls came down, but Dave Synnott never appeared. I hung on for him for about three hours and eventually he arrives in. Initially he was very cool but after a few drinks, it was OK. We got on grand.

Because of what happened, I never went back with the team to the Ashbourne House that evening. I stayed with Dave, and later that night our sales manager Michael Gilroy had a party in his house for about 40 people, and we all went back there late. What happened then? I wrote off my car. It was a Bank Holiday Monday the next day and I had to do a promotion in Gibney's of Malahide. And who came with me and did all the promotion, helped me with transport, but Dave Synnott. A year later, Dave was at my stag party. He brought Charlie Redmond with him, who was actually on crutches at the time. He had crashed on the way home and wrote off his car! Now that's a story of two company cars!

We still meet up and get on very well. I would probably mix a bit more with that Dublin team than most of the Meath fellas. Working with Dave as well, I knew a lot of the Dublin lads. That night of the stag, there was a cow strayed out from a field, about half four or five in the morning, and he wrote off the car. We were in the Boyne Valley Hotel in Drogheda. They all stripped me and put me out on the street. We were all good pals.

Not like Mayo and Meath in '96! The moaning was unbelieveable after that All-Ireland final. But Mayo would have had a name in GAA circles. They moaned a fair bit. That's the one thing with Meath and Dublin. No matter how lucky or unlucky you were to win or lose, it was all over and forgotten.

The last few years, Meath have become easy with the media. But go back to the late '80s and the early '90s, some of the stuff that was written about Meath was just incredible! I remember going into the replay of the '88 League final. We had been away on an Allstars trip – we went to America in between the two matches – and some of the stuff that was written at home about the fighting out there, stories about Kevin Foley and Ciaran Duff, was just dreadful.

Some of the articles were kept for us when we got back. I remember going out in that League final replay against Dublin and we said that if we won, we wouldn't open our mouths to the media, that we'd shove it up to them. From around '87 to '91 the media really were on our backs. In '91 that changed because of the way we won friends that year, but we lost the All-Ireland!

I could not put into words the hurt and the disappointment of the '91 defeat by Down. Even today, now, it hurts talking about it. You could get over Cork beating you in a final because you had beaten them a few times, but the '91 defeat, it probably would have been one of the greatest All-Irelands ever won – the games against Dublin, the comebacks – and yet we lost!

I'll never forget the feeling among the squad that night, and on the Monday. I remember going home on the Tuesday and my mother still crying. She hadn't moved out of the chair at the cooker from Sunday night. When I walked in the door she just started up again. I remember walking straight out of the house. I couldn't face it. It took months and months. A lot of us never got over it.

It wasn't worth anything, all those ten games that year. The Meath team and Sean Boylan were realists. There was no bullshit. When you were beaten, you were beaten. And if you didn't win it, you didn't deserve to win it. There was no feeling sorry for ourselves, but we messed up against Down. And no disrespect to them, they played very well on the day, but if it was any other given Sunday we would have beaten them.

In the All-Ireland semi-final, Meath were found guilty of putting their feet up near the end of the contest, as the team led 0-12 to 0-2. Then Liam McHale scored a goal with a shot from 20 yards out, and then Anthony Finnerty got a second goal, followed by another goal by McHale beating Liam Harnan in the air and flicking the ball to the net. Luckily, the third Mayo goal was disallowed, but Meath were still in total disarray in the closing minutes of the game. The final score was 0-16 to 2-5, but the good of the win had been eaten away by Mayo's fightback.

Four weeks later, the defending All-Ireland champs were still nervy and unsettled. Cork dictated large portions of the game, and they also got stuck into Meath in no uncertain manner. It was 0-12 to 1-9 at the finish, but Colm O'Rourke looked an old man back in the team hotel as he still felt the effects of a shoulder charge to the chest and head from Barry Coffey. Stafford had five stitches inserted into a cut over his lip after one tackle by Niall Cahalane, and Dinny Allen's elbow had connected with Mick Lyons's jaw and the Meath full-back also retired to bed early with a pounding headache. Nobody could say that Cork were deliberately dirty, but they had got some big hits in! They also played some great football from the opening bell. Teddy McCarthy received a great cross-field ball from Dinny Allen and slotted the ball between Mickey McQuillan's legs in the opening minutes, but four points from Staff and two mighty efforts by Rourkey had Meath in front, 0-6 to 1-2, at half-time. Larry Tompkins was enjoying more freedom than the previous year, wandering deep into midfield, winning the ball and racing at the Meath defence. He finished the game with eight great points, but he was also wide with two or three scoreable frees which would have completed one of the greatest one-man shows ever witnessed in Croke Park on All-Ireland final day. Stafford, who quietly also scored eight points for himself, levelled the game with the last kick of the day, after David Beggy was adjudged to have been fouled by Dave Barry. Kerry referee Tommy Sugrue got a blasting from every Cork footballer on the field after he blew the final whistle, but in their hearts the Cork team knew that one iffy decision by the referee should not have been crucial. They had not finished Meath off, and three weeks later they were asked to repeat their outstanding performance.

PADRAIG LYONS: *I played well in the first half of that All-Ireland, but I will never forget the feeling at half-time in the dressing room – my legs went! I should have called Sean to take me off during the second half. Maybe the whole thing had just sunk in – nerves, whatever – I don't know. But I'd be no more nervous than the next guy. I felt great in the first half and was going well. But I went in at half-time, sat down to have the cup of tea, a bit of talk going on, and I could actually feel the power draining out of my legs. I'll never forget it. And running out then, it was like running out on legs that weren't my own. I knew that there was a problem. I regret not going off. I said it to Sean a long time afterwards and he said, 'Why didn't you tell me? I'd have got you right.' But I never said anything at the time. I remember Paul McGrath going round the long side and I even cut off the angle and still couldn't get to him, because there was nothing there. I wasn't the fastest in the world, but I knew how to get from A to B! I would have got the run-around from Paul McGrath in the second half. And that was the nail in my coffin for the replay.*

I'd say Michael told me I was being dropped for the replay. 'There's bad news coming.' He probably said something like that. In between the two games, we went up to Ballymascanlon Hotel in Louth, and played a harem-scarem match up there. We played a match among each other and hammered the daylights out of each other. There were locals up there who couldn't believe what they were seeing. And this the next morning, after going drinking, and going to the disco! We knocked seven bells out of each other. A couple of lads went off with knocks on the leg, there were a few late tackles, and plenty of cross words.

I felt by that stage that Sean had lost confidence in me. I could feel it – I just knew it! Anything that I did wrong seemed to be picked up, whereas in the early years it was as if I could do no wrong. I felt that any time I had a sub-par performance, I got hammered for it. Sean doesn't like to meet those things head-on. He did come out to me one night. It would have been '88. I think I was dropped for the Leinster final, but there was an injury to someone and I got back in. Michael was here in the house the same night. Sean was told, 'You'd better come out.' Michael and myself were here when he came in the door and I remember saying, 'Why can't you just leave me alone to get on with it?' That comes back to always feeling under pressure. It got the better of me that night. I went off to my room and he followed me up. I cried the same night. Sure he didn't know what to say to me, and I didn't know what to say to him. It wasn't anger at him. But he says, 'Give yourself a night to think about it. Take the night off.' So I did. And then went back on the Thursday night.

There was no question of Michael going out in sympathy with me. I would have no time for that. Michael would have been as annoyed as me, but he would have got on with it and done his own thing.

I quit the panel at one stage. It's an episode we all have a great laugh about now, but it was after the All-Ireland years. We flew down to Farranfore to play Kerry for the opening of a pitch. Meath had played a match the week beforehand in Summerhill and I was playing. So off we went down, and I togged out. Everything was grand – and then I got a sub's jersey. 'That's fuckin' it', I thought. I had the boots and everything on me when I picked up the jersey. I was actually putting it on when I saw all the numbers on the back of it! I knew straight away that there was a number too many on it! So I put my clothes back on me, left the jersey down between my feet and walked out, without saying anything to anybody. I went to the airport and I came back on the early plane. Jesus, I must have been so annoyed. I hardly remember coming home. There were two flights, an early flight and a *late flight. Don't ask me why we were divided between them. Maybe they were small planes, but Pat Reynolds and a few of the lads were on my one, with the bulk of the lads on the later flight.*

Well, the boys laughed more at that. I didn't go training for say a fortnight. It didn't go on too long. You realise after two weeks there is only one loser here. Everything carries on the very same as if you were never there. I don't even know if I got a call or word got back to me that I was wanted, but I went back to training anyway.

Joe Cassells started his first Championship game of the season in the All-Ireland final replay, and also took over the team captaincy from Mick Lyons. Padraig Lyons, Kevin Foley and Mattie McCabe paid the heaviest price possible for the entire team's dismal performance in the drawn game, and were replaced on the team by Terry Ferguson, Colm Coyle and Cassells. Six and a half minutes into the game, Gerry McEntee was sent off for giving Niall Cahalane a slap in the jaw, and Meath moved P.J. Gillic out to partner Liam Hayes in the middle of the field. The changes didn't matter a great deal. The team had a different face on than three weeks earlier, and was in a completely different mood for a game of football. Tompkins would score eight points from frees before the final whistle was heard, one more than Stafford this time. Cork would also lead 0-6 to 0-5 at half-time, having used Tony Davis as their extra-man, and used him quite intelligently. This time, however, it was Meath who started dishing out the punishment early on. Cork seemed surprised. And when, like a long distance runner, Meath made a break for the finishing line in the last quarter of the game, Cork were slow to respond. It was 0-8 each after 50 minutes, but suddenly, in a breathtaking move up the field,

Bernie Flynn latched onto a cross-field ball, beat his man and stroked the ball over the bar from 30 yards out. Meath were three points in front with nine minutes left, and the lead had stretched to four points with seven minutes remaining on the clock. In the last five minutes the Meath legs began to buckle. Every last man headed for defence. Dinny Allen pointed, Tompkins pointed, Barry Coffey pointed, and the final whistle sounded. Meath left half-back Martin O'Connell was named 'Man of the Match', but there were few other compliments waiting in the wings for Marty or anybody else in green and gold. Among those with a frown on his face was GAA president John Dowling, who revealed that he was 'disturbed' by what he had just seen on the field and promised a top level investigation. 'While I was not happy with some of the happenings on the field of play yesterday, this is not the place to deal with it', the president told both sets of players as they looked down at their lunch the next day in the Royal Hospital. 'I will deal with it at the appropriate time and place.' When John Dowling visited Meath two months later to present the players with their All-Ireland medals, Liam Harnan and Gerry McEntee refused to step on stage. Three other players took their medals from the guest of honour but refused to shake his hand.

P.J. GILLIC: *The first All-Ireland was special. The second time around there was a lot more pressure. You start to feel it then and start thinking, 'Jesus, do you want to do this again and finish up losing?' Whereas the previous year when we were in an All-Ireland final, it was another step along the way. If we win it, great but if we don't, it's still another step along the road. We had won the league title straight after the All-Ireland in '87 so we were becoming the team that everyone* *wanted to beat. With the bunch of players we had, and the team that Sean had built, I think we underachieved a little. I know it's easy to say we should have won another one or two All-Irelands, but then we were lucky to beat Cork in '88.*

We definitely came out the worst of the whole thing. We were labelled as 'dirty', which was unfair, and that definitely left a sour note for a while afterwards. I never had any problems with any of the Cork lads. They were a fantastic team at the time. I suppose the first year, in '87, maybe they were carrying a few fellas that weren't up to scratch whereas in '88 they came back a lot stronger. You have to say that we were very lucky to survive the drawn game. After that game we had a meeting in Malahide the next morning. We took a hell of a bruising in the drawn game. Cork really hockeyed us. There were a couple of incidents where we felt that they had gone over the top a little, and had got away with it, so the next day we decided that we weren't going to be pushed around, weren't going to be bullied, that we were going to fight our corner. The training for the couple of weeks between the drawn game and replay was pretty savage stuff. I remember fellas saying that the training was a bit lackadaisical before the drawn game, that we were pussy-footing around, with fellas afraid of getting injuries. At that meeting we agreed that we were going to train the way we intended playing the next day. There was this thing in the media after the replay that we were the aggressors, that we caused the whole situation, but there were two teams involved.

I actually was one of the lads who didn't shake hands with John Dowling, and it's something that I regret to this day. It was a childish thing to do looking back on it. I went up there and took the medal off him but just didn't shake hands. He didn't say anything. I think there were three of us that didn't shake hands, apart from the two lads who didn't go up at all. I think the whole thing was wrong that particular night, it was badly organised and it was something that shouldn't have happened. I wouldn't say it took away from the All-Ireland win. It was just very hard to accept being branded as thugs. It was as if Sean had said, 'Look, you're going to go out here and you're going to be over-physical and win this game by hook or by crook', which wasn't the case. Definitely we decided that we weren't going to be pushed around, that we were going to match Cork physically the next day, but it was nothing more than that. We weren't going to go out and just hit lads.

BERNIE FLYNN: *Apart from Colm O'Rourke the first day against Cork in '88, nobody played well. Yet in the second match, we all knuckled down and worked hard. People forget we were defending an All-Ireland with 14 men. What were we supposed to do when Gerry McEntee was sent off so early on? I spent the last 20 minutes of the match at right half-forward. What Gerry did, it just happened! If you look at the video, he hardly touched him. If Gerry McEntee wanted to really hurt Niall Cahalane, he would have known all about it. I would hold Gerry McEntee above anybody I played with, as a great human being, as a friend, as a leader. Even down the road and since, McEntee was special. All that mattered to Gerry McEntee was that Meath won. He didn't care how, when or where. He sacrificed more than anybody. What he put on the line for the Meath jersey, in his profession over the years and his family and everything, can't be underestimated. He went to America, he went to Limerick, he went to Newcastle – and he still performed for Meath. All he wanted was to win. Nothing else mattered. McEntee took his football so seriously, it was frightening at times. It was coming up to one of the big games in '90 or '91, and he was dropped after a team meeting. There were big steps up to the house in Bellinter where* *we used to eat after training, and I remember Gerry storming out of the place after the team was announced. Well, the first thing that he met was Pat Reynolds' new Merc. Pat was a selector, and Gerry drove his boot into the side of the door as far as he could and sped off, stones going for a good 100 yards after him. McEntee had a huge influence on the team. If Gerry opened his mouth, everybody would listen. The same couldn't be said about everyone else. He was good at talking to opposing players on the field too. In the Dublin matches, some of the stuff that was said on the field – God, it was terrible!*

GERRY McENTEE: *There has been too much talk about the Meath-Cork match, and the less said now the better. It has all boiled down and we have met and talked since, and they are no different to us. Too many people said and wrote things that shouldn't have been said or written.*
For me, the strangest thing between the draw and replay was a trip we took for the weekend. We had a game up in Cooley. We went up there because Sean thought it would relax everyone. He was completely wrong because we were so uptight waiting for the replay that it didn't work. We played a game among ourselves and nearly killed each other. The people from Cooley came out of Sunday mass and were looking at us, and I think they thought we were gone mad! There were three, including myself, hurt. I got a knock from Liam Hayes during the game and it was quite sore. Liam was being his usual temperamental self and when he wasn't allowed to catch the ball cleanly like he wanted to, he got thick, lifted up his knee, and gave me a dead leg – and only it was the Sunday before the All-Ireland final he would have got one back.
I deserved to get sent off in the replay. Nothing on the field really led up to the incident. It was more to do with the three weeks building up to it and I went out on the field in the wrong frame of mind. There was

nothing personal between Niall Cahalane and myself. For me, 1988 was not as enjoyable as the previous year. The whole saga of getting sent off ruined it. But, then again, for others it was wonderful. For the 14 fellas who stayed out on the field that day and who played really well, it was terrific.

MARTIN O'CONNELL: *I thought it was harmless enough what Gerry McEntee did. They were fired up. Gerry was fired up, and it just happened. Everybody piled in. You could understand Cork piling in because they were after losing an All-Ireland and didn't want to lose another one. To lose two in a row! We went through that ourselves, and it's an awful feeling. We didn't panic though. Everybody put their shoulder to the wheel even harder.*

There was a bit of bad blood between the teams, and it was stupid on both sides. We both went on holidays to the Canaries the following January, and they'd be sitting on one side of the swimming pool and we'd be sitting on the other. I certainly wasn't mixing with any of them, for some stupid reason, just the bad blood from the All-Irelands. You'd see them and you'd just look at them and keep going.

The thing that changed it all was John Kerins's death. Gerry McEntee was actually treating John for his illness and I remember him telling me, seven or eight months before he died, that it didn't look good. Then he rang me when John died to say that a few of the lads were organising to go down to the funeral. There were eight or ten of us that went. A lot went down on the plane on the Thursday night for the removal, and myself and Mickey McQuillan drove down together on the Friday morning. Gerry McEntee was down, Liam Hayes, Bob O'Malley, I think Bernard Flynn as well, Joe Cassells and Colm O'Rourke. Unfortunately it took a death to break the ice between Meath and Cork.

That puts it all in perspective, and that only happened last year, so it took nearly 14 years.

The Misery

Chapter Five:

1989
1990
1991

Martin O'Connell was probably the happiest man in County Meath. He had his No. 7 jersey, and he had a 'Man of the Match' award from the 1988 All-Ireland football final, but the next eight years were about to grind themselves out for Sean Boylan and the Meath football team. When Boylan led a younger, smaller, faster, fitter Meath team to a third All-Ireland title in 1996, Martin O'Connell was still there, seemingly still having the time of his life. Only O'Connell and Colm Coyle would display the supreme act of faith in the Meath boss. The darker and more miserable years of Sean Boylan's reign would include two more provincial crowns and two additional National League titles, but when Meath lost by ten points to Dublin in the 1995 Leinster final, it did appear that the team was now reversing through the same tunnel it had been progressing since 1989. Martin O'Connell? Whatever was to become of the Meath football team, Martin O'Connell was only a short distance away from having his portrait on the nation's postage stamps after being named at left half-back on the 'Gaelic Football Team of the Millennium'.

MARTIN O'CONNELL: *I wouldn't have known anything about Sean really. I wouldn't have known him at all when he became manager.*
I remember actually playing against Dunboyne in a junior match in the summer of '82 and actually marking Sean Boylan. He was corner-back and I was corner-forward. I could have scored two or three points that day and it was only a short time after that that he got the job. I reckon he called me in because I gave him a roasting! I would have been 19 at the time.
I always wanted to play for Meath, since I was a young fella. I remember going in and looking at the likes of Colm O'Rourke and Gerry

McEntee and Joe Cassells and Mick Lyons, who were all household names. They were the fellas you looked up to and to be in the same room as them made me step back and think. Sean had that way with him, even back then. You knew he meant business. Meath football was at such a low at that time. They lost to Wexford in '81 and Longford in '82, so they couldn't go any lower. He was gathering us all in and we kind of all looked at each other and thought, 'This guy wants to win.' Everybody was equal that night, the younger and older lads on the panel. Everybody was tuned in on what he was saying, what he wanted. However, when we won our first trophy, the O'Byrne Cup, a few months into 1983, I was taken off in the final after playing centre-back. I had been out on the Saturday night before the match. Sean took me off, and rightly so, because I wasn't able to walk. But that was my first and last time ever doing that.

It wasn't a local disco I was at. I think it could have been a butchers' dinner dance. Sean found out after the match, maybe a couple of days afterwards, but, in fairness to him, he didn't make a big issue out of it. He called me to one side – I think we were down in Roscommon the week after, we were opening a football pitch down there – and said to me, 'Look, I know you were out. I heard you were out. Were you out?' I couldn't deny it. I said, 'Yes I was.' And he just told me, 'Look, we mean business here. This has to stop'. So I told him it definitely wouldn't happen again. You always get caught once and I got caught early on in my life, which was a great thing. He warned me, and that was the end of it. Any game I ever played since, I never had a drink on me, ever.

I didn't make the Championship team in '83. I just couldn't get in. When we won the Centenary Cup I played the whole way through at left half-back, and that trophy was a massive thing for us. Every county

Brendan Reilly, June 15, 1997

Barry Callaghan and Dermot Flanagan, September 29, 1996

wanted to win it. It was actually a glass trophy so there was no drinking out of it, or bringing it around the pubs! Dublin were after winning the All-Ireland the year before with only 12 men. They were household names at that stage, the Barney Rocks, the Ciaran Duffs. A little bit of inexperience probably cost us the Leinster final in 1984. We missed the penalty and they got a couple of goals. One of them, the ball hit the crossbar and came out to Rock and he just pulled on it to the back of the net. He was well known at the time and I was marking him. I remember my mother at home saying, 'You're marking Barney Rock!' Sean's approach though was, 'He's not going to come down the field with ten pairs of legs. He's only human like the rest of us.' I think he only scored one point from play on me that day. You'd be happy enough with that, but when you lose the game you're not happy. It's all about winning, isn't it? Nobody likes losing.

The next year was the start of the three selectors! Tony Brennan and Pat Reynolds were in that year. Sean didn't agree with the seven-man selection committee. He just wanted himself and two selectors which I thought was the right thing. Seven fellas in a dug-out trying to make a switch! Sure the game would be over before everybody would agree.

This was the start of it for me. When the seven selectors were there, I was always left half-back. Even going back to '83 I was left half-back. When the two new selectors came in, maybe they didn't see what the others were seeing, maybe they thought, 'He's not fitting in here.' Maybe one of them didn't get on with me. The story was going around that Pat Reynolds didn't rate me. Pat Reynolds never came to me and said this, or Sean Boylan or Tony Brennan, but every dog on the street had it. This is what I was hearing back, but I never heard that directly from Pat Reynolds.

I was the type of fella that would never question the selectors or manager and say, 'Sean, what the feck are you doing here?' That's just the way I was. I felt that if I did a thing like that, the pressure was going to be on me, that if I went out playing wing half-back someday and got a roasting, suddenly, I'd be under extra pressure

It was a lot harder as a forward. I think you have to have something different to be a forward, you have to be a natural, and I was never a natural forward. I always liked meeting the ball. I could feel comfortable anywhere in the backs, corner-back or full-back or right half-back or anywhere along the line. Centre-field, I wouldn't feel comfortable, even though I play a lot there with my club, but up front definitely wasn't my scene. I found myself running around like a headless chicken really, running here, running there. And the more times you run, the less ball you were seeing, and then the ball was kicked in and you weren't there. Basically, it was down to the fact that I couldn't really read the game as a forward compared to reading the game as a back.

I remember we played in the quarter-final of the National League against Galway in 1987, down in Portlaoise, and they played me wing half-forward. I thought I was doing well enough but they took me off at half-time. That was enough for me. I said to myself, 'Look, I'm not going to get back here.' I remember talking to Mick Lyons in the Killeshin Hotel afterwards and I said, 'Mick, I think I've enough of this. I think it's time for me to pack it in because I'm not going to get back.' Mick didn't say to me, 'Hold on', or 'You're right.' He said nothing really. And that was it. So I didn't go back training on the Tuesday night. I said nothing to anybody, just didn't go back training on the Tuesday night. I suppose I thought the easiest way was just to get out. It was probably the wrong way in the end, but it was the easiest way for me.

I thought once I walked out, that was it! I suppose it took a fortnight or *three weeks for it to register with me, to realise that I probably shouldn't have done it. Four or five weeks later, Sean actually rang me at home, to see would I come back in, and I was glad I got the phone call. But again when I got back in, there was nothing said about where I wanted to play. At the time, I felt that I had made a stupid mistake. I thought to myself, 'If I get on the Meath team, I'll grab it, no matter where I'm playing.' I remember training in Dalgan Park on the Saturday morning after I came back and Sean gathering us all together, and Gerry McEntee was in like a shot, 'Are you gathering us all around just to welcome Martin back?' A lot of them took a while to welcome me back. I'd say there were a few guys who were putting in the hard effort themselves, and didn't like what I had done – me walking away – and it was the old campaigners who found it harder to accept me back. That's the impression I got.*

We played Kildare in Tullamore in the semi-final in 1987. Colm O'Rourke was injured and they played me corner-forward. We were after playing a few challenge matches and again I was playing in the forwards. I passed no remarks. I said, 'I'm not going to walk away again. I'm going to stick here, and if I'm playing, I'm playing.' I remember the team being named for the Kildare game and I was a sub. But O'Rourke took sick two or three days beforehand and in the hotel beforehand in Tullamore, Sean comes over and says, 'Colm is sick. Will you go in corner-forward?' So I says, 'Fine Sean, no problem.' Once I was in, I said I was going to give it a hell of a go. I think Frank Foley then got injured and they brought me back from corner-forward to left half-back in the same game. Obviously, they saw something in the way I handled it and that's where I stayed.

Martin O'Connell never looked back. All-Ireland medals in 1987,

'88 and '96 earned him the reputation as one of the greatest Meath defenders of all time. Other observers of Gaelic football, however, went some distance further than that and deemed O'Connell one of the six best defenders ever to try their hand out at the old game. An operation on his back in 1997, however, deprived him from finishing off his career with a fourth All-Ireland medal and becoming the only Meathman to hold that amount of GAA gold!

MARTIN O'CONNELL: *I trained on the Tuesday and Thursday nights before the Leinster final in '97. The game was on the Saturday, but I just couldn't get out of bed on Saturday morning with my back. I was after playing on Thursday night and there wasn't a bother on me. I remember meeting Sean up in the Sisters of Sion out in Bellinter and I said, 'Sean, I think I'm in trouble'. I got a pain-killing injection, thinking I was going to be OK, and togged out and all, but as the day went on, it was worse I was getting. I had played every game up until then. We were short four players against Offaly that year, and I was injured as well, so with the suspensions and everything else, we were well beaten. I played again in '98 after the operation on my back to have the disc removed, played League matches and challenge matches, but never got onto the Championship team. I was a sub in '98 for the Leinster final against Kildare.*

I knew then that was the time to get out because I wasn't going to be on the team for that Championship. And then we played a few challenge matches under lights, building up to the League campaign in October or November, and I remember being up in the dressing room and Sean naming the team for the Clare game, down in Clare. I remember saying to my wife, Samantha, that if I didn't get in for a League match against Clare, there was very little chance I'd be part of this for the

Championship and the remainder of the League. And that was it. I went to Sean, told him I was going, and that was the end of it. I said, 'I'm going.' He just said, 'Fine.' I didn't go to Sean and say, 'What the fuck is going on Sean? I'm after busting myself to get back after my operation, and do you want me?' Nothing like that. I could have gone to Sean and reefed him out of it. But I didn't. I definitely thought I had another year or two in me. I had trained hard to get back. I might have lost a little bit of pace but I always maintain that that's where a little bit of experience comes into play. I know you have to mark a man, but you have to mark a bit of space as well. You have to know when to go and when to stay, and I thought I still had that.

Of course it was tough. I watched the 1999 All-Ireland final from the Cusack Stand. There's never a good time to leave. The thought of winning four medals went through my mind. I'm not saying I was going to be on the team, but if only Sean had given me a chance to prove myself. He never gave me that chance. Maybe he had his reasons, maybe he was right. He never wanted to play guys who had bad injuries. I never got a phone call a few weeks later. If I did I would have gone back in. Oh, absolutely! If I got a phone call tomorrow, Id probably go back.

The Millennium award was a shock really. I suppose you could pick ten teams and there would still be controversy over it. I thought the way the GAA did it, though, was very poor. It was kind of shoved under the carpet. All the nominations were in the papers, and everybody had to pick a team. Now, I thought that there would be a big function for all the nominees, like the Allstars, but that's not what happened. What actually happened was a joke, and was typical of the feckin' GAA. The function was actually on a Tuesday at Croke Park. The team hadn't been named at this stage and I got an invitation saying that I had to be at this function. I thought that all the nominees were going to be at it, so I remember ringing Colm O'Rourke, because he was nominated – Bob O'Malley was another – and I remember ringing him saying, 'Will we all go together and make a day of it?' But they had got no invitation. Only the team had got an invitation, but I didn't know that. So I went up to Croke Park that Tuesday with Samantha, drove in round the back of the Cusack Stand thinking I might see some of the Meath cars. I was still thinking that they just hadn't received the invitations in the post or something. It still hadn't dawned on me. But no Meath cars. In fact there were feck all cars around!

I was a bit late due to work, and got stuck in traffic, and I think they had the goalkeeper named when I walked into the bar in the Cusack Stand. That's a fact. There wasn't 200 people at it. I was sure it was going to be a big bash but that was all that was at it. There wasn't even 15 of us footballers because, of course, a lot of the Millennium team were dead, so you had representatives up. What they had done was put on a buffet, but it was all gone, of course, when I went in, so I ate nothing. I remember going up to the bar and the bar was closed, so I couldn't get a drink either. It was only when they were naming the team then that I realised that I was actually picked on it. No one had bothered to ring and tell me before it. They just sent me an invitation to be in Croke Park at one o'clock as they were announcing the Millennium team. They never said I was on it.

We went out onto the pitch to get our photos taken, the lads that were still alive! I remember then saying to Brendan Cummins from LMFM radio that we'd go for a pint, because we couldn't get one in Croke Park. So we went into the Tolka House, had two pints and went home. And that was the celebration for the 'Football Team of the Millennium'.

Martin O'Connell was one of the lucky ones – he got a call back from Sean Boylan, and answered that call. Others were making their minds up about their careers at this same time, amongst them one of the most astonishing young talents in Meath football, Packie Henry. The 20-year old from the small parish of Cortown had the same skill level as Bernie Flynn, and he was five years younger than Flynn! He had already pocketed an All-Ireland medal from 1987, had toured the Canaries and the United States with the Meath team, and was awaiting the opportunity to prove himself worthy of a Championship place when, inexplicably, he told Boylan that he had had enough. Packie Henry never got a second call; there was no second chance.

PACKIE HENRY: *I remember sitting in the Nally Stand with a friend of mine for the All-Ireland semi-final when Meath played Kerry in 1986, and there was this huge big pillar in front of us. We couldn't see a thing so we had to get up out of our seats and stand in front of the pillar for the entire game. We weren't meant to be standing there, but no official or pillar was going to stop us watching Meath play in an All-Ireland semi-final. My first time to really talk with Sean was about three or four weeks after Meath were beaten by Kerry. Liam Creavin rang me and asked me if I would come up to Dalkey in Dublin for a challenge match, and of course I said yes. The game was on a Saturday, so I went along and we were all meeting in Clonee. I was a couple of months short of my 19th birthday and was gob-smacked to be involved with the Meath seniors. I had spent the previous summer sitting in Croke Park and other grounds in the country looking out at these guys. I was a fan behind the fence and Sean was carrying me over that fence, and putting me face to face with the Meath team. When I arrived in Clonee I wasn't sure what* to do or say, but the first man that came over to me was Sean. He had a big smile on his face and gave me a huge hand shake and introduced himself. He welcomed me on board and told me not to be nervous. He then introduced me to a couple of the lads and made me feel comfortable. The following day we played Offaly in Summerhill in another challenge and he came over again just to make idle chat, but when I look back now he obviously realised I was young and nervous as hell, so he was looking after me and making me feel more at home. He didn't have to do that for me, but he did and I appreciated him helping me relax.

The night Sean Boylan resigned, I remember going up in the car with P.J. Gillic, Brian Stafford and Terry Ferguson to a training session in Dalgan Park. Sean had organised a last-minute session. We arrived in Dalgan anyway and it was in complete darkness, and we were all wondering what the idea was of bringing us up here at this time of the evening, in March! So the four of us sat in the car for a few minutes not knowing what was going on. Some of the other lads were sitting in their cars also and everybody looked bemused. It was pitch black outside. Eventually we were all called into the dressing room and Sean got up and spoke. He said he was resigning. We could not believe it. It was the last thing we thought was going to happen that evening. I mean Meath had won a Leinster title in 1986 and we were confident we could emulate that feat and even go a couple of steps further that year. Sean just said, 'Now, you can have a chat about it and if you want me back, you come back to me.' Then he stormed out.

We did win the All-Ireland that year, and Mick Lyons's block that day on Jimmy Kerrigan was just phenomenal. It changed the flow of the game, and Colm O'Rourke's goal was fantastic. All the players on the bench just jumped spontaneously out of their seats when Colm scored that goal. We jumped out almost onto the pitch. We were hugging each *other and everything. It was a vital goal, but the calmest man on the sideline was Sean. We were all celebrating, as he was handing out orders to the lads on the field.*

We went on an Allstar trip to America after that and at one of the games Bernard Flynn got injured and I went in at corner-forward. I will never forget it. I got the ball about 40 yards out, turned and I started to solo towards the goals. I took a shot from about 30 yards out and it rifled into the top corner of the net. It was my moment of fame, but I thought everybody had forgotten all about it. Then a couple of months ago (2002), at a club game in Meath, Sean came over to me and we were chatting away when suddenly he says to me, 'Packie, I always say that you scored the best goal I have ever seen, over in America on the Allstar trip in 1987.' That meant a lot to me. He hadn't forgotten me. I suppose I had let him down a bit by stepping off the panel, but he never held it against me. Anytime he sees me now he reminds me about that goal.

I broke my jaw during an Under-21 game in Summerhill towards the end of 1987. That put me back about five or six months as regards the Meath team, and I lost a lot of fitness. I came back in on the panel in June or July but I knew straightaway that I was way off the pace. There was no way I could reclaim the fitness I had lost, to get on a par with the lads in such a short space of time. Meath were preparing for a Leinster Championship and Sean had them ready, so I just said to him that I was withdrawing from the panel. I told him there was no point in me carrying on, but he asked me to reconsider and told me to stick with it, and that my chance would come. I will never forget that he promised me a starting place in the League. Sean turned to me and said, 'Our first game in the League this year is likely to be Dublin in Croke Park, and I guarantee you now that you will be No. 15. However, as regards playing before then, no, you are not fit enough.' I knew I wasn't ready for the Championship, but I just felt so far behind the rest of the team that I stood by my decision to step down. Sean tried to stop me and maybe I should have listened to him – I mean, I was young at the time, only 20, and probably didn't appreciate the situation I was in – but that's just life. Sean was not too happy at the time because the way he saw it, he had put almost two years of work into me, building me up and helping me mature on the panel. I was kind of like one for the future and I had thrown it back at him. Of course, I sometimes regret it now and when you get on in years you start to wonder, 'What if', but there is no point dwelling on things like that. The day I was pulling out of the panel Sean probably realised that some day I would live to regret my decision. He genuinely tried to talk me out of it, but I was young and wanted to go out with my friends and do the things that other 20-year olds were doing at the time.

That same year, I played in the All-Ireland junior final against London, which provided the curtain-raiser to the senior final replay between Meath and Cork in 1988. We won, and afterwards we all sat in the Hogan Stand watching the senior game together. Anyway, Sean came over to all of us after the game and congratulated us on our success. I appreciated him coming to congratulate us in his personal moment of triumph.

I played in an All-Ireland junior final again in Croke Park for Meath before the final game in the 1991 saga between Meath and Dublin. We played Kerry but lost. It was great to be participating in an All-Ireland final. I scored eight points that day, but obviously it would have been nice to have been involved with the seniors, especially after our defeat. Sitting in the dressing room, deflated, I wanted to be next door. We passed the lads and Sean on our way out, and I wished them the best of luck. I watched the game with the rest of the junior team as a Meath fan. The score that sticks in my mind from that series is P.J. Gillic's last-gasp effort at the end of the first game. We were behind by a point. Meath were kicking into the Canal End, and P.J. got the ball and kicked it from under the Hogan Stand, over 30 yards out, towards the goal in injury time and it hopped over the bar. John O'Leary had come out to gather it, but the ball bounced over his head and behind for a point. It could just as easily have slipped into the net. The referee blew the whistle on the kick-out and it finished a draw.

In 1996, when Meath drew with Mayo in the All-Ireland again, I remember sitting just over from P.J. Gillic at the game and looking over at him when Colm Coyle's point bounced over the bar in the dying seconds. Neither of us could believe it. We thought it had slipped away. It was a great feeling and it gave us a second chance.

I remember so much about my days with the Meath team. I remember getting a lift with Sean to a challenge game in Mayo one afternoon. Gerry McEntee was in the car also and he sat in the front with Sean. I was in the back on my own. Sean had a Mitsubishi of some sort at the time. Anyway, it was a sports car and boy does Sean like sports cars! Jesus, it was like a Formula One race driving to Mayo that day. I was being tossed about in the back of the car like a rag doll as he flew around corners. It was a real white-knuckle ride. We were doing well over a 100 miles per hour I'd say, but he is a great driver, always in control. Still, I was wishing he would slow down a little going to Mayo. I was the young fella in the car. I should have been the one urging for more speed – not Sean Boylan. It was unbelievable. Himself and McEntee just chatted away as if they were out for a Sunday drive while I clung on for dear life in the back.

Even though Meath lost six games out of seven in the 1988-89 National League campaign, and experienced a humiliating drop down to Division Two, there was already talk in the county of another All-Ireland triumph. Three in a row! The team was unhappy, naturally enough, with all the abuse which was directed its way after the controversial All-Ireland final replay against Cork. Of course, some players and officials did not help the situation by stepping out in public on a regular basis and announcing that they were not one little bit sorry for one single act which had occurred on the field the previous October. Refusing to accept All-Ireland medals from the GAA president was also misunderstood and misrepresented in the national media and, all told, the Meath team was a marketing and public relations disaster all through the winter. In the team's final game in the League campaign, in Newcastle, there was some good news for a change. After losing six on the trot, Meath trailed Down by 3-1 to 0-1 after just nine minutes of their last competitive outing before the defence of the Leinster and All-Ireland Championships. Then, things turned, Liam Hayes scored a goal either side of half-time, P.J. Gillic kicked over nine free-kicks in the absence of Brian Stafford, and Meath won 2-12 to 3-4. After their 'winter of ungratefulness' the Meath team was in lively mood that evening on their way home, but in the early summer Mick Lyons broke his leg and despite a spectacular effort to regain full fitness he was forced to sit out the Leinster final on the Meath substitutes bench. It was the second time in six years that Lyons would have to sit and watch a Leinster final between Meath and Dublin, and it was the second time Meath would lose to their greatest rivals, 2-12 to 1-10.

The defence of the Leinster crown got off to a satisfactory start in early June against Louth in Navan, Meath winning 1-15 to 0-13 and holding enough in reserve to completely demolish Offaly in the provincial semi-final three weeks later on a 3-11 to 0-9 scoreline. Bob O'Malley wore the No. 3 shirt against Offaly, but Lyons's first cousin Liam Harnan took the famous shirt back into 'the family' for the decisive meeting with Dublin.

The loss of Lyons was undoubtedly colossal. The story is told of how, one afternoon, as Mick Lyons took up his position as guardian of the Meath goalmouth, a large number of young Dublin fans started shouting at him to come up onto the Hill where they would sort him out. An older Dublin supporter was stretched across a barrier listening to this for a while and, eventually, felt compelled to shout over at the gang of brave men dressed in blue, 'Jaysus, you all want him up here. Why doesn't one of you go down?' Even without Lyons, however, the 1989 Leinster final was a game which almost every Meath footballer who took the field that afternoon still claims should never have been lost. With Harnan in the No. 3 shirt and Terry Ferguson in the No. 6, and with the whole of the Meath defence guilty of looking at one another in the opening minutes, Ciaran Duff took advantage of the situation to race down through the middle and plant the ball into the back of the net from 20 yards. Duff was moving so fast, that he took eight or nine steps without soloing the ball, but nothing was said by the referee or his officials. With Lyons missing and Dublin thinking of scoring goals again in the Leinster final, Meath knew there was trouble looming. However, Meath held on, stayed close, close enough to make a Mattie McCabe goal in the final minutes of the game and move them back into the lead by one point. Meath would have won too, but Dublin scored a second goal, from Vinny Murphy, seconds later.

GERRY McENTEE: *I came home from America for the Leinster final in '89. The late Noel Keating footed the bill, but it was a mistake, a big mistake. Even though I had done a good bit of training over in America and kept myself in good shape, the flight home was a killer. My legs started to cramp about 15 or 20 minutes from the end and I ran out of steam. It was a mistake. There was no way you could fly in on a Saturday afternoon and play in a Leinster final the following day.*

I don't agree that it was an unbelievable commitment, as some people say, to come for the game. Any of the other players would have done the same, the very same. They would have flown home from America for the game, all of them. I wanted to play and so did all the others and there isn't a single one I think who would not have come home. The mistake was that I should have come home four or five days before the game, not the day before. It was a bad call and I was more to blame than anyone because I should have known better myself.

I remember the game well. It started at about 100 miles per hour. Keith Barr was starting his first big game for Dublin that day and before the game, as the teams were kicking balls around beforehand, you could see he was up for it all right. It was a scorching hot day and we fell behind but Mattie McCabe scored a goal, set up by Liam to put us ahead with only a few minutes left. Then Vinny Murphy got a goal that deflected off Martin and went into the net. After that, they kicked a few points and it was all over. Afterwards I flew straight back to America.

P.J. GILLIC: *Had we scraped over Dublin that year, I think we would have gone on to do the three in a row. There was a lot of talk about Murphy's goal at the end, but it's another incident, Ciaran Duff's goal, that actually stands out more in my mind. Duff scored a goal up the Canal End, and he probably took a lot of steps, and Bob O'Malley came* *running out signalling to the referee for over-carrying. Now, I felt Bob should have nailed Duff coming through instead of letting him in. We were without Mick Lyons that year as he had broken his leg. Mick had done terrific work to come back and I think he was ready to play. I'm sure he was togged out that day, and maybe if he had been brought in for the last 10 or 15 minutes, when we were right back in the game, we might have been able to salvage a draw out of it. It would have given the whole team a lift to see him come back in.*

DONAL SMITH: *Colm Coyle should have been taken off that day, because it was obvious that he was going to get sent off. I would hope that Sean learned more from that game than any other. From where I was sitting he was certain to get sent off, because the entire Dublin half-back line kicked and thumped at him every time he moved for a ball. It was obvious that sooner or later he was going to react. As well as that, P.J. was not playing well that day and they launched Mattie McCabe on for him with 20 minutes to go and maybe they should have brought him on earlier. He scored a goal when introduced. I just remember Mattie's punched ball heading for the top left-hand corner of O'Leary's net. Everybody talks about the great Kerry team, but I have no doubt that we were on for the five in a row in those years.*

MICKEY McQUILLAN: *When Mattie McCabe scored near the end I think Mick Lyons should have been introduced. The second John O'Leary put the ball on the 21 yard line Mick should have shot straight out onto the pitch to the referee. The atmosphere would have lifted and the players would have responded. I think that might have knocked the stuffing out of Dublin to see Mick run out. Then they got the deflected goal and there was nothing I could do about it. The ball just hit off*

Martin O'Connell and into the net. We were all devastated afterwards because we knew we should have won the game and had thrown away the chance of three All-Ireland titles, but that's football I suppose. Sean tried to cheer us up and, fair play to him, he took the defeat well, but there is nothing that could be said to us that would have made us feel any better.

MARTIN O'CONNELL: *Dublin's second was a flukey goal that went in off my elbow. It came from a ball that Vinny Murphy caught. It was probably the tamest shot he ever kicked, but I went up to catch it on my chest and it hit off me and went over Mickey McQuillan's hand. If I hadn't touched it, Mickey would have saved it. There was only about five or six minutes left. Mattie McCabe had come on and scored a goal to put us a point ahead and then they came along and got that goal.*

TERRY FERGUSON: *I played centre half-back that day. We were missing Mick Lyons. Dublin got the run at us but, in a way, we were glad to get a little bit of a break and start to enjoy ourselves. The appetite was not going, we just felt a little burned out. We had been visiting so many schools and making presentations, we were exhausted, and it finally caught up on us against Dublin.*

The Meath team was undoubtedly at a crossroads after the 1989 Leinster final defeat, but Sean Boylan was not going to allow his group of footballers to sit around all by themselves, weighing up the future. Three long, victorious, delirious, argumentative years had taken their toll on the older footballers, and the younger footballers! No doubt, the team had tired. Appetites were no longer what they had once been, and half the team was heading

Martin O'Connell, July 28, 1996

P.J. Gillic, May 1988

towards 30th birthdays, while Lyons, Cassells, McEntee and O'Rourke had already been there, and had their cake! The team needed some new blood. Problem was, any young man entering the Meath dressing room was made to feel that he had walked into a far off pub, in a far off village, and the place was absolutely jammers! There was barely a seat left for the young man. Nobody was going to move for him. Boylan always had a great big welcome, but Boylan was a busy man. Everybody else preferred to be greatly suspicious and, God forbid if Boylan heaped any praise at all on the young footballer, he had to be quick to come out of his shell and score a few points, sing a few songs, catch some high balls, do something! And do it quickly. Brendan Reilly, from Boylan's neck of the woods in Dunboyne, had been introduced in 1988, Tommy Dowd appeared in 1989, Colm Brady was brought in early in 1990, and Alan Browne, Sean Kelly, John McDermott, Terry Connor and Hugh Carolan came in, mostly together, over the following 12 months. The new boys helped out, and with victories over Louth (quarter-final), Cork (semi-final) and Down, Meath were National League champs once more the following spring. The team was on the move again. When Meath defeated Dublin, 1-14 to 0-14 in the 1990 Leinster final, Reilly was left half-back, Brady was in the middle of the field with Liam Hayes, and Dowd was on the half-forward line. In addition, Donal Smith had taken over the No. 1 position from Mickey McQuillan, beginning a tug-o-war match for the goalkeeper's position which would continue, controversially, on and off, for the next four years.

Smith's clean sheet meant that Meath enjoyed a fairly comfortable afternoon, once again, in the company of their nearest and dearest rivals. Dublin, on the other hand, were struck down by a Colm

O'Rourke goal after just 25 seconds. A high centre from Colm Brady fell between John O'Leary and O'Rourke and the latter somehow managed to bundle the ball into the net without raising any great objection from Westmeath's Paddy Collins. It was 1-7 to 0-2 ten minutes from half-time, and Dublin looked like a team eyeing up the exits. There were five points in it at half-time. Three points from O'Rourke, Stafford and Flynn restored an eight-point advantage three minutes into the second period, but with six minutes remaining there was only one point between the sides. Dublin's courage, and desperation to hold onto their Leinster title, definitely surprised Meath in that second half and almost overpowered the team, before Gerry McEntee was introduced close to full-time. One mighty fetch from him stopped the entire Dublin team in its tracks, and made absolutely certain that Colm O'Rourke would be a winning Meath captain.

BRENDAN REILLY: *Before I came onto the senior team I wouldn't have been a mad Meath fan. In fact, I had only ever been to one game before I started playing myself. I played all around the pitch during my career. I hadn't a good run in '88. I played in the first round of the Championship against Louth in Drogheda, but broke my nose and got a generally good seeing-to. I was out for about two months after that. I came back in for the All-Ireland semi-final with Donegal, but by that stage lads had established themselves in the team and it was a lot tougher to get in.*
The fact that Sean was a Dunboyneman helped, I suppose, in my regard. There may have been other lads coming in from further down the road, or the opposite side of the county, whom he wouldn't have known as well. But it wasn't any great help at the end of the day. Sean was always a

private enough man. None of us would have moved in the same social circles as him.

The training was difficult for myself, coming from a junior club background. Even being asked onto the panel was a bit of a shock, really. After that you'd always be asking yourself, 'Why should I be here?' There was stuff I'd never done before, like the training down at the Hill of Tara was a real eye-opener. There was the training over in Bettystown beach, too, getting the balls frozen off you.

We had a great run in 1987, and when I came into the squad in '88. But I think the one that we really left behind us was in 1990. I think Cork just had the greater hunger that year. I don't know. I think they just weren't prepared to lose three All-Irelands to Meath. They were great teams, those Meath and Cork teams. In 1991, I came on in two of the Dublin games. I really broke into the team from the Leinster final onwards, when Bobby O'Malley broke his leg. It happened early enough, after 10 or 15 minutes, and I got a good run for that game. In the All-Ireland final against Down it all went sour. It was a case of let me out of here quick! We had played Down in the League that season and Kevin Foley had marked James McCartan. I don't know if maybe I should have stayed on James that day or maybe Kevin should have done it, like in the League. It didn't go too well for me. I think maybe, in hindsight, I wasn't mature enough or cunning enough at the time to mark a player like McCartan. There was a lot of stuff going on in that match, with that player and if I had my time again I'd do it all differently I'd play a different game. I just wasn't cute enough.

TOMMY DOWD: *The first night I went in to train with Meath was a Tuesday. The lads were after getting a hammering that weekend. I think it was from Antrim. Joe Cassells and Mick Lyons were there in the* dressing room and, when I went in, I remember them saying, 'The seniors are in next door!' It was as much as saying that they were so bad in that match, there were no players present who deserved to be called 'senior'. That message always stuck in my mind.

I was a Meath minor sub-goalie, in '87, I think it was. I had always played in goals when I was younger, I'd say up until under-12 or so, but on the Meath senior panel I was never made to feel inferior. Once you were in on the panel, you were there to do a job and that was it. It took some of the forwards a while to trust you, to pass you the ball. O'Rourke, Flynn and Stafford – there were a few players there who would kind of give it to themselves before they'd give it to you, even if you were in a better position. But I think they just didn't trust you to get a score, because they were so accurate themselves.

The night before my first Leinster final in 1990 there was a bit of argy-bargy between Hayes and Sean. It was some tactical move they were talking about, and Hayes wasn't happy about it. I was being taken off a lot at that time. It was my first major start. In front of a big crowd, you would be nervous, but if you do it against Dublin, you'll do it against anyone else! Until you do it against Dublin, you haven't really proven yourself. It was very important to go out and do well. There was a lot of talk about Keith Barr, one of the main figures on the Dublin team. He was playing very well, and was strong as a horse coming out with the ball. All I was worried about was getting out in front of him and winning the ball. If I got it, there were lads around who could score.

He was definitely one of the toughest players that I ever marked. He wouldn't be intimidating you, jawing at you or anything. But if he saw a chance where he could go for you – and get away with it - he would. You would be always sorer after a Dublin game from all the hard-hitting involved, no exaggeration. There was so much at stake between Meath and Dublin, it was as good as an All-Ireland, the next best thing. I got dropped for the All-Ireland that year McEntee came in. I was brought on for the last 10 or 15 minutes, but I was very hurt not to be playing from the start.

They took me off again at half-time in the Leinster final against Laois in '91 when I was doing OK, and brought McEntee on. I was hurt over that too. It was demoralising. That would have been Sean's decision, even though they said O'Rourke used to pick the team! Maybe he felt that there wouldn't be as many ructions if I was taken off, compared to some of the other lads. In the All-Ireland semi-final against Roscommon, I got 'Man of the Match'. I felt I had a point to prove that day. It always took a couple of years to become a regular on the team. You were never going to come in and get straight onto a team like that, so I suppose you have to take it on the chin and accept it. It was very disappointing at the time though. I don't know whether I was being made a scapegoat or whatever.

We had known that Down had never been beaten in an All Ireland final. A team like Down, you never know what to expect from them. O'Rourke being absent, that was a lift for them more than anything else. If we had had him from the start, I've no doubt we would have won the All Ireland. That was the second All-Ireland I was beaten in. I thought at that stage that I'd never win one.

That team was getting on in years and it was very hard to see anything coming through. I suppose, when you're beaten in two All-Irelands, you say, 'This isn't going to happen. I'm not going to win one of these.'

In the Dublin games, at the beginning of '91, things went well for me. In the first game I scored a couple of points off Tommy Carr. Everything ran for me. The next day I went out, I thought I was going to do the same again, and he roasted me! I didn't get a kick of a ball off him. He would have been a lot more focused, and I might have been a bit naive at the time. I thought the fact that I went out and did well the first day, that I was going to do the same, but I never got a smell of the ball. I really didn't. I wasn't at the races at all. Those games were so close, it was nip and tuck throughout. We were just happy to get away with a draw on a couple of occasions. Apart from winning the All-Ireland in '96, the fourth game against Dublin is my greatest memory, just the way we came back and beat them. In fairness to them, they never whinged about it. That's why you really have to admire Dublin. Compared to any other team in the country, once it's over, they wish you the best of luck. I know for a fact – the girfriend of a Dublin player told my wife, Geraldine – that they couldn't look at that game for weeks and weeks after, it was so hard on them. If it was ever on when they went into a pub, they would turn on their heels and walk out. Yet they never, ever said a word about it.

COLM BRADY: When I was young, I used to work on my uncle's farm out in Bellinter for the summer, and I have very vivid memories of listening to Meath on the radio, invariably playing Dublin, and cursing and swearing Dublin because, you know Meath would be so close – a point ahead, or one down – and the only name I wanted to hear getting the ball was Colm O'Rourke. Once Colm O'Rourke got the ball, something could happen. The way you're visualising the game, Colm O'Rourke might be 40 yards away from goal, or 70 yards, it didn't matter. In your head it was a scoring chance. A lot of swearing would have been done on that farm, most of it aimed at Dublin. We were always close, but even if we ever managed a draw, we would have been beaten by a point in the replay. And then when it was over, it was just another beating, another game that got away, where Meath could have *broken through but let it slip.*

Then, I ended up being taught by O'Rourke at St Pat's in Navan. Economics! He used to use very, ehem, what's the word, 'unusual' teaching methods for helping you remember things. Some of the lads in the class wouldn't have been particularly bright. In economics you would have demand curves and supply curves and Rourkey used to always give the supply curves of french knickers or that type of thing in relation to demand, this type of stuff, in the hope that it might stimulate the lads, make it interesting for them. 'Can we use that as an example in the Leaving Cert, Sir?' That would have been the usual question from us.

Something that I found difficult to deal with was the guys I was coming in to play with – they were Gods to me! They were the guys who, in '87 and '88 you were going round chasing autographs for, they were the household names. After being a source of inspiration to you, suddenly you're in there playing on the same team! I specifically remember an intense desire to prove myself. Once you're in, you forget about all the rest of it and it's like you want to prove that you're as good, that you're worth your salt.

O'Rourke would have been particularly good to the likes of me. I could definitely say, particularly in the early challenges, that when you were just coming into the team he'd be giving you the pass that he didn't have to. It was difficult coming in because they were established at that stage. Any of our lads who were brought in from the Under-21 squad weren't making the breakthrough. They weren't getting into the team. It was demoralising, yeah.

The difficulty initially was trying to cope with being played out of what you felt was your natural position. That's what I found the most diffi-cult. I would have always been midfield with my club, but Boylan would always try you in a variety of different positions. You'd be expecting to go in to your familiar position, but he mightn't necessarily pick you there. So he experimented with me in the forwards, half-forward, corner-forward, everywhere basically. I felt I wasn't doing myself justice in games. My positioning, I just couldn't read it. I was mad to be out in the middle of the field contesting the ball when really I should have been staying in the forward line, trying to pick up breaks. I remember relishing the chance to get a crack at the Dublin household names, Barr and Heery, those two in particular. Any chance to meet them 50-50, that's all you wanted, because it was a real test. Having yourself worked up to such a state, and such a level of preparedness, you nearly lost a sense of reality, that it was like life or death, when in actual fact it wasn't. It's so far from that, but that's how it felt at the time.

I got my chance in 1990. A Leinster final is the noisiest game you could ever play in, and it was as bad as an All-Ireland that day. Quite early in that game I went for a score. Sean would always have talked about the wind in Croke Park, the swirling air, pockets of air, all this kind of stuff, and the lads used to be smirking as he mentioned this. But I remember kicking that ball as hard as I could kick it and when it rose to a certain level towards the Canal End there was a point where the wind seemed to just catch it and it just started to go more vertical. O'Rourke was able to see that. 'This ball is not actually travelling anywhere. It's just going to go up and come back down.' And he was the quickest to respond to it. He palmed it or fumbled it over the line.

It was great. The thing about Meath and Dublin, whoever scores the goals in the Meath-Dublin matches tends to win. Having discussed that, and then the goal going in, you had that added confidence. It was so easy that day against Dublin for so long, if my memory is right. And then they came back and ate into our lead. They just kept coming back.

As a unit though – I remember talking about it afterwards – everybody felt that it could be taken up a gear, that we were going to win that day. It was just one of those days. I can't remember too many more of those days in my football career where I had the same sense of certainty.

Its a laugh now looking back on it, but the Meath team meetings were notorious in nature at that time – a lot of people would have talked about them – the length and the nature of the conversation, and some of it would be quite harsh, quite close to the bone. It would be controlled by team management, but they would very much let you air your views, if you had anything to say. Hayes and myself, at different times, would have come under fierce pressure at team meetings about the nature of the ball that was delivered in, the number of breaks that weren't being picked up in midfield, one thing or another. Whatever about Liam, as a gasun at that stage. I was a little bit reluctant to stand up and start fuckin' Brian Stafford out of it. So you just didn't!

As a player, I used to put in extra training myself. I used to cycle from my home in Navan over to Ann Bourton's, the team physio over in Slane, which is probably seven miles away. I'd cycle to her, I'd cycle home, and I'd cycle to training. And I'd train and cycle home. Boylan used to reprimand me for over-training. He'd be trying to get me to try and take it easy and slow down, not train as much. Fitness-wise, I'd be lapping some of those players on the Hill of Tara. Running was always no problem.

When the All-Ireland final in 1990 came along, Gerry McEntee was looming. I remember an interview prior to the match – it was all 'Gerry McEntee and Brady'. Every question I was asked related to Gerry McEntee, every question. 'Do you feel any pressure?' At 20 years of age, in my first All-Ireland final, of course I was feeling the pressure. I was suffering from an awful dose of shin splints at the time, and that was bugging me. It was another thing that was in the back of your mind.

'McEntee, McEntee, McEntee' – *it was all I heard. And, 'Would he be fit?' For an All-Ireland, all the loyal supporters would be hedging toward the older lads, the established firm. I remember being interviewed by RTE and being asked again about McEntee and I spoofed out the usual, 'It's all about the team, and whoever is good enough for the team, they should be on and if Gerry is on the team, I'll be delighted for him.' The truth was, I wanted to be on, and that was it!*

Myself and Hayes had formed a good partnership at midfield. Tommy Dowd was a forward. I didn't regard myself as a forward, but for the final McEntee came in and I ended up wing forward. I think it was a mistake. The night that the team was due to be named, on the way out to training, it was put to me, 'If you are playing in the All-Ireland final, but not playing at midfield, how would you feel?' Well, Jesus! When it was phrased like that, the answer was that I just wanted to play in the All-Ireland final. Looking back now, Tommy Dowd lost out on his position. Tommy Dowd was a better forward than me. Sure I was never a forward! The whole balance of the team went out the window that day. I ran around like a headless chicken. I didn't know what I was supposed to be doing.

I remember the team meeting prior to that game. We could have broken the door down with the commitment and passion that was built up in the room during this team meeting, the level of intent. It was mentioned that Meath had beaten Cork in this game and that game, '87 and '88 were brought up, and the semi-final of the League earlier in the season when we played them off the pitch. And the words that we used at the time were, 'Cork don't beat Meath!' When you put something that definitive in the heads of the players, or if you try and convince yourself of that, it's setting yourself up. I remember at the time thinking, 'Jaysus, that's a dodgy thing to be saying.' That came from within the players. Looking back, that haunted me, that, 'Cork don't beat Meath!'

I was after going so well in the latter stages of the League, forming a great relationship with Hayes, and really looking up to him. At that stage, he really was instrumental in my development. Before a match, he used to spend a couple of vital minutes with me in the dressing room and during the kick-around when he'd see what midfielders were playing. He would invariably have played against them and he'd come to me and say, 'You're marking so and so. This fella now, great fielder of the ball, I suggest you just break, don't try and catch with him, outrun him, he can't run.' Whatever little bit of advice he'd have, I'd follow it, and it worked to a tee. Liam was the fielder and I was the runner. I ran for Ireland and Liam fielded for Ireland, and it was just a great partership. And it was going really well.

I was named 'Man of the Match' in the League final against Down with Liam at midfield. I had played there against Cork in the semi-final where I was marking Teddy McCarthy and I outplayed him. These were times that, as a player, you were going, 'Jesus, this is brilliant. Teddy McCarthy! Jesus! It's so easy to play against him.' And then to be moved! I knew that I had been tried before in the half-forward position and didn't perform, and here I was now on the biggest day of my career on the half-forward line again.

A week after the All-Ireland, we had a junior final with the club, and we won that, and that was great. I was captain of the team then, so everything was flying, everything was great. The following week we had an Under-21 match and I tore the cruciate ligament in my knee. I was trying to keep a ball from going over the sideline, but I managed to go across the sideline by about a foot and a half. The linesman put up his flag to indicate a sideline ball, and I reckon had the ref's whistle blown when it should have, it wouldn't have happened. This guy came across *me, my leg was outstreched, and he just pushed it to the side. My right leg, cruciate gone! From then on, the one word I would attach to my football career was 'frustration'. Running in straight lines was fine, but turning? I was on crutches 13 times, had six operations, missed League finals, missed Leinster finals, you name it.*

I was on crutches 12 months later when Meath played in the 1991 All-Ireland final. I had my flags with me as a supporter, and my crutches! I was at the ground when the team bus arrived in. Boylan spotted me and, Boylan being Boylan, brought me onto the bus. Instead of just waving, or winking, or nodding, he came off the bus without any lads getting off and brought me on. He's very intuitive like that. He would understand the mental anguish you would be going through on the day. It was a very emotional time.

In the 1990 All-Ireland semi-final, Donegal made all the moves, but rarely looked like scoring very much. The Ulster champions had two outstanding goal chances in particular which went west! Seven minutes before half-time Joyce McMullen was racing through the Meath defence, after receiving a great through ball from Martin McHugh, but he dithered and waited and eventually fluffed his shot. Midway through the second half, when the teams were all level, McHugh also had the goal in his sights, but he did not make good contact with the ball and Kevin Foley blocked his shot. It was a disappointing afternoon for the mercurial McHugh, who was face-to-face with Kevin Foley in the Meath No. 6 shirt in the continued absence of Liam Harnan. McHugh hardly got a second kick of the ball in the second half, though Donegal did manage to kick the ball wide 12 times as they went down 1-7 to 3-9. The Meath performance was not as complete as the scoreline might indicate, and without P.J. Gillic, who kicked four points from play, Donegal would have been in with a shout right to the very end. Two goals within 60 seconds of one another, 10 minutes from the end of the game, also allowed Meath to escape a dull, patchy performance overall. Brian Stafford and Bernie Flynn got Meath's goals, both of which were supplied by Colm O'Rourke, who had an afternoon that was barely more memorable than McHugh's day out. Midway through the second half O'Rourke was being hailed off – the first time he would be substituted in his great career. Gerry McEntee was running onto the field, but O'Rourke was not making the opposite dash. In the end, in absolute confusion, Meath took Colm Brady off the field instead. Donegal would have to learn from their big day out and come back two years later to claim an All-Ireland title, when Gary Walsh, Martin Gavigan, Anthony Molloy and Co. proved that they had been expert students in 1990. Cork had won the All-Ireland title they most surely deserved in 1989, seeing off Mayo in a tight enough contest, and they would defend their crown against Meath in the 1990 All-Ireland final. Unfortunately, unlike the rest of the country, there was precious little respect or admiration for the Munster champions anywhere in County Meath! And the Meath football team, more than any other group of Meath people, felt in their hearts that the team Billy Morgan had been grooming for the previous three years would not want to answer the really tough questions which should always be posed on All-Ireland final day. Neither Cork nor Mayo, actually, were top of the class in Meath players' minds. It was a costly miscalculation to be carrying into the final game of the season. And, it was the Meath team which had nothing much to say for itself at the end of the 1990 final.

There were only two points in it at the finish, 0-11 to 0-9, but there was never any stage at which Cork looked like losing. Midfielder Shay Fahy was their match-winner, scoring four points from play, and winning the 'Man of the Match' award and every other end of season trophy which was available over the subsequent months. Cork had Colm O'Neill sent off for striking Mick Lyons early in the first half, but even if Meath had extra men on the field it is doubtful if they would have been able to dismantle the Cork defence. On the day the Meath team never raised much of a gallop at all.

COLM O'ROURKE: *We struggled in 1990 and, apart from playing well in the Leinster final that year, we never really played on form. We were poor enough against Donegal in the semi-final and were fortunate enough to get through to the final. I was captain that year and still thought we would win it even though we were not at our best, but we played very poorly in the final. That really was one of the worst performances of all. We kicked an awful lot of wides and just didn't get going at all. In saying it though, I wouldn't have begrudged it to Cork because they were the better team. The policy that the Meath fellas had was that as soon as it was over and you were beaten, you said well done and went home and never complained about anything. And nobody was allowed to do that. Any player who would have dared complain about a ref or anything else would have been told to shut up! You never complained, and that was that!*

LIAM HAYES: *Shay Fahy was one of the most decent, easiest-going lads I ever met in the 12 years I spent on the Meath team, a real gentleman. However, I always felt that I could take Shay. We'd played against each other since we were 18-years old and I always felt faster than him. I always thought I could jump higher, pass better, and going into the game I distinctly remember thinking that this was my chance to score a hatful! I was thinking three or four points, maybe a goal thrown in for good measure. Turned out to be the most humiliating experience of my whole football career, because no one else was marking Shay that afternoon. Only me! I took the blame. I wasn't to blame for all the scores because, for two of them, I was chasing other people's men. Gerry Mc's man Donal Cullotty was loose for the second Fahy score and I went to cover him and the ball was passed to Shay. Then, for his third score, I was racing down the field about 500 yards ahead of Shay, belting it down to the other end of the field, when Marty miskicked his clearance and guess where it went? Straight into Shay's arms. He scored four points, and Cork won by two! You didn't have to be a genius to work out who had the dunce's cap on at the post-match banquet that night. That really was the end of my career. I never recovered fully from that, and even though I was captain in 1991 and got through some good games in that run the next Summer, I always felt I was playing catch-up – as if I owed everyone else a giant apology, and would never have time enough over the next few years to make up for it. I've got to say, though, that if there was one other midfielder in the whole country I would have chosen to subject me to such a mortification, it would have been Shay Fahy. He was a good guy and a great footballer.*

Donal Smith had just completed his first full year as the Meath No. 1, but he was not afforded the opportunity to build on his performances in 1990. Mickey McQuillan was back on Sunday duty the following year. Smith's roller-coaster ride with the Meath team would continue for another four years. The big, gentle garda from Navan O'Mahonys had been the complete team player during his years on the Meath squad, and his ready good humour rarely deserted him, even when he was living morning, noon and night on the substitutes bench.

DONAL SMITH: *It was agreed that during the League that season Mickey McQuillan and myself would play every second game. It was going fine until before Christmas. However somebody said to Sean that it wasn't fair on Mickey because he had done nothing wrong. Then, all of a sudden, it changed overnight and Mickey started two in row! We went down to Wexford and played them in Wexford Park where they scored four goals. Then, in the next game, which I expected to be playing in up in Antrim, Mickey started again. Yet again, we conceded four goals! In fairness to Mickey, he was unlucky because the backs were playing bad and he was made the scapegoat.*

When we got to play Down in the League final in 1990, I was playing and I remember one incident in the first half in particular. Liam Austin was running down the field along the Hogan Stand side of the pitch and Ambrose Rogers was coming straight down the middle of the park, and I could see what was going to happen before the ball was kicked. So I ran out as the ball was centred. But I knew I didn't have the time to get the ball into my hands, so I pulled on it and it went out over the sideline on the '45' metre line on the Down side of the pitch. When I turned back around, I noticed I was 30 yards from goal. Everybody in the crowd must have had heart attacks.

Something that nobody realises about Mick Lyons is how adaptable he was to the players he shared the field with. Mickey McQuillan and myself were two very different goalkeepers in style. Mickey's reflexes were so much better than mine, and he just remained on the line and did the business! But I used to come out and meet the ball, and try to command my area. What Mick Lyons used to do was, if I was playing, he would drop in behind me because he knew I would go out to meet the ball. But if Mickey McQuillan was playing, Lyons would go and meet the ball. We never talked about it or decided to do it. I think Lyons was just such a good player that maybe, even subconsciously, he programmed himself to adapt to whichever goalkeeper was playing.

We conceded a penalty against Donegal in the All-Ireland semi-final later in the year. It was a really wet, miserable day and I got my hand to it, but the ball hit off the butt of the left post and into the net. Manus Boyle celebrated but I was annoyed. I nearly had it but it skidded off my glove. It was the first goal I had conceded in the entire Championship. An article in the Evening Herald *a few days later absolutely lambasted me. It said that Meath would never win an All-Ireland with Donal Smith in goal! I have to admit, I felt under pressure after the article. There was a team meeting called and some of the players on the team suggested that I was coming out too far. At that meeting the video of the match was put on and there was only one performance analysed, and it was mine! The entire panel were sitting there in Dalgan Park analysing my performance. I was cringing in my seat. It was a severe ordeal to have to go through. But lucky enough any decision I had made on the day turned out to be right. A couple of times I came out about 14 yards and blocked the ball, and there was nobody else about as far as I was concerned. It's just because they were used to Mickey's style in the goals. We went training the following night and what the public never realised was that I had dislocated two middle fingers the week after the semi-final. The two fingers were shoved right back into my hand, right out through the back. For the couple of weeks prior to the final I was under serious pressure to prove I was fit. Every time I went to catch a ball people were coming over asking me if I was minding my hand. I always felt that they wanted any opportunity to give Mickey the chance to play and I'll always regret that, coming up to an All-Ireland final. I never knew until the Thursday night that I was playing – after playing the entire Championship and conceding only one goal, and that from a penalty! The annoying thing about it was that no selector, or anybody, came near me except to put me under pressure. Anyway, that night at training, after the video of the semi-final, there was one of the lads kicking a ball over to me and there were three selectors lined up to see how I was catching the ball.*

Now, when I look back at it, is it easy to say I was probably too quiet and didn't stand up and fight my corner. Maybe I should have taken the bull by the horns and said, 'Listen, what's the story?' But I didn't. Some people would take that as a weakness, but I look on it as strength, that I was happy in my own ability. I got a lot of criticism, and that's fair enough, but people forget that I played all my football in goal – for club and county. Mickey only played in goal for Meath, which meant that it was always likely that I would make more mistakes than Mickey because I played in goal week-in week-out. If I conceded a goal in a club game it would be highlighted, but Mickey didn't have that pressure because he played outfield for his club.

I will never forget going from Malahide to Croke Park on the bus on the morning of the All-Ireland final, and Sean approached me. 'Well, how are you Donal?' he asked. 'I'm fucking great Sean.' He asked, 'What do you mean?' I told him, 'How many footballers in this country are playing the game 20 years and have never played in Croke Park, and here I am playing in an All-Ireland final today. I feel great.'

I remember Colm O'Neill's effort before he was sent off. The game was about ten minutes on when O'Neill grabbed possession just behind the

21 yard line, and he turned and ran towards my goal. But Mick McCarthy was in the corner and I was sure he was going to flick the ball over to him, so I wasn't expecting a shot. Next thing, the ball just walloped off the crossbar on my right-hand side. I never even saw it and the ball then went about 25 feet up in the air and it fell into Kevin Foley's hands, and he kicked it downfield. To tell you the truth, I was scared at that moment. It was an incredible shot. I also recall Colm O'Neill striking Mick Lyons in the face and getting sent off. Mick came into me after getting hit and he asked me what was happening. And I said, 'O'Neill is getting sent off.' He just lifted his head, looked at me and said, 'Aw, fuck it!'

Mick was standing in front of me for most of the match. Then, about ten minutes into the second half Cork brought on Paddy Hayes at wing half-forward marking Martin O'Connell. So I said to Mick that he should go and mark Hayes, because Mick Lyons is a marker and that would let Martin do the roving. So Mick was on his way over towards Hayes when the men on the line returned him to full-back. Then John Kerins kicked out three balls to Paddy Hayes and he caught every one of them. They were looking for an outlet and he was the man they were picking.

I played all the League games in 1991 until we went down to Killarney to play Kerry, and coming off the train in Killarney my knee just went. It was a shocking pain. There was obviously a serious problem and to this day I believe if I had been Mick Lyons, Colm O'Rourke or any of the bigger names, my knee would have been sorted out within three weeks. It was a cartilage problem. I didn't get my knee operation until after the first of the Dublin games in the four-game saga. I felt then, and I still feel now, that it suited them for Mickey to be back in goals. For some reason, whether it's the way I took risks or that I wasn't standing on my line, they wanted Mickey! But neither Sean nor anyone ever told me they wanted me to change my style or stay on my line. I got no encouragement. Sean would never turn around and say, 'Listen, you are not playing well and I'm dropping you.' Basically you just found out when the team was announced. And that is the thing about Sean – as a person, a more amiable fella you couldn't meet, but he hated confrontations.

MICKEY McQUILLAN: *In the late '70's I quit the panel myself. There were about seven or eight selectors at the time. I wouldn't say things were bad but they were just not as smooth as when Sean took over. There were always disagreements and nothing was done on the spot when it should have been.*

Then, several years later, 'Scubs' (James Whyte) who had been driving the team around for a long time, for two or three decades, called over to me one night and asked me did I want to go for a spin with him on Sunday, so I said, 'Grand, yeah, no bother', because I thought it was just to go to a football match with him. But then he told me to bring my boots. 'We are playing below in Arva against Cavan', he said. So I was obviously delighted but on the day of the game I was kind of nervous as well. I remember the team was having tea before the game in a pub-type shop in Arva. Anyway, Scubs opened the door and the first two people I see sitting on the stools were Jimmy Fay and another goalkeeper. Therefore, Sean Boylan had his two goalkeepers on the panel present and I thought to myself, 'Oh shit! What's going on here?' Anyway, Sean was late, so Pat Reynolds picked the team and I was started. I played quite well and coming off the field I heard Pat saying, 'At least we've got a keeper.' Now that is no disrespect to the two other boys, but it was good for my confidence.

When we won the Leinster in 1986 I was back in goals, and I played a lot of the All-Ireland semi-final against Kerry with a broken nose. That happened after that famous clash between the three of us. The ball was kicked in and as it came I shouted, but you wouldn't hear anything with the crowd in the stadium. Mick Lyons and Joe Cassells went for it also. I remember getting my hand to the ball, but when I touched it I heard a bang and hit the ground. Ger Power just tapped the ball into the net. I knew the nose was badly broken. Anne (Bourton), Sean and Gerry McEntee ran over to me and sorted it out until half-time. In the dressing room Jack Finn, the Doc, bandaged it up but it kept bleeding afterwards. But that was only a minor thing. I mean, it was an All-Ireland semi-final and I wanted to play.

And I played right though until 1990. That year there was an arrangement that Donal and myself would alternate games in the League and that happened for a while. One day before a match Sean came up to me and said that Donal was starting. Sean said he was concerned that Donal was not getting enough games and in case I got injured he was giving him a run. I said it was fine and that was how it was left. He didn't say I was dropped, but obviously I was. There was a match in Antrim where I let in four goals. I certainly was at fault for the first goal and I hold my hands up and admit that, but I probably took the brunt of the blame. But I wasn't told I was dropped, just that Donal was getting a game. If I was told I was being dropped for a certain reason, bad kick-outs or poor handling, then fair enough, I would have worked at that. I remember just saying to my wife, Angela, after two or three weeks, that I was going to be back next year and win an Allstar. And I did! I worked extremely hard. I trained two nights with Meath but also three nights in Gormanstown College with my brothers. They were kicking balls at me and it paid off in the long run.

DONAL SMITH: *We trained in Gormanstown swimming pool for three months during the summer of 1991. We were wearing buoyancy suits and people thought we were mad. But, you look at those four games against Dublin, and not once was fitness a problem for Meath. I remember sitting on the bench after Foley's goal in the fourth game. Liam Hayes had the ball and got it across to P.J. Gillic. Everybody on the bench was roaring, 'Shoot! Shoot, Don't give it to Beggy. Don't give it to Beggy.' Anyway, he did give it to Beggy and Jinksy knocked it over the bar and we all looked around at each other in stunned silence that he was after scoring.*

My opinion is that the selection of the team for the All-Ireland final that year in '91 was all wrong. On the Thursday night the team was named with P.J. in midfield and AN Other at corner-forward. Now P.J. Gillic was of the opinion that he was marking Barry Breen and he studied videos of him and all, so everything was fine. Then on Saturday evening we were told that Colm O'Rourke was not starting and that P.J. was going into the corner, and Gerry McEntee would start along with Liam Hayes in midfield. Now, I don't know if Sean was subjected to pressure to play Gerry, but anyway, Breen scored the goal for them. But, from where I was, I could feel that pressure was put on Sean to play Gerry. From whom or where I never knew, but I realised on the Saturday night that it was the wrong move. As for P.J., he didn't perform at all. He had mentally prepared himself for Breen in midfield and the switch left him disorientated. It was impossible for him to retain his focus. For weeks he expected to play in midfield and the day before the game, all of a sudden, he is playing corner-forward.

Barry Breen's goal was a blow because Mickey Linden was coming down along the sideline and Lyons went for him, which is fine. But Mickey McQuillan followed him. He went about three yards towards that post

Ollie Murphy, June 6, 1999

Darren Fay, August 29, 1999

and the ball came to Breen, and although it may not have prevented the goal, at least if he had remained where he was it might have provided a challenge in the air for the ball. But mistakes like that happen.

MICKEY McQUILLAN: *In 1991, I got back in and was delighted because I knew there was a lot of football left in me and I wanted to get back playing Championship football again. But those games against Dublin that year would leave you drained. For me, playing against Dublin in the Championship is sometimes the most important game Meath play all year. Sometimes it is bigger than an All-Ireland final even. I think we were very lucky to get a draw the first day and I came off the field very, very happy. I was mentally drained though. I remember waking up on Monday morning thinking, 'Oh no, I have to go through this again', but at the same time I was very happy to be still involved.*

The set-up Sean had when the late Noel Keating, the boss of Kepak, was involved was absolutely fantastic. The weekend we went to Scotland during the four game saga with Dublin in 1991 was genius. It actually took us away from the pressure. The wives and girlfriends came along, and we played golf and so on. I think he flew over earlier on in the week and checked out this place and booked it for the panel. So, we were in Scotland one of the nights and we were drinking away. Sean was there drinking Rosemary tea and water, and at about half twelve he stood up and said, 'Right lads, I will see you in the foyer at nine o'clock for training.' The following morning he ran the absolute guts out of us. The hotel ran out of water! We enjoyed ourselves out there but worked damn hard also. I think bringing us over there was an inspired, classic decision. Keith Barr's penalty in the fourth game was the best peno ever taken on me that didn't go in! He actually struck the flag at the post. I went the right way but it would still have beaten me if it was inside the post. It was hard and low, and I have not seen many better penalties, but thankfully it went wide. Even if I had got a hand to it, the ball would have gone back out to him and he probably would have scored.

Kevin Foley's goal showed the character within the team. It started across from me on our own end-line with Martin. He could have lashed it up the field but didn't, likewise Mick Lyons and Harnan! Mattie McCabe told me afterwards that he told Kevin to keep going on because Dublin would pick up Mattie quicker than they would Kevin. If Mattie had made that run he would have been picked up straight away because he was a forward. But Kevin was different. I mean, once he got over the half way line he was lost, in a different world altogether. But he just kept going and was there at the end to score the goal. Then when Liam Hayes got the ball, Dublin were still thinking about the goal, and Jinksy got it and fired over the winner. I was standing in the goal looking at it all happen and couldn't believe my eyes, but when the final whistle went, boy, was I happy! The only man I really hugged after a game was 'Scubs'. I knew he was at the 21 yard line at the Canal End with water. He came running out and he had two bottles in each hand and they were flying out, and I headed straight across for him.

If the All-Ireland final against Down had been played two weeks earlier then we probably would have beaten them. As it turned out, we were left idle for almost a month. I remember Breen's goal. I came out and thought McCartan was going to shoot, so I tried to narrow the angle, and Mick had come across as well and then McCartan flicked it to Breen and he just palmed it into the net. I narrowed the angle and expected the shot but he was clever enough to spot the free man.

The ten games Meath played in the summer of 1991 would have

brought any other team to its knees. Undoubtedly, there was something very special about a team which could go four punishing games with Dublin in the first round of the Leinster championship, make a meal out of beating Wicklow over two games immediately after, blitz Offaly, win the Leinster crown by toughening it out against Laois, beat Roscommon with a late sprint in the All-Ireland semi-final and then, after falling 11 points behind Down in the last game of the championship, make an almighty charge until only two points separated the two teams at the season's final whistle. How did Sean Boylan do it? That summer was, undoubtedly, the greatest undertaking of any manager in the history of the GAA, especially when it is considered that Boylan began the ten-game series with a roomful of crocks. Meath had spent the final week of April and almost all of May in the swimming pools of Navan and Gormanstown. Eleven players were struggling to recover from a variety of injuries as the clock counted down to the 2 June meeting with Paddy Cullen's Dublin in the first round of the Leinster championship. Boylan resolved to stop the casualty list from rising any higher and, instead of cotton wool wrapped around his squad, he chose water. It was a brave and brilliant decision, as it turned out. Meath, obviously, were not as fast out of the blocks or as sharp on the ball as their opponents when the first Sunday in June finally arrived, but Boylan had a clean bill of health, at least.

Dublin, however, were already in mid-stride when the two teams began their five-weeks battle. They had been crowned League champs by defeating Mick O'Dwyer's new Kildare team, and all through a fierce, wearying contest Meath seldom managed to get shoulder-to-shoulder with their opponents. Heart and wit, and not a lot else, carried Meath along from week to week. Until Dublin, with the finishing line in sight on 6 July, suddenly, inexplicably, slowed up. The Meath team then put its head down.

On 2 June, Dublin were five points up at half-time, but when Mick Deegan was dispossessed running out of defence in the final minute the ball was taken by P.J. Gillic, who completely fooled John O'Leary with a lofted kick from 40 yards which hopped over the bar. On 9 June, Meath led by three points at half-time, led again by three points in the first period of extra-time thanks to a David Beggy goal, but were denied victory when Jack Sheedy punched the ball to the net. On 23 June, Dublin were back to being five points up, with 15 minutes remaining, but a Bernie Flynn goal saw Meath through to extra-time, where Colm Coyle scored Meath's second goal with a rasping shot and Paul Clarke scrambled home a Dublin goal three minutes later. On 6 July, Meath led by two points after 16 minutes, Dublin led by two points at half-time, Dublin led by six points after 50 minutes, and Dublin still led by three points with 60 seconds remaining. It had been a strange and wonderful experience, for both teams on the field, for their sets of supporters, and for every football team and football supporter watching all over the country. And then came the ending, an ending which, over the next decade, would be talked about and analysed, and feasted upon more than the whole body of the four games put together.

MARTIN O'CONNELL: *It was probably one of the worst games I ever played for Meath. I just couldn't get going, for whatever reason. At the very end, I remember this ball coming in, and it was rolling and rolling along the end-line, and I just happened to pick it up. Declan Sheehan tackled me and I flicked it to Mick Lyons and it all started from there. I could have let the ball roll out over our end-line but for some reason I* didn't. I just kept it in. It's probably two or three years since I last looked at the video of it. You just could not see it happening. We were three points down with, what, two minutes to go? I remember someone asking Foley, 'Was that the best goal you ever scored for Meath?' And him saying, 'It was the only feckin' goal I scored for Meath!' Sure it was David Beggy who kicked the winning point! And you know David kicking the ball? Sure it could go anywhere, but lucky enough it went over the bar. But, sure, what is it now only a memory? If we only had to play Dublin once and win an All Ireland, you would have swapped it straightaway for those four games.

P.J. GILLIC: David Beggy was probably the cause of those four games. He scored the winning point, but he also made the point which levelled the first game with Dublin! Mick Deegan was coming out with the ball down along the Hogan Stand side and if he had blasted the ball out over the roof of the stand we were probably gone. But he chose to solo it out, and Jinxy got a great tackle on him. We both went to tackle him at the same time and Jinxy got there before me and, as the ball broke, I picked it up. I can remember getting around Deegan and going along down the Hogan Stand side and having a look in to see what was going on in the square. I could see Tommy Dowd was bombing it through the middle and John O'Leary was coming out to cut off the angle. So I wouldn't say I was going for a point, but I was definitely lobbing it in, and hoping something would happen. I was delighted to see it go over, even if initially I was a bit disappointed not to see it drop into the net. But, it could have popped wide just as easily.

In the second game, I had a great chance of a goal. We were after making a great move up the field. Martin O'Connell was after carrying it past one or two and hand-passed it in to me, and I was aware that John

O'Leary was coming out. I remember gathering myself up into a ball, waiting to get clobbered, and whatever way he was off the ground when he hit me, he just rolled off my shoulder. I was left with a wide-open goal and I blasted it right over the bar. I can still see myself going, 'Aw, Jesus, there you are again! if it was Flynn or O'Rourke, that ball would have been in the back of the net.'

It would be unfair to blame Keith Barr for missing the penalty near the end of the last game. It was a rocket of a shot, and just went out by the foot of the post, and Mick Lyons running up alongside him. Barr, though, never made anything of it. I don't think Lyons being there would have affected him. It was a fantastic hit – it just went the wrong side of the post.

We were dead and buried by the end. Even before the game, there was a sense that everything was going against us. We lost Sean Kelly before the game for some reason; Terry Ferguson seized up in the dressing room taking his trousers off; Padraig Lyons tore his hamstring badly about 15 minutes into the game and had to go off; Rourkey got knocked out and had to go off for a few minutes; and Bernard Flynn went off after half-time. Things were going really badly for us that day and we showed great character to get back into it.

Whatever about the goal, the winning point was also strange. It was strange because myself and Jinxy set the ball rolling with the ball that hopped over the bar five weeks earlier. Liam Hayes kicked the ball across to me and I can remember Eamon Heery coming to meet me. I wasn't aware of what Meath fella was running alongside me. I actually thought it was Flynn, and when I saw that it was Jinxy I passed it to, I thought, 'Oh shit!' I had actually got round Heery and could have kicked it myself, and I can remember thinking, 'What am I after doing?' I'm not sure if I saw it go over. I thought he was going to balloon it wide so I closed my eyes.

TERRY FERGUSON: *Before the last game against Dublin, we went over to Scotland and Sean nearly killed us with training over there. We went over on the Friday and stayed in a place called Drymen, near Loch Lomond. It was a lovely quiet spot, lovely facilities. We trained on the soccer pitch and we had a couple of great nights out also. We got up the first morning after being out the night before and Sean said just go out and have a bit of a run-around – and he kept us out for four hours! Almost killed us! Naturally enough, we all headed out again on the Saturday night because we said to ourselves there is no way Sean is going to do it to us again – no way he's going to bring us out training on the Sunday morning! Sunday morning came and, lo' and behold, Sean had us out from 11 a.m. until 3.30 p.m. He absolutely killed us all over again, but we knew it had to be done. We really wanted to beat Dublin. I remember we had a players' meeting and Joe Cassells stood up and got talking, and he couldn't shut up. He started talking about this and that, not necessarily football all the time, and he just couldn't shut up! He must have spoken for a good half an hour. Sean got up then, and said, 'Right, that's enough', and that was the end of the meeting.*
I was in the dressing room taking off my trousers before the last game and I pulled a muscle, had a muscle spasm in my back. I had trouble with my back before but not like that, right before a game. I remember sitting beside Bob, and I had just one leg of the trousers off, was standing on one leg, and the muscle in my back just locked! I held myself up with my two hands. I couldn't really sit. In fact I couldn't move. I asked Bob to get Anne (Bourton) or Jack (Doc Finn) over, that I was in a little bit of trouble! And he shouted over and one of them replied, 'Yeah, I will be with you in a minute.' I said to Bob, 'Get them, I want them over

now.' Bob shouted again, more urgently this time, and then they came over. Naturally enough there was a bit of hassle in the dressing room and everybody was a bit concerned. I was in severe pain. Sean Kelly also couldn't play and things just seemed to be going wrong everywhere. I was up on the table and, Jack being Jack, said, 'Aw, we'll give you something for that.' No matter what was wrong with you, Jack would say, 'I'll give you something for that.' After a while, all the boys were ready and there was a bit of a team talk, and they went out. I was left sitting on the table. Mockie Regan, who was the masseur, stayed with me but it was a very lonely time. He helped get my tracksuit on because I couldn't dress myself, such was the pain. So I hopped out to the dug-out, and it was not a good place to be. I felt out of the whole occasion. I have had back trouble ever since. I have had an operation and had a disc removed

During the game then, O'Rourke got a bang and he came into the dug-out and I remember looking at him and he was extremely dazed. He was concussed and Jack and Anne were trying to bring him back with smelling salts. Sean was going to replace him but Jack said, 'No, give him a minute', and somehow Colm went back on and played a blinder after that. I'll never know how he was able to continue, but it was just one of those days. The goal, of course, is something nobody who was there will ever forget. It was brilliant. The way we won the game was superb. The poor Dubs couldn't believe it and, I suppose, we could hardly believe it ourselves. When we scored I wanted to jump up and celebrate like everybody else but I physically was not able to. I just sat there and looked on. The whole stadium erupted into a mass of green and gold. I was in total disbelief. Brilliant. Then Jinksy got a point and the game was over before the Dubs knew what had happened.

For the next game, I remember doing a fitness test. I think it was before *the Wicklow game. Sean had myself and Jinksy in for a test and yet again he nearly killed us for 25 minutes. We had to do a lot of short sprints and running around in circles. I didn't want to miss out on it because we were on a roll at the time. Even when my back was at me later in the Championship, I didn't say anything. I didn't let on. I just wanted to be involved. We were lucky to get past Roscommon in the All-Ireland semi-final and I was taken off that day. It was the one and only time I was substituted. Derek Duggan scored a famous goal that day and although he wasn't my man it looked bad, and Sean gave me the long finger. But I understood. I was having a bad day. Tommy Dowd was great. However, sitting on the bench again didn't feel nice. I never liked the damned bench, ever.*

PADRAIG LYONS: *Terry Ferguson got injured and I was in for the last Dublin game, but after about 10 or 15 minutes I tore my hamstring – tore it to shit. I tore it in the middle, tore it off the bone under my backside. Ah, it was just a freakish thing. The ball came in, and myself and my man headed off. The boys always say I was actually getting ahead of him but there was something amiss – I was going too fast for the rest of me, and that was the end of it! I don't think I togged out for Meath ever again after that. I played outfield for the club for about two years after that, but if I got a little tear in it, it would take me twice as long to get it right. Then a vacancy came up in the goal with Summerhill. I always had a good kick-out, and I told them, 'I'll catch anything that comes in, but don't expect anything spectacular. There'll be no diving or anything like that!'*

DARREN FAY: *I was at the third and fourth games in 1991 against Dublin. The main memory I have, obviously, is the goal in the fourth* *game from Kevin Foley. But, aside from that, I always remember P.J. Gillic's point in the first game – he kicked the ball late on and it hopped over the bar for the equaliser. I was in the Canal End at the time and I remember watching it going towards the goal, and being so sure that it was going to drop underneath the crossbar for a goal. We were kind of disappointed that it bounced over because when it cleared John O'Leary in the Dublin goals it looked a certain goal for Meath. But it hopped over the bar in the end, and for me that is the real moment that sticks out in my head – standing in the Canal End watching Gillic's point hop over. I was there with a few friends at the time and we all looked at each other for a split second, thinking the same thing, that it was going in for the goal which would have won the game. We were so close to winning at that stage.*

GERRY McENTEE: *I watched the first two games against Dublin in the stand and although I came back for the third game I had wanted to return for the first game. I was down at the training sessions prior to the first two games but didn't think I was fit enough or sharp enough because I had been training on my own which is not the same. The mood was also really bad in the camp in the lead-up to that first Dublin game. The attitude was awful and everybody was just fed up. They had had enough and were fighting with each other and were not playing well. Everybody was crabby and there didn't appear to be any real enthusiasm for it at all. Training was bad and things didn't look good. In fact, it looked like Colm O'Rourke and Mick Lyons were going to be dropped. That's how bad things appeared.*

I don't think Sean asked me to come back after the first two games. I think I asked him. The whole momentum seemed to be snowballing at that stage and I wanted to get involved. My memory of the final game was that it was Dublin's best performance. They played brilliant football and scored some brilliant points. They were six points up at one stage and Niall Guiden was kicking some great points. Of all the games, that was the one where they were really on top of us. I remember Terry Ferguson's back getting stuck taking his trousers off before the game, and he could not move! That was a big blow before the game even started, but Padraig Lyons replaced Terry in the starting 15 and was marking Declan Sheehan. When the ball was played into the corner early on, he was so determined to play well that he made a mad burst to get out past Sheehan to the ball when he got a dreadful pain and he knew exactly what was wrong straightaway. He was in agony and had to come off. Colm was brought over to the line early on also, after he got dazed in a tackle. He was out of it for several minutes but we didn't put on a sub. Keith Barr, who was playing centre half-back had nobody to mark. He should have gone up the field and punished Meath. He had five or six minutes to do it, but he didn't. He never moved! They were about to put in a sub on the sideline when Jack Finn said, 'Hold on Sean, I think he is coming to!' So they stood Colm up, and although he was still groggy they put him back out on the field. He didn't know where he was for a good ten minutes, and still Keith Barr didn't go up the field! Colm came to and then in the second half was very involved in the lead-up to the goal. I thought Dublin were coasting towards the final whistle. They actually took off Charlie Redmond and replaced him with Vinny Murphy. In the end it was a bad move because Redmond was not there to take the free-kick that Jack Sheedy missed, which could have drawn the game. Vinny Murphy gave away a bad pass when he came on and Martin O'Connell collected it on our end-line. He passed it to Mick. Someone came to nail him, but Mick saw him coming and just set himself and squashed him into the ground. He passed the ball on and it worked its way down the field. You could never see it ending up as a goal, especially from Kevin Foley, because he never went forward in his life, never! And, of course, when he scored the goal there was no celebration, no arm in the air, no nothing! He just started to run back down the field. Then Liam Hayes hit a great ball to P.J. Gillic, who in turn gave it out to Jinksy and he put it over the bar. It was a great feeling, and it was only the first round of the Championship.

CORMAC SULLIVAN: *I was there at all four games in Croke Park in 1991. At times you felt that we were gone. In the end it was Kevin Foley's goal that brought us back into it in the last game. It was one of the best you'll ever see. It should be used as an example to kids around the country who are being taught the game. It was the perfect example of teamwork and support play and what started off at the back ultimately ended up in a goal. It was the perfect goal. To score it in any match would have been a great achievement. But to score such a goal at such a crucial stage of the game, and Championship, was just unbelievable. Those games created a serious buzz around the county. It was unbelievable to be living only a quarter of a mile away from Dublin but to be on the Meath side of the border! I only live about two miles away from Balbriggan so there would have been plenty of local rivalries there. Even when I was in school in Gormanstown College it was always 50-50 in terms of support for Meath and Dublin, and that added to the attractiveness of the ties.*

Maybe the players thought they had a god-given right to win that All-Ireland final after the four in a row. It was always liable to happen (letting Down get too far ahead) considering that Meath had always managed to come back in the past against teams after giving them big leads. I remember Colm O'Rourke coming on as a substitute and changing the game. If there had been another five minutes, then I believe that we would have won. We were nibbling off their lead all the time. But we just ran out of time.

FRANK FOLEY: *It got to a point in '91 where I was sick of the sight of Croke Park because I seemed to be up there all the time watching Meath! Myself and my wife, Mary, got married the week after the All-Ireland final loss to Down in 1991. My brother Kevin was the best man and I was starting to think to myself, 'This is going to be a quiet wedding.' Kevin hadn't really talked much to anybody between the Sunday and the Wednesday. It worked out OK, however, and he opened up after a while but it was on my mind that it might be a bit much for him so soon after the Down game. I remember our mother was quite sick at the time in 1991. There were some stupid rumours going around that Kevin was only playing as a last request to her. It was ridiculous! At the time there was a train going from Navan up to Croke Park and by all accounts, from what I've heard, someone started the rumour in Navan and by the time they got to Croker it was the word of the Bible. It was rubbish really, totally untrue.*

I didn't go to the first round game in 1992 because our mother was even worse at that stage. Meath were beaten by Laois in Navan and you know my mother was actually happy that they were beaten. Kevin had just got married to his wife, Geraldine at the time and my mother thought it was time for him to be settling down and looking after the kids, and all that.

I remember sitting beside my sister in the crowd at Croke Park and watching Kevin's goal go in against Dublin in the final game of the four. I turned and told her that Kevin had just scored, and she just looked back at me and said, 'Did he?' I don't think anyone expected what happened to actually happen. I remember looking at a picture in the Sunday World taken from around the President's seat in Croke Park looking back towards the Hill after Kevin's goal. There were no Dublin hands in the air at all. Some of the fans' hands were on their heads in a kind of agony. But apart from that they were all completely still, and the flags were all hanging by their sides. It was as silent as the Hill has ever been, I'd say. Kevin never mentioned the goal at all since. I think the lasting memory for any of the players involved in '91 is that they didn't win an All-Ireland medal. I'd say, speaking for Kevin, he'd much rather have not scored any goal but won the final against Down. Most of the players are like that.

JOHN McDERMOTT: *I came on in the second game against Dublin, caught this magnificent ball, turned around and said to myself, 'By Jaysus, I'm flying here' and hand-passed it straight to Ciaran Duff, who put it over the bar. I'll never forget it. I just wanted the ground to swallow me up. I was left on for about 15 minutes. It could have been in extra-time of the second game, I think.*
I made a mistake, but at least I was trying. Against Offaly, a few weeks later, I came on and scored a goal with my first touch of the ball, with five minutes to go. So my first two Championship experiences consisted of coming on and being taken straight off again, and then coming on and scoring a goal. What about that! It wasn't a very spectacular goal. I just dribbled it over the line.
You don't really think about getting into the team for those Dublin games. You just do your best and if you're good enough to get in, fair enough. If not, well, you did your best. I'd be like that. I wouldn't be looking over my shoulder. I'd be looking to see what I can do. You felt part of it all and, at the same time, you didn't! You were part of the panel and

bursting your arse along with everybody else, but that team was after winning two All-Irelands, and you weren't part of that. At least I can say that I played in one of the four matches, even if I don't want to pick through the bones of it.

I'd prefer to be beaten in a first round, than a Leinster final or an All-Ireland final. The longer it goes on, the whole year becomes a waste then. You'd be looking round you back then in 1991 and you'd be saying, 'Jesus, we just mightn't have too many All-Irelands left in us.' There was no Trevor Giles, Darren Fay or Graham Geraghty around then. So you'd be saying, 'Hold on a minute now. I mightn't be winning too many of these, and I'd like just one in my back pocket.' To rub it in, I was hit with a six-month suspension at the end of that year. I was working with at fella at the time from Garristown and he said, 'C'mon over and play with us.' It was a real Mickey Mouse affair. There were no team sheets even handed in and I thought it was a challenge match. I only found out afterwards that it was a tournament game. So, I came out then after the Dublin game in '91 to be banned for six months because I played with another team outside Meath. I had to go down to the Leinster Council and stand up and do my bit! I appealed it, and got it down to three months.

There's no doubt about it, playing Dublin at any time is the biggest game of the year, whether it's the first round or the Leinster final. You're going to fill Croke Park. Even more so after '91. That whole saga still affects Dublin. You very rarely see a Dublin player talking or doing a piece in a newspaper without mentioning Meath in it. They could be in an All-Ireland final against Tyrone – but they'll still mention Meath! They would see it as the ultimate test.

BRIAN STAFFORD: *The mood certainly wasn't great coming into the*

Dublin games. There were certain lads who weren't going well, probably myself included, and I started No. 13 for the first game, which was kind of foreign to me, to be honest. In truth, Dublin could have and probably should have won each of those four games, but it was just that old fighting spirit and never-say-die attitude that got us through.

Sean's decision to bring us to Scotland after the third game was brilliant. It was totally against the rule book almost to bring us away before such a big game. I don't know where he came up with the idea or whose idea it actually was, but it was a super weekend. We did some training over there, but mostly tried to drink the place dry. We did a bit of training on the two mornings, but it was harmless and I even remember lads falling over each other. I wear contact lenses and remember actually getting up the first morning and trying to put the lenses into my eyes, and it was a disaster. I couldn't even see my fingers, never mind my contact lenses! But it got everybody together. We trained in a local soccer field and we were sending a fella up and down to the hotel like a yo-yo for water, we were so thirsty. It was just unbelievable. I scored a goal the fourth day, which Rourkey put on a plate for me. There was a high ball knocked in by P.J. Gillic and Colm caught it and ran towards the goal at an angle. He fisted it over to me in the centre and I just closed my eyes and hit it, and thankfully it found the back of the net. I remember with about ten minutes to go we were four points down, and although I had scored a goal and five points I hadn't played particularly well. Then we won a free on the Cusack side shooting to the Hill on the 20-metre line. I was kind of half-reluctant to take it but went over to kick it anyway. It was probably the hardest free-kick I ever took in Croke Park, but luckily enough it went over the bar and shortly after Foley got the goal and Jinksy got the winning point. Kevin Foley scored one of the greatest goals ever. I was right behind him, if he had only let it go, Jaysus! I would have got all the glory if he had let the ball come to me. Seriously though, at training we would be working on those kind of moves, but I guess that was the one and only time it really worked.

TOMMY DOWD: *There was a reception in the Mansion House for both teams after it all, and Tommy Carr was nearly in tears with the whole emotion of it. That's what it meant to both teams. I wasn't supposed to be playing in the final game. My clubmate Sean Kelly was picked ahead of me for the game, but then he picked up an injury. That's how I got in. During the movement for the goal, P.J. caught the ball and gave it to me. I gave it to O'Rourke, and he gave it back to me. I didn't think he would. I thought he'd turn around and blast it himself. But he did. I saw O'Leary coming for me. Now I would never take a shot at John O'Leary if I was ever in that sort of position. I would either try and give it to a man outside, who was in front of the goal, or try and get round him. I would never try and take a shot because he was such a good shot-stopper. I didn't even know who was outside me at the time. I just saw a green jersey and Foley happened to be there in that position. It could have been Stafford for all I knew at the time. Sure none of us could believe that Kevin was there, above all the lads! He was involved in the move as well and he just travelled up the field. Fair play to him, he was brave enough to keep going. A lot of lads when they made the pass would have run back down into the defence to pick up a man, but he kept going. I suppose he threw caution to the wind. He said once, that the reason he went forward was because he saw the stewards circling. It could have been the case. That's like something Foley would come out with.*

I remember Hayes running down the wing with the ball under the Hogan Stand. He kicked it across to P.J., who gave it in to Beggy, and Beggy kicked it over the bar. Beggy was a very under-rated player. He got an

*awful lot of important scores for Meath. He had great speed – it was just
that his ball control mightn't have been brilliant. A Meath selector told
me one time, and I won't name him, that if I was ever playing with
Beggy, make sure to run behind him because he was guaranteed to drop
the ball. Beggy was always a man for a bit of craic, a bit of music and
a few pints as well. He still is. All he wanted to do was go out and have
a bit of fun. He was also very dedicated at the same time. He'd really
put it in when he had to. He wouldn't be drinking now the night before
a game or anything like that.*

The four historic meetings between Meath and Dublin brought the
financial gain of the Leinster Council to over one million pounds.
Almost 250,000 people attended the six hours of football over a
five weeks period, as Meath scored six goals and 44 points and
Dublin's tally came to three goals and 52 points (1-12 to 1-12, 1-11
to 1-11, 2-11 to 1-14, and 2-10 to 0-15). Once again, the
No. 1 rule in the handbook of every Meath footballer, as written by
Sean Boylan, had brought the team through a brilliant but harrow-
ing battle – score more goals than Dublin, and victory is almost
assured!

'The incredible saga which lasted almost as long as four World Cup
soccer finals, nine World heavyweight title fights and three
Olympic marathons produced a remarkable finale at Croke Park
yesterday, with Meath finally solving the puzzle which had taken
more twists and turns than a rally circuit', wrote the always astute
and authoritative Martin Breheny in the *Sunday Press* on Sunday,
7 July, 1991, adding, 'In normal circumstances, 340 minutes of
football would have been enough to get a team into the last ten
minutes of an All-Ireland semi-final, but not this time. Since

2 June, the finishing tape has so often been a mischievous mirage, coaxing each team to breast it before gleefully dancing off into the distance, that one suspected it might take a toss-up to eventually prize the teams apart.'

Four weeks later, on 10 August, Sean McGoldrick, now of the *Sunday World*, was also doing his sums after Meath had claimed the Leinster title with a 1-11 to 0-8 victory over Laois. 'Croke Park is now quiet, save for the hum of two lawnmowers and the sound of bottles being brushed off the terraces', he wrote, continuing, 'An hour or so has passed since Liam Hayes cradled the Leinster trophy in his long arms. After more than 10 hours of football, Meath's endeavours have finally earned them a piece of silverware. Meath won back-to-back All-Ireland titles in 1987 and '88 after 11 games of football. Now it has taken them eight games, two of which went to extra-time, to claim one provincial title.' Eight days after freeing themselves from Dublin, Meath had played Wicklow in the first round (Dublin and Meath had been a preliminary round tie!) of the Leinster Championship and Wicklow fully deserved their draw (scoring 12 times to their opponents' 1-9). In the replay on 21 July, Meath had three points to spare at the end (1-12 to 1-9), and on July 28 the team summoned up an incredible amount of strength and sheer will power to conquer Offaly (2-13 to 0-7). That, however, was the only time in the ten games that Meath were allowed to put their feet up late in a game!

LIAM HAYES: *There were not too many funny or light moments that summer. For starters, as captain, I had to make ten big team talks before each game, and that was so like the Bill Murray movie, Groundhog Day, where he keeps waking up and experiencing the same day over and* *over, and can't escape from that damned day. But I'll never forget the seconds after we had beaten Laois in the Leinster final on the Saturday afternoon – it was strange enough playing a Leinster final on a Saturday to begin with! I was standing around trying to get the lads together so that we could go up onto the Hogan and get the trophy, and Mick Lyons walked past me, and didn't really stop walking. 'Just go up and get the fucking thing', snapped Mick. Do you know something? Meath teams had spent 16 years trying to win a Leinster before we managed it in 1986, and here we were just a few years later, walking up a few steps to take the Leinster trophy and it was being considered a pain in the backside! Is life strange or what?*

Meath beat 14-man Laois 1-11 to 1-8 in the Leinster final in front of a paltry attendance of 28,157, and thereby brought home the fifth Leinster title in six years to their loyal supporters. The biggest cost of the day for Meath was the loss of Bob O'Malley, five minutes into the contest, with a broken leg. Pat Roe, Martin Dempsey, George Doyle, Denis Lalor and Tony Maher were outstanding for Laois all afternoon, but they lacked the necessary strength in depth to fully wrestle control of the game for long stages. David Beggy shot the all-important goal in the first half from only five yards out. Five points in the last 12 minutes completed the day's work. Eight days later, in the All-Ireland semi-final, Roscommon put up a gallant fight for three-quarters of the afternoon before their own insecurities and self-doubts allowed their opponents to walk quite easily through to the final game of the epic season. With Martin O'Connell moving back to corner-back to give close attention to Derek Duggan Meath settled into the game, but it was Brian Stafford at the other end who brought

Meath home safely. He had scored three points over 55 minutes against the hard-grafting Pat Doorey, but he added a further six in the last 15 minutes of the game (five in the last three minutes). Roscommon could have been 2-5 to 0-0 ahead after ten minutes, such was their early superiority, but their interval advantage was only 1-7 to 0-7 thanks to a Duggan dropped-kick rasper of a goal. Meath trailed by five points with 17 minutes still left on the clock. Stafford ensured it was 0-15 to 1-11 at the very end against the heart-broken Connacht champions.

After so many matches coming so quickly and so fast all summer long, the Meath team had a full four weeks to prepare for the All-Ireland final against Down, and Sean Boylan and his team hardly knew what to do with themselves. Time dragged and then, in the final days before the game, Colm O'Rourke went crashing down with viral pneumonia. The season had been playing tricks on the team all year long, but O'Rourke's illness was a final, dastardly card to have thrown in their direction. Bob O'Malley was still on crutches nursing his broken leg, and now O'Rourke! Fifty-two minutes into the game, Mick Lyons would also have to make his departure from the 1991 stage after suffering a bad blow to his leg. Down led 0-8 to 0-4 at half-time, and Meath captain Liam Hayes, once again, would share a few short, angry words with Sean Boylan in the dressing room. It was 1-16 to 1-14 at the finish, and Hayes, like his Skryne clubmate and long-time friend Colm O'Rourke before him 12 months later, would have to walk away from Croke Park without Sam Maguire. He would also have to live with his prepared captain's speech forever locked up in his head.

COLM O'ROURKE: *I was knocked out for a while early on in the final* game with Dublin and had to go off for an amount of time. I think Stafford tried to set me up to be killed with a high hand-pass and he pretty much succeeded. I came back on but didn't remember much of the first half after that. But I remember the entire second half when we were playing badly, and looked like we were in big trouble. I was involved in the build-up to Kevin Foley's goal. I gave a bad pass to Jinksy out towards the Hogan Stand side of the pitch and he collected it and worked it up towards the Dublin goal. Tommy Dowd came running through and, at this stage, I had run forward and he hand-passed to me and I gave him a hand-pass return. He passed to Foley then and that was that. So I was involved in it a couple of times. It is the one moment of all my years with Meath that, whenever I see it again, I still feel like jumping up and punching the air.

That was another one of the great days. If I were to take out two days I would say the 1986 Leinster final and the 1991 win over Dublin. You should never look back on life with regrets, but it certainly would have been nice to win the All-Ireland in 1991. I had pneumonia the week before the game, but I was always hoping against hope that I would be able to play – but I just wasn't getting better. I remember coming on that day. Sean basically left it up to me at the time. He just asked me would I go on and if I had said no I don't feel there would have been a problem about it. He just said to me, 'Will you go on?' and I said I would. I think at that stage the game was getting away from us and as soon as I came on Down got the goal. I got a good bit of ball when I came on, but Flynn was playing really well that day and I gave a couple of balls to him because he was on fire. It was just a matter of giving the balls to him because he was the man scoring.

GERRY McENTEE: I had come on as a sub against Wicklow the first day and started the replay against them. Then I played against Offaly because Liam was suspended, but I was dropped for the Laois game and shouldn't have been dropped. I was absolutely flying and should not have been dropped. Sean told me on the Thursday night that I was dropped. I had played well on Padraig Dunne of Offaly and also played well against Wicklow, so the logical thing was to leave me there when I was playing well. And I did nothing wrong in between to deserve to be dropped. Liam had been suspended and could have been left sitting on the bench for a while and then brought on, but Sean dropped me instead. We exchanged words over it, but it was left at that.

Down deserved to win that All-Ireland. I will never forget their support. I remember Hill 16 was a sea of black and red. They were also a very sporting group of supporters. When our bus pulled into Croke Park that day from Malahide, the Down supporters clapped us into the dressing room. There weren't too many fans from other counties prepared to do that. We had a lot of ball early on and not enough scores to show for it. Also James McCartan was starting to run riot. At half-time we were a couple of points down, but that never bothered us before. Then, after the break they scored a flurry of points and, then, my man Barry Breen got the goal, but we just kept plugging away.

I think the 1991 All-Ireland final was lost tactically. Brendan Reilly was picked to play on James McCartan, but everyone, absolutely everyone knew the man to mark McCartan was Kevin Foley. He had played him before and was the type of player that could always play him, but Sean insisted on putting Brendan Reilly back in the corner on McCartan. Brendan was a very good attacking wing-back at the time but had no experience marking a dangerous corner-forward like James McCartan. At training on the Tuesday night before the game, when the team was announced, Mick Lyons actually asked if it was Brendan or Kevin that *was going to mark McCartan. Everyone on the team just presumed that Kevin would be marking him.*

There was absolutely no complacency with players or management but, I think that a lot of people, Meath people in particular, believed that because we had played so many games we were almost destined to win it that year. There is no such thing as destiny, however. You have to play on the day to win it. I think of all the summers, of all the years of Championship football, that was the one year to win it. It was my greatest disappointment. Indeed, I would say losing the 1991 All-Ireland final was the only regret I have from 16 years playing. We didn't deserve to win but it was just so disappointing. I never played with Meath again.

LIAM HAYES: *When Down were 11 points in front of us with 20 minutes left, it definitely looked as if we were completely gone, but what was happening with the team that year was that every so often one of our players would do something, something remarkable or outrageous, and the entire team would suddenly jump back into action. That was how the final went too. Rourkey coming on was the spark, but Bernie Flynn was scoring every time he got the ball. I think he scored six in all, and with him buzzing, we never threw in the towel. Tommy Dowd then hit a brilliant pass to me from a quick free-kick and I scored a goal. That brought it back to five points or something, and Down immediately had a fantastic chance at the other end but Mickey Linden made a complete mess of an open goal chance. Watching a hot-shot like Linden fail to keep his nerve told every Meath man on the field that we were still in with a chance. Linden was their best forward at the time and he always promised more than he ever delivered against us. He only got one point that afternoon! It was like Down still did not believe they were capable of winning the game.*

Enda McManus, August 29, 1999

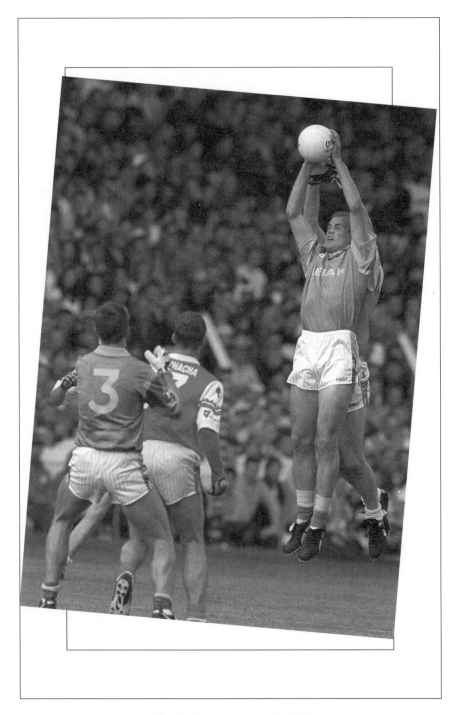

John McDermott, August 29, 1999

People have written about that game for the last ten years and they always say Rourkey turned things around on his own. It's not true. His appearance made a massive difference, but the rest of the team actually had the winning of the game, especially Bernie. He was having the game of his life, and I'll never forget the great goal chance he had near the end. I could not believe it when the ball went wide or was saved or whatever. Bernie should have had it in the back of the net, and if he had scored then we would have beaten Down by two or three points at the end. It would have been like the All-Ireland semi-final all over again. Nobody could blame Bernie, however, because without him we would have been nowhere near Down, Rourkey or no Rourkey coming off his death-bed. But they won, and they deserved to win on the day. Ross Carr came up trumps for them, and Breen and Eamonn Burns in the middle of the field, and later Liam Austin, had us scrapping for every ball. There was hardly any clean catching all day. Down had done their homework, and they also had the hunger. They were a fine team, and any team which wins two All-Irelands in four years has to go down as one of the great teams of modern times. So we were beaten by a great team which was well tutored by Pete McGrath, but that's little consolation.

That was my last time to start a Championship game for Meath. I knew I was close to the end, because I had never made any secret of the fact that I would retire at 30. I'd given 12 years to the Meath team, and I was beginning to begrudge the time I was away from my family. Also, work-wise, I was unhappy and I wanted to do something else. I wanted to start my own business and I wanted to start making some money for my family. I was penniless the day I stopped playing for Meath. I hadn't a bob in the bank. In fact, the bank manager was being very kind to me. People who often commented that I got out early have no idea of any player's personal circumstances.

As it turned out, I broke my arm in about half a dozen places a few months after playing my last game against Laois in 1992. I made a complete mess of it, playing for Skryne against Walterstown in a stupid tournament game. My last words before leaving the dressing room were to Trevor Giles. I told him to look after himself, for some reason! The injury had me in plaster, off and on, for the next 12 months because the bones would not come back together, despite the fantastic work of Tim Scannell in Navan Hospital.

Nobody's career ends on the perfect note, and mine certainly did not. I was dropped for the Laois game in '92 for the first time in about ten years. I came on when John McDermott was knocked out and then was sent off in the final minute of the game. McDermott was the next 'big man' for Meath in the middle of the field. It was easy to see what a fantastic athlete he was even back then, and he had a great head on him. He was as serious a footballer as I have ever seen walk into the Meath dressing room. It was definitely his turn. The team was in good hands. It might have helped if I stayed around the place for a couple of years, but I wanted to at least start thinking about getting my own business up and running. I always wanted to have my own publishing business, and it took me three years to realise that dream. You can't do that and play football. Anyway, I made the right decision, because John McDermott showed that he was the best midfielder in the country for the next ten years. He was fantastic, and every time I watched him playing for Meath I realised Gaelic football was a young man's game. At 30 years of age I was already feeling an old man! It was hard watching Sean Boylan build an entirely new team, watching him with McDermott and Graham Geraghty and all the new boys. It was like sitting in a movie theatre watching our decade all over again, except the main characters on our team were replaced by actors! It's hard to explain it, but that is the incredible genius of Sean Boylan. He is a man of immeasurable warmth and giving, and he gave everything he knew in his heart and head to our team for ten years, and then turned around and started giving of himself all over again. As I said earlier, he always makes the person in front of him feel No.1. Not many people can genuinely do that, but Seanie would, and he was always genuine, completely and utterly genuine.

He's been lucky over the years, no doubt about that. Like, there are very few Gerry McEntees! They come around once every 100 years. McEntee's an incredible person. I've never seen anyone with such passion for anything! He was not the greatest footballer in the world, and I always enjoyed playing against him, because I knew in training or in club games, when he wasn't acting like a maniac, that I could beat him – I always felt I could beat him. But try beating him for a ball if a Leinster final or an All-Ireland final depended upon it! Then, McEntee would be the last man in Ireland I would choose to go up against, even though nine times out of ten I'd be confident of taking the ball off him. That was Gerry. He just did not know when to give up. He didn't know when to retire. I actually wanted him to retire a year or two before he did, because he was getting in my way. I was trying to build a new Meath midfield and Colm Brady was my first choice partner. But even after putting in a great first year, the carpet was pulled out from under Brady because Gerry came back into the picture. Meath needed a new midfield partnership, but in the 1991 series against Dublin I played those games with three different lads, P.J. Gillic the first game, Sean Kelly the second game, Martin O'Connell the third game, and P.J. again the fourth time. By the time of the All-Ireland final it was Gerry and myself again. It is impossible to build a winning midfield partnership with that sort of swapping and changing.

When you look back, you think how could we not have been successful with the likes of McEntee, O'Rourke, Stafford and Flynn and so on. But Sean Boylan brought all of those players to an individual excellence, and it is no sure thing that we would all have made it without Sean. Or without Sean's team, because Boylan was not just a manager, he brought a whole team of great people with him. There was Anne Bourton and our Doc, Jack Finn, and Mockie Regan, the greatest masseur and confidant any team could ever have. Then there was another dozen great people who also surrrounded the team, like James Whyte or 'Scubs', a fantastic friend to any footballer. We were lucky men to have such a great team of people around us, the luckiest team in Ireland, I'll tell you.

Chapter Six:

1992

Sean Boylan's tenth anniversary as Meath football manager was a short-lived, forgettable day out. On 24 May, Meath were beaten 1-11 to 2-11 by Laois, in their own Pairc Tailteann in Navan, but several days before that shocking defeat Boylan had already made it known that the good ol' days were no longer going to count for anything. The medals on a man's chest would no longer allow him to march onto the Meath team. So, Enda McManus had been named at left corner-back for the first round of the Championship, Alan Browne was handed the No. 6 shirt, John McDermott and P.J. Gillic were asked to team up in the middle of the field, and Brendan Reilly was centre-forward and the leader of the attack. After the pre-match warm-up and kick-around, Bob O'Malley, Colm Coyle, Liam Harnan and Liam Hayes trotted off towards the Meath dug-out. The game would turn out to be Mick Lyons's last appearance in the magnificent No. 3 shirt to which he had restored great fame. Gerry McEntee was in the stand once again, looking on, but he would never again leave his seat and tell Boylan that he wanted to be back on the team, that retirement could still wait a little bit longer. There never would be any tenth anniversary party. And, for the next four years, there never was an overwhelming reason to celebrate anything in the Royal County. Neither was there the hint of an All-Ireland title around the next corner.

With the old team quickly breaking up, new boys in the Meath dressing room were made to feel perfectly at home from their very first evening in the place. The old seating arrangements in that room were no more. Nobody could book their place on the team any more and, therefore, nobody was going to make a song and dance if some young upstart happened to be disrobing in the favourite corner of a crusty, impatient, two-times All-Ireland winning Meath footballer. In 1993, when Meath extracted suitable revenge in Portlaoise by giving the home team a 1-12 to 0-7 whipping, Graham Geraghty and Cormac Murphy would make their Championship debuts for the team either side of Martin O'Connell on the half-back line, Jody Devine was on the half-forward line and Larry McCormack and Trevor Kane would also be called into action before the afternoon was out. In 1994, Thomas Hanley, Jimmy McGuinness and Trevor Giles would be on the chosen 15, and twelve months later Conor Martin, Evan Kelly and Ollie Murphy would answer the call and take up their places on the team. All of these new faces, however, did not appear to be any closer to putting a winning, and permanent, smile back on the Meath football team. John McDermott, still, had no sight of an All-Ireland medal.

JOHN McDERMOTT: *I was always brought to Meath games. I went with the O'Connors, Butch and Gerry, and a couple of the lads from* *around. They used to always go. And then back to the Ashbourne House Hotel, where the team would be, always stopping for chips or something as kids on the way home. As a young lad back then, I was starting to drink. You'd have the craic back in the Ashbourne House, but you'd nearly genuflect in front of O'Rourke and Lyons – when you're 17 and 18-years old, these guys were gods. The Centenary Cup year was the first year I was plugged into it. The big joke going around was, 'We'll win the next three in a row.' You had lads taking bets on it.*

By the time Meath had won the Leinster title in 1986, I was big into football. I was playing with St Mary's, the Christian Brothers' School in Drogheda, and we had an absolutely fantastic football team. We had Colin Kelly and Johnny Bell and some really great players. I'll never forget the slagging we gave O'Rourke. We played St Pat's of Navan in a championship game in Duleek when he was over them, and we beat them by 22 points. Even then, though, you'd be a bit star-struck saying, 'Jaysus, there's O'Rourke!' I started off on that team as left full-back. I was big then, but eventually in the final year I made it out to midfield. We won out in Louth every year. Even though the school is in Meath, we played in Louth. I actually broke both of my ankles with the school. I went to six Meath minor trials, three the first year, and three the second year, but I was never put on the field once! I'm deadly serious. I sat in the dug-out for all six! I went for Under-21 trials the first year and by default I got on the team. I'll never forget it. It was down in Kells, Mattie Kerrigan came over and said, 'Where the fuck have you been?' They had never even heard of me. I got in at corner-back and then they sent me out to midfield. Kerrigan was in charge of the team and, in fairness, he was brilliant. He took this young fella from nowhere. When I went to the minor trials, it was, 'Where are you from? Curraha? Ah, good luck!' You had nobody touting for you at all. I have to thank Mattie for getting me on a team. He's the best coach-manager I've ever worked with. Sean Boylan doesn't coach fellas – he manages them more than anything. I was playing in Rathkenny against Cavan in an Under-21 game, when I was taken off shortly after half-time. That was a Saturday. Boylan was outside the railing with Pat Reynolds and he asked Mattie to take me off because he wanted me the next day. So I played against Cavan on the Saturday and lined out for the seniors against Dublin, in the middle of the field, in the National League on the Sunday.

It was incredible. I flew it! Jaysus, sure it was one of the best days in Croke Park I ever had. I caught feckin' everything. I was marking Declan Bolger and it went like a dream. And none of the family were there to see it! It was Mother's Day and they didn't come up because they said, 'You'll just be a sub.' Before the match I was brought up to the Ashbourne House for lunch and was introduced to all the lads. I had never met any of them before and they had never seen or heard of me.

Oh, McEntee just could not get over this, the fact that I had come out of nowhere. After the game, I was flying, on a high. We went up to the Cat and Cage pub and McEntee says, 'Who the fuck are you?' I said, 'John McDermott, from Curraha.' And he replied in a flash, 'Where's Curraha?' He thought this was great craic. I had played alongside Hayes, and the whole day was surreal. I had to come home and milk cows after it. I remember far more about that day than I do of my Championship debut the following year, against Laois. All I know is that I was knocked unconscious in the first 20 minutes.

You began to think, as the years passed, that maybe that's the share of All Irelands handed out, that you missed the boat, and that there's nothing you can do about it. There were good lads coming through though. You had Trevor Giles, Graham Geraghty, Darren Fay and Enda McManus.

My first conversation with Sean Boylan was a quick, 'Hello and goodbye', across a room. It was at Brian Stafford's wedding. That was when I met him first. But, sure Boylan is some character! In 1996, when we won the All-Ireland, Tommy Dowd was captain and I was vice-captain. Then, I was captain in '97. Every week, Boylan would ring me, asking, 'How are things going pal? How are you doing?' And I'd say, 'Grand Sean, grand.' He'd be just seeing how you were feeling. But, he'd have these long silences and you'd rush in to fill the silence. So one night, I knew what was coming and I said, 'Fuck this, I'm not saying a thing to him.' The next thing the silence came and I just got pig ignorant and sat at the end of the phone saying nothing. I swear, over ten minutes went by, I'm not exaggerating. I just refused, thinking, 'No way am I giving in!' And then, after ten minutes, I hear him say, 'Oh fella, fair play, fair play!'

Mad as a brush! But he's such a nice fella. When you see him after a game and he's nearly apologising for beating the other team, people say to me, 'Ah, he's too nice. What's going on?' But that's the way he is. In the 10 or 11 years I was there, I saw him lose the rag maybe half a dozen times. If you were doing something wrong, he might feck the whistle at you and say, 'If you want to manage the team, then you do it!' We used to always say that he makes up the training as he goes along – Bob O'Malley will tell you that. O'Malley used to be there in training, saying under his breath, 'He's mad, he's mad!' He had some client, for instance, that hires out bikes and he got a trailer load of about 30 bikes one day. And off we went one Saturday up the Wicklow Mountains. With Boylan, you think he has a master plan. Now whether he has or not, nobody quite knows. You'd be at training sometimes and you'd be thinking that if anyone saw us doing this, we'd all be locked up.

The maddest day we ever had was the time we were all told to meet at

Kepak at six in the morning. So we all headed off thinking, Lanzarote or somewhere with a bit of sun! The next thing we arrived at the Ferry Port. Holyhead was where we were going! I had food poisoning that day, and this is a week or two before the All-Ireland final in 1996! From the moment we landed over there, I didn't eat a thing. We went to a pitch at the back of some housing estate. I ran across the field twice and nearly died. Denis Murtagh had the jeep over there with all the gear so I ended up sitting there for the whole day. We went back to a hotel then for a bit of grub - I didn't eat anything for the whole day – got back on the boat and came home. I wasn't back home until about 12 o'clock that night and Michelle says, 'What were you at?' The second time we landed at the Ferry Port we went, 'Oh Jesus, this gig again!'

I'll never forget our trip to Florida after 1991, the time the lads nearly drowned – Harnan, Foley and O'Rourke. That morning, before anyone got into trouble, I was on the beach and Boylan was paddling, about ten foot out. And he shouts, 'Mac, give me your hand!' Then he shouts, 'Save me!' I thought he was messing, but I just walked out, grabbed his hand and dragged him in. He was there panting, 'I couldn't get in!' The rip-tide was pulling him out. That was early on in the morning. Later on that day, the lads went out. It was the last day of the holiday. And the same thing happened O'Rourke. He got into awful trouble. He told me afterwards that he stuck the head down and swam as hard as he could for 30 seconds and when he came up for air, he was further out from the shore. He said himself that he thought he was a goner. Thankfully, the 'Baywatch' guys came running across the sand and saved the day.

Boylan? He's going to go on for ever. Otherwise, he's going to have to be taken outside and shot! He's a great little man. How he does it, I don't know! There are guys on the Meath panel now who weren't even born when he took over the team. There's no way of defining him. Sean is Sean. He doesn't coach that much, he doesn't man-manage that much. He's just such a nice fella. If you have a boss who's a tyrant, you're going to find ways to get around him. But if you have a boss who's a hundred per cent behind you, you'd die for him.

I was never dropped while I was on the team – I got out before I could be! I didn't get out for that reason though. I just had enough of it. There are men who were dropped who'll probably say the guy is ruthless. But I never found that at all. The Meath success wouldn't have happened without him but having said that, the Fays and the Gileses and the O'Rourkes, they don't come around too often.

However, tactics were out the window with the Meath team. When we were going bad in the early '90s, it was, 'Hit Tommy Dowd with everything!' If Tommy was shut down, we were gone! The previous year it was, 'Hit O'Rourke with everything!' But at least when O'Rourke had a bad day, there was Stafford and Flynn who'd step up.

COLM O'ROURKE: *Tommy Dowd scored a goal against Laois in '92 to get us back into the game, but then we gave away a goal down the other end. However, I don't remember it as being abject disappointment or anything like that when we lost. Some of the players went after '92 and I was going to go at that time, but played on for a few years, and enjoyed it. We had a couple of close shaves against Dublin in Leinster finals, and won a League against Armagh, and at the time I played for enjoyment, not necessarily to win anything.*

We had played badly in the first half of the Leinster final in 1995, but came back in the second half before Dublin got an avalanche of scores near the end. At one stage in the second half it looked like Meath were going to actually win it, but we didn't and it brought the curtain down on a lot of fellas' careers, mine included. It was pure enjoyment that kept me playing for all those years, just pure enjoyment. I wish I could still play.

MARTIN O'CONNELL: *I was actually captain that year when Laois beat us in Navan, and I was captain again in '95. So my captaincy of the Meath team reads: beaten in the first round in Navan, and beaten by ten points in a Leinster final! It was probably coming towards the end for a lot of fellas. The team was breaking up. Liam Hayes was dropped, Bob O'Malley was dropped, Liam Harnan was dropped, Colm Coyle was dropped. As to whether we underestimated Laois or not? I'm not sure. After doing so well in '91, everyone thought, 'Here we go again'. But we got caught.*

BRENDAN REILLY: *That defeat in 1992 was a disaster. I played centre half-forward and it was the beginning of the end for many lads. At that time Laois were formidable enough opposition. I always thought they loved the physical challenge and looked forward to playing us. They weren't put out by Meath at all. It was a shock, but then again Meath going out in the first round is always a possibility because we've generally been slow starters. Sean never came under pressure at the time. The one time I thought he may be on thin ice was ahead of the 1996 Championship campaign. I thought that, possibly, if we went out in the first round of the Championship he might be under pressure. He won the All-Ireland that year though and proved everyone wrong. He was golden after that. It's like Tommy Lyons with Dublin in 2002. Once he beat Meath he was guaranteed his spot for another two or three years, no questions asked. Preparing for Carlow in the first round of the Championship there was talk that this was the worst Meath team ever.*

We beat them well and coming home on the team bus afterwards I said to Enda McManus, 'Don't let us be the players that are known for being on the worst ever Meath team.' It was never like that though. Things just went on in leaps and bounds after the Carlow game. We were excellent all year and I think the worst match we actually played was against Mayo in the All-Ireland final.

DONAL SMITH: *I remember Mick Turley's goal in the first half in '92. I went out and dived at his feet. Bob O'Malley dived across him as well, but it hit Bob and just looped over me and went into the net. I always regretted that. All I recall about their penalty was this white figure standing in front of me and realising it was their goalkeeper. But he slotted it past me. At the time, I was still annoyed at the first goal we had conceded.*

ENDA McMANUS: *I had first come into the squad about March of 1991. My Dunboyne clubmates Brenny Reilly and Peter Reilly were going to Drumbaragh to play for Meath in a challenge match against either Derry or Armagh. I was only out of the minors, I was 19 at the time. Apparently, Sean had just told Brenny to ask me to come along and bring my boots in case they were short of players. So I stuck the boots in the bag and went along. When we got to the pitch Brenny and Peter headed into the dressing room and I just sat in the car. I was sitting there waiting for the game to start when I turned around and noticed Peter running out towards me. So he gets to the car and tells me to get my gear and go to the dressing room. In I go, anyway, and all the boys are sitting down around the room on the benches – Mick Lyons and all these lads I had gone to see playing in Croke Park only months earlier, just sitting in front of me. And I remember walking in and* *thinking, 'What the hell!' I was only about 5'11" tall. I headed for the nearest space I could find and got changed. Sean came over to me and told me to give it a go, and do my best. 'We're not expecting anything of you. No pressure', he said. So I ran out onto the field. I played corner-back and I walked away as the 'Man of the Match'. Sean came over to me after the game, easy-going as always and said, 'You know there will be a bit of training now during the week. Sure, you may as well come down.' And that was that. I was on the panel from then until two weeks before the four-in-a-row games against Dublin, when I got dropped.*

I was not involved for the rest of the summer and it was difficult watching the lads I had trained with, out playing in Croke Park in all those big games. Foley's goal summed up those games though. End-to-end stuff! I watched the All-Ireland final of '91 at home on TV. Terry Connor and Hugh Carolan had been kept on, so there was no place for me on the panel. I would like to have been involved but it was not to be that year. Meath were very unlucky. A few more minutes and we might have pegged Down back.

So Laois in 1992 was my first ever Championship start for Meath. I lined out at corner-back instead of Bob O'Malley. I remember going out onto the field in Navan and I was marking Michael Lawlor. The two of us were the same age. I was substituted, though, and Bob replaced me. Michael Lawlor came off two minutes after me and Noel Roe went on. It was a bad afternoon to begin the Championship scene.

TERRY FERGUSON: *Losing to Laois was the beginning of the end for some of the older guard. Some of us had burn-out. Liam Hayes came on that day and then got sent off. He hung up the boots after that, that evening, as did a lot of the lads. I hung up mine as well – gave it up.*

But Sean asked me back just to give a bit of experience. I think he was right to bring in the young lads for the game against Laois. Others disagree, but he had to build for the future. The sparkle some of us had in the late '80s was gone and he tried to freshen it up. I remember sitting on the line, when I came back after '92 and, as ever, it wasn't a pleasant place to be, and I didn't really want to be there because I knew my time was up. It was time to go. I went back because Sean asked me to help out and I wanted to repay him for the great faith he had shown in me through the years. But I had nothing left. I got out and I remember sitting watching the Leinster final in 1995 in Croke Park. I was in among a load of Dubs, and they knew who I was and gave me plenty of stick and grief. It was a bad performance but every dog has its day and ours was to come the following year in '96.

Terry Ferguson stayed on after the early failure in 1992, as did a handful of his older colleagues, who did not fancy calling it quits after losing two All-Ireland finals and then a first round Leinster Championship game! Bob O'Malley, Kevin Foley, Liam Harnan, Colm O'Rourke, Brian Stafford and Bernie Flynn all wanted to give it one more year, at least, in one last effort to arrive at a suitable ending to their Meath careers. Ferguson and Harnan stuck around for a year or so, but the remainder actually stuck around a little bit too long for their own good and, following the fairly sickening defeat to Laois, they would endure three Championship defeats on the trot to Dublin. Bernie Flynn, in particular, fought as long and hard as anyone to bring his Meath career to an appropriate resting place. The tantalising corner-forward was struck down by injury after 1992 and did not play any part in '93, but he fought his way back onto the team in 1994. With Colm O'Rourke taking up duty on the '40', Flynn teamed up with Brian Stafford and Tommy Dowd in the Meath full-forward line, but by 1995 he was out of the picture for good.

Flynn had scored six points in the 1991 All-Ireland final, but at the end of that year, as he examined his career to date, it was not just the serious business of collecting cups and medals that occupied his mind. He had always enjoyed a unique relationship with Sean Boylan. In addition, he had never denied himself the fringe benefits and the fun bits of being an All-Ireland winner! Bernie Flynn had a lot of unfinished business.

BERNIE FLYNN: *Losing Bob O'Malley was a big blow to us in 1991. I know everybody talks about Colm O'Rourke not starting, but O'Malley's absence at corner-back was crucial. He was a massive loss. We could still have won the game. I remember getting in with about ten minutes left and the keeper saving it. There was a good bit of time left after that, and when O'Rourke came on, a lot more seemed to happen. It's totally irrelevant how much you score yourself. At the end of the day, you're better off scoring nothing and the team winning. One things sticks out in my mind from that game. Watching the size of the Down lads, their legs and stuff, I could see they were so up for it. I remember even saying to myself running out, 'Jesus, these lads do look strong.' They were so fired up. At the same time, we probably took it a little bit for granted. We were in an All-Ireland final, we knew what was coming. We were overwhelming favourites going into it, and with all the matches we had played there was so much hype. You have to remember, the four matches against Dublin and the comebacks we had produced. We were seven or eight points down against Roscommon in the semi-final, and we came back. So we had played a lot of football.*

That game still hurts. I'll never forget that morning in the hotel, and Gerry McEntee came down. A few of the wives were there for the breakfast and a few of us were there together, looking at each other, not saying anything. And the next thing he sat down and just burst out crying. He was inconsolable for about half an hour. He cried like a child. And I'll never forget feeling so sorry for anybody. He knew it was his last hurrah. What he'd given the day before – he had given his last ounce on the field. His performance was incredible. Incredible. McEntee's performance that day was something to behold for a man of his age in Croke Park. And the job he was in, and the effort he had put in! I can still see his face in the Grand Hotel crying. I'll never forget it. It was so sad to see a great man like that so hurt.

In defeat, Sean was a great manager. Absolutely brilliant. When you were beaten, if you had played bad or even if it wasn't your fault, he'd be there with the arm around you. He was never one to lecture fellas on where they went wrong. All the lads are drinking on the Sunday after a bad game like that. You're together, close together, and it's not so bad. It's the Tuesday, Wednesday and Thursday, when you go back to your family and work that's so lonely. It's terrible. However, having said that, the lunch on the Monday after the All-Ireland final that year was a famous meal. We were so down and disappointed, but one thing sticks out, and that was David Beggy. He had a few jars on board, and he somehow spots a piano in the lobby of the hotel and within half an hour he has the whole Meath and Down teams around him, singing and playing the best '60s and '70s music you'll ever hear. He's a dog on the piano. It broke the ice. The Down fellas were so gracious that day, but as we were so sick, it took Beggy to break the ice. And we parted with the Down fellas and got on the team bus in good humour.

When we were away during all of those years, any chance I could get to

269

room with Beggy, I would. I used to love it. We were rooming in America one time, in Boston on an Allstars trip. Fr Sean Hegarty was the manager of the Allstars team and he would be a fairly straight-laced enough fella. He had the team for training, but one of the nights we went to a big function in the Park Plaza Hotel. I'll never forget it. There were about 1,600 people there to greet everybody. It was incredible. Sean says to us, 'I don't care what you do tonight, how much you drink or whatever, but I want you all back here training in the morning at 10 o'clock.' Lo and behold, myself and Beggy ended up going on an unmerciful rip. Guess what? We never appeared back at the training. We didn't come back until late the next day and there was Sean, waiting for us in the lobby of the hotel, and we in the same jackets and shirts and ties! Oh, we were the worse for wear. Well Sean got the two of us up in a room. All I can remember was getting an awful lecture, but he told Beggy that he would never wear a Meath jersey ever again. He did.

Beggy was massive fun. He was the best character you could ever meet. Tell a joke, sing a song, he was unreal, unbelievably funny. Beggy was one of the few Meath footballers who, while he was disappointed, could get over defeat like nobody else. Within an hour or two, there he'd be, fag in his mouth and a pint in his hand. He didn't give a shit! And I mean that in a good way. He never let it get in on him. Ah, he was a great character. Beggy added a whole new dimension to the team. The points he scored were a breath of fresh air. We needed someone to take on defences, particularly Dublin. Himself and Eamonn Heery had some real ding-dong battles at the end of the '80s. You couldn't coach David Beggy. Genuinely. You couldn't coach him. If you tried to coach him, you would just end up annoying yourself. And you would take away the very thing Beggy had, that unpredictability. If he had been coached, I don't think he would have been half the player he was.

The game was different then. There was a lot of holding and messing, especially in the Dublin matches. If I was moving across the field there would be a lot of kicking. I wouldn't even be marking some defender or other but there would be verbals going on, a kick in the ankles, a kick in the back of the shins. Funnily enough, with Dublin you were always guaranteed a good bit of possession. Dublin defenders probably weren't the tightest. Mick Deegan, for example, would get a lot of ball, but you'd get a fair amount too, whereas the Cork defenders would sacrifice their own game more to keep you quiet. The best marker I ever came across was probably Niall Cahalane. I had some great tussles too with D.J. Kane of Down.

The only big game in which we got it all wrong was against Cork in the 1990 final. We lost the focus against them, definitely. But we bounced back the following year. We got to four All-Irelands in five years, which is fair going. There were all types of guys on that team which made it all possible. Like Harnan. Harnan is very intelligent, but he's a tough, tough man. He hated bullshit. Probably myself and O'Malley were looked on as a bit cocky, and Harnan didn't like that. But Harnan was also the wittiest guy on that squad, and he'd make you pay for any indiscretion, no matter how small.

Any trips that were going, myself and O'Malley would be there in a flash. Didn't we get a chance to go to Toronto, myself and O'Malley! The Allstars trip was in a few weeks time but we got going as guests to do an advance three-day PR package. We had to do three big live TV shows, which would have been the equivalent of the 'Late, Late Show'. We were going for three days, so we were effectively missing only one training session. Now, we were playing Dublin the following week in the quarter-final of the National League, so we checked it with Boylan and he said we could go. But we stayed five days! We were treated like royalty, limousines everywhere, picked up from our five star hotel to do TV and radio shows. Well, the boys got wind of this, and it wouldn't have gone down well - 'Flynn and O'Malley off again!' O'Malley and myself could just hear them. So we arrived home two days late. We flew back in on the Thursday, the night when training was on, and I remember parting company with O'Malley at the airport and him saying, 'Neither of us had better miss training tonight or the shit will hit the fan.' And I said, 'Bob, I can hardly walk, let alone run.' Sure we had hardly seen a bed for four or five days. So I went home, got a couple of hours sleep and went training. Well there wasn't a word when I went into the dressing room that evening. You could cut the tension with a knife. I looked at O'Malley in his corner, and he looked at me. We went out to training – it was a wet, pissy night – and I said, 'Malley, we're going to get the shit kicked out of us tonight'! And it was Liam Harnan who bet the living daylights out of the both of us. But, when the training was over, we were picked on the team for Sunday. Well, I slept Thursday, Friday, Saturday night like a baby, and O'Malley says to me at the team meeting on Sunday morning, 'We'll get ten minutes here and we'll probably be gone out the door!' But both of us played really well. We won and we were lucky. But it took a long time for the lads to forgive us for that.

If you ask Harnan or McEntee or any of the boys now, they'll tell you we were dead right to go on the trip. Any trip that was going though, Flynn and O'Malley would be on it. We'd go anywhere.

It was perceived at this time that Sean and I didn't get on, but I always had a great relationship with Sean Boylan. We might have knocked sparks off each other an odd time, or hopped off each other, but most of it was healthy and constructive and good. He knew how to rile me, get me going to try and get the best out of me, but I never had any problem

Tommy Dowd, July 20, 1997

Trevor Giles, September 29, 1996

with that. The way I finished up between injury and that, though, probably wasn't the greatest. I was in a bad way with pain when I finished. Before I finished up in '94, I was getting injections and pain-killers and tablets for a few years, for my knee and my hip. I was literally playing the last year or so on pain-killers! It was crazy. I knew I couldn't keep it going, I couldn't do it any more. And I probably felt at the time that my situation could have been handled a bit differently. But I've no qualms. When you're gone, you're gone! You move on.

I had the utmost respect for Sean Boylan. Still do. But the two of us starting drifting, and it started when I began writing for the 'Evening Herald' in '95. There was a headline when Dublin hammered Meath by ten points in '95 – it was my first column for the 'Herald' – and in the article it was said 'Sean Boylan must go.' That was in my article, as if I had said, 'Sean Boylan must go, for the future of Meath football.' Now, I never said those words at all. I now do all my own stuff, but for the first couple of years my column was ghost-written – I don't mind saying it. I know Sean had a serious gripe about that headline. P.J. Cunningham was the sports editor of the 'Herald' and I got on to P.J. the following week and said, 'I never said that.' And he said, 'Well, I'll set the record straight.' And I said, 'Don't bother. Sean knows me well enough to say whatever he needs to say.' It was never discussed between me and Sean, but I knew he had a serious, serious problem with it.

He knew me well enough, and had met me several times after, but hadn't mentioned it. Yet I knew from other third parties that he was very unhappy about it. I was probably wrong that I didn't go to clear the air. I didn't say anything though because I felt that he should have said it to me and, knowing me, that I wouldn't have said it in the first place.

Do you know when Sean Boylan found out I didn't say that? Last November (2001)! I didn't know this at the time, but P.J. Cunningham picked up the phone after six years. P.J. would say, 'Some day I'm going to ring Boylan', and I'd say, 'You can do what you like', and he seemingly rang Sean. There was a 'This is your Life' done for me, and Gerry Farrell, who is a close friend of mine, asked if the Heart Foundation that he was involved in could do a video of me, with the proceeds to go to charity. So they put on this night and wanted somebody to launch it. I rang Sean to launch the video himself, and he came down that night. After all those years, he came down, made his speech, and in his speech told the story of how he had just found out about that 'Herald' article. And we still never spoke of it! Even afterwards, it was never discussed.

We definitely would have had a few barneys, myself and Sean, over the years. I would say what I felt, and we had our moments, no doubt about that. But it was healthy There was one incident when I didn't make training and I couldn't get through to Sean. I was down in the pub I owned in Laois at the time, doing 100 hours a week working, and driving up and down. And it was killin' me. One night I didn't make the training. Boylan will tell you himself that I missed very little, but this one time I couldn't get through to him, so I rang Martin O'Connell's house and gave his wife Samantha the message. I went in the following night to training and before it started, Sean rattled off his phone number in front of all the lads – a bit smart I thought at the time! So I said, 'I rang Samantha. I couldn't get through. I rang Samantha!' And he said, 'Samantha doesn't pick the team!' With that I replied, 'That's a load of bollox!' And Sean shouts back, 'Are you calling me a bollox'? I said, 'No. That's a load of bollox!' We were over near the wire on the football field, and people were leaning over listening to this.

That's the sort of thing that would happen between myself and Sean. There was another incident. We were playing Down, in a challenge in Cullen and I was after killing myself getting to Cullen, right? I arrive at

Cullen and the man at the gate says, 'The match is cancelled!' And I says, 'What?' So, I'm like a bull and I shoot in to Navan, thinking that that's where they're training instead. Then I meet Tony Brennan, our selector, who tells me training is in Dalgan Park. So I fly up there. No one had fuckin' told me. So I arrive, drop the balls, and a row starts between the two of us. Well, I fucked him out of it, and he fucked me out of it. I remember going in then to tog out, and he knocked sparks out of me in training that night. That was me and Sean.

He would have a go at me in training, he would have a go at O'Malley, and he would have a go at Beggy. But he never had a go at the older fellas in the same way. I don't mind saying it, that used to rile the shit out of us. O'Rourke could do what he fuckin' liked, I used to tell him. And O'Rourke used to play on it. Aw, he'd be very funny, very witty, stirring it the whole time.

One night we went training, and Sean could sense the tension in the camp. It was around '88, when we were training hard for the Championship. I remember being huddled under the stand in Navan after what was a ferocious session, everyone a bit fed up with each other and the whole thing. And he gathers us together and says, 'Throw those bags of gear in the corner and come with me'. What does he do? Brings us straight over to the Chinese restaurant in Navan, where we had a nice few pints and a bit of craic – and Sean looked after the bill himself.

That was the amazing side to the man. He was very good to a fella who was going through a bad patch, in his personal life, job-wise, or anything like that. And he was great at helping the guys get a start. That whole squad all did fairly well out of football. He was never around his players much when they were drinking. If they had a few jars he let them off. He never put himself in the situation of discussing anything with drink. He was brilliant at keeping his distance. He knew when to be there, and when not to be there.

Chapter Seven:

1993
1994
1995

Bob O'Malley's bar in Trimgate Street in Navan had opened for business a few weeks before Meath lost to Down in the 1991 All-Ireland final. It was not the greatest timing in the world for a Meath footballer, but O'Malley's actually became the most popular haunt in the town for the next few years, for football fans, for the young crowd who were looking for a cool place in which to hang out and, occasionally, for Meath footballers trying to work out the best way in which to bring their inter-county careers to a halt. Working all hours did not help Bob's football career enormously, but Sean Boylan was happy enough with his work ethic, and his appetite, and appointed him team captain in 1994. That summer, like the summer before and after, would be entirely forgettable, but 1994 also went down in history because it would mark the most ruthless act of Sean Boylan's 20-years career as Meath football manager. It was the year in which Boylan took out the axe! The implement did not fall on some young fella or some imposter who had been taking up space in the dressing room for a couple of years. No, it fell on Donal Smith. The Navan O'Mahonys goalkeeper had been on the Meath team for eight years. He had fought long and hard to gain the No. 1 position from Mickey McQuillan and, after a temporary residence in the Meath goalmouth in 1990 and '92, Smith gained his just reward at the beginning of the 1993-94 season. He played through the National League, started the first round of the Leinster Championship when Meath once again took care of Laois on a 0-20 to 2-10 scoreline, and was on duty in Croke Park when Wexford were beaten decisively by 4-14 to 2-6. In the weeks counting down to the Leinster final against Dublin, however, Boylan told Smith he was off the team, and off the Meath squad!

The early 90s, undoubtedly, were the longest and loneliest period of Sean Boylan's time as Meath team boss. After losing the 1989 Leinster final to Dublin, then losing two All-Ireland finals, falling flat on their face in the first round of the Championship against Laois in 1992, and failing to Dublin in the Leinster Championship in 1993, '94 and '95, the Meath football team did not comprise the happiest or most contented bunch of people in the whole country. Those seven years of misery contained two Leinster Championships and two National League titles, but entering 1996 the team looked to be in enormous trouble. Boylan, however, didn't act like a man who was even remotely aware of any pressure. Generally, he wished the very best to the retiring stars from the '80s and early '90s, and gave absolutely no impression that he ever considered joining them on the short journey from the dressing room to the relative comfort of the stand! Those defeats, in 1993,

'94 and '95 came fast and furiously, but Sean Boylan barely flinched, or at least none of his players ever saw him batting an eye-lid.

When Dublin defeated Meath by one point in the Leinster semi-final in 1993, 0-12 to 1-10, there was still considerable hope that all was not lost. Enda McManus had acquitted himself more than adequately in Lyons's old No. 3 shirt, Martin O'Connell had done fine directly in front of him, and Graham Geraghty and Cormac Murphy looked quite at home either side of the new centre-back. John McDermott and Colm Brady were the new midfield pairing and they too looked happy with one another, and very definitely won an even share of the possession against the slightly more experienced Pat Gilroy and Jack Sheedy. Up front, Colm O'Rourke played like a 2-year old that afternoon and enjoyed probably his finest game in a decade against his favourite football team in the World. Dublin led by five points early in the second half, but Rourkey hit five points in total that afternoon, the last coming from long range and perfectly dissecting the Canal End goalposts. It looked like another draw, another replay to look forward to, as time was up on the clock. But Dublin got possession quickly from the kick-out. Charlie Redmond went to shoot the winning point, but Bob O'Malley bravely threw himself at the foot of the Dublin centre-forward. The ball darted over to Sheedy, who immediately dispatched a wonderful and accurate strike from well over 50 yards out. With Meath out of the Championship, O'Rourke chose to immortalise the latest Dublin battle by naming a 2-year old horse after the game. The horse was called Tragic Point.

After Meath saw off Laois and Wexford in 1994, there was

another, equally tragic one-point defeat by Dublin in the Leinster final. But this time there was no horse! There was no soft underbelly this time around. It was 1-8 to 1-9, and the result really hurt. Nobody had any interest in keeping it alive on the back of a horse. It was a game Meath could have won, should have won! And if Donal Smith had been in goal, would Meath have won? That was a question which could not be avoided. Sean Boylan had recalled Mickey McQuillan to the Meath team in the weeks leading up to the 1994 Leinster final and, in the finale to the game, McQuillan had inexplicably allowed a long-range free-kick from Charlie Redmond to squirt through his hands on the goal-line. Dublin were suddenly five points to the good. Meath fought back after that, and it was the new boy on the block Graham Geraghty who led the charge more than anybody else, crashing the ball past John O'Leary close to the end. Trevor Giles also looked like a winner that afternoon in his first Leinster final. The kids had found their feet on the team, and the oldies had proved in 1993 and '94 that there was no more wobbling in terms of ambition or desire. Going into the 1995 Leinster final against Dublin, with victories over Offaly (1-15 to 1-5), Longford (4-15 to 0-10) and Wicklow (3-14 to 0-9), Meath had every reason to be hopeful of ending their losing run. Eight goals in three games! Confidence was at the highest point it had been in six or seven years, and nobody in the Meath camp had reason to consider a complete and utter demolition job. But on 30 July, 1995, Dublin would enjoy their greatest victory over Meath in 15 years, winning 1-18 to 1-8, and playing like men against boys on the field for the last ten minutes of the game. Meath actually led by one point early in the second period, but once Dublin began scoring, they couldn't stop! Paul

Clarke punched home the Dublin goal and, for all intents and purposes, his fist landed on the chin of the opposing team. Meath had been floored, buried!

MICKEY McQUILLAN: *Sean rang me before the 1994 Leinster final and asked me would I come back in on the panel. He told me I had a fair chance of playing, so I said I would. Conor Martin was there at the time and there was talk about Brendan Murphy from Trim, and I wasn't really happy about that because I didn't want it to be a case of him not being able to make it and then Sean falling back on me. It worked out that it was between Conor and myself, though. Charlie Redmond's goal from under the Hogan Stand that day was a simple goal and I thought I was going to catch it. But unfortunately I didn't! I was almost looking at who I was going to kick the ball out to, because I thought I had it covered. I went up too casually for it because it was a handy catch. But it just didn't happen. The ball went into the net, and all I could do was take it out, put it on the '21' and get on with the game. I made a mistake but the lads were always behind me and we had great team spirit. Sean came over to me after the game and told me I wasn't to blame for the defeat and he probably took a big responsibility himself because if he hadn't called me in, it might not have happened, but who knows? He was big enough in the dressing room to say I wasn't to blame and that we had kicked 14 or so wides. But I knew myself I had let the lads down. All I could do was place the ball, and kick it out.*

Like any goalkeeper, I got a bit of stick from fans behind the goal in Croke Park. I was called the usual names, and with the Dublin fans I got it moreso because I was living just beside Balbriggan. But after a couple of games it doesn't get to you at all – in one ear and out the other! There would also be money and golf balls thrown. I remember picking up a load of copper and silver coins one day and I must have had about 40 pence, so I went over to one of the umpires and said, 'There you are now. Any square ball that comes in, you know what to do! Put the money towards a pint.' It was great to play in front of the crowd on Hill 16 actually, and when the ball went wide and you went over to pick it up along the wire you could look up at them and smile, especially if you were winning.

I still keep in contact with Sean, and we play a bit of golf together. He mightn't be great at it – he's definitely a better manager than he is a golfer! He is always late for a round of golf and would have you under pressure straightaway. Not that that would worry him, because Sean was always a very good-humoured manager and was great at getting the best out of players, whatever the situation or pressure. He is a very strong man, and I will always admire him. OK, he will be late for this, that and the other, but that's just Sean.

DONAL SMITH: *I will never forget playing in the Canal End goals in the 1994 National League final against Armagh. Ger Houlihan got the ball about 40 yards from goal. The Armagh fans behind me start chanting, 'Houli, Houli', and the closer he was getting to the goal the faster their chanting went, 'Houli, Houli, Houli'. I could almost feel the crowd coming in on top of me. He was getting closer and they seemed to be getting closer. So he shot and the ball hit the crossbar, and the crowd behind me all sighed simultaneously. The noise was just incredible. I also saved a penalty in that game. It was probably the best save I ever made anywhere, it was real top-corner stuff. It was down in the Hill 16 goal and it was the last kick of the ball. I had been wearing a faded blue cap for the second half because of the sun and I remember taking it off and throwing it on the outside of my left post before the* *penalty was taken. The game as a contest was over, but I wanted to save it anyway. I just guessed the right way and clawed it out of the top left-hand corner. A lot of people might say it didn't matter, but it mattered to me!*

The week before the Wexford match, a month or so later, I got a head-butt in the face working as a garda over in Slane. It was the night Ireland played Italy in the '94 World Cup in America, and I suffered with a bit of whiplash afterwards. Anyway, I went and played in the Leinster semi-final and during the game I was sick and felt terrible. In hindsight, if I had pulled out of that game I probably would have been playing in the Leinster final against Dublin. I made a few mistakes that day, but we won, and afterwards in the County Club in Dunshaughlin I went over and told Sean my neck was sore. So he had a quick check and said I had pulled discs out in my neck. He told me to call over to his house the following day and he would sort it out. I went over and he put the discs back in and didn't give me any hint about what was to happen the following day.

Tuesday night, I arrived at training and next thing Sean jumps into the car beside me. I had come togged out and ready to train. Suddenly he turned around and said to me, 'Donal, I'm dropping you!' As you can imagine, I was stunned, but I replied by saying, 'Oh, hopefully I can work hard and get myself back into the team.' He said, 'No, I'm dropping you off the panel altogether.' I asked him why, and he said that himself and the selectors had lost confidence in me. I couldn't believe what was happening. I hoped I was dreaming. I told him that it was all well and good dropping me off the team, but dropping me off the panel seemed a bit extreme. I went from first choice goalkeeper to being dumped from the squad altogether! But I said, 'Fine Sean, you're the manager, you make the decisions, and you live and die by the decisions you make.' The only thing I asked of him in the car was to give the young lads a chance. I asked him not to bring back Mickey McQuillan. I told him to give Conor Martin a chance. McQuillan had not played in goal for 12 months. I thought it would be unfair on Mickey, and on young Martin. So we sat in my car talking about what was going wrong for about 25 minutes. I talked about the big gaps in front of the goals and how we needed to sort it out. I still hoped it wasn't really happening.

Sean brought Mickey McQuillan back for the game. I decided not to attend and went to a friend's house in Drogheda, and we had a barbecue. It was coming up to throw-in time and I asked him was he not putting the game on the radio. He was afraid to put it on because I had been dropped. But I told him, 'I'm a Meath man. I want Meath to win!' I remember sitting around listening to the radio and when I heard Mickey had spilled the ball into the net my heart genuinely went out to him. Mickey played outfield for St Pat's and had not played in goal for 12 months. It was a wet day and the pressure of playing in Croke Park in goal, where you had not been in over a year, well, it's a nervous feeling.

MARTIN O'CONNELL: *We won a National League title against Armagh when I was full-back. It was different, but I enjoyed it a lot more than playing full-forward, or anywhere in the forwards. I remember Mick Lyons was sent off in one of the Dublin matches in '91 and I was put back there, so it wasn't completely new to me. To be beaten by ten points in the Leinster final in '95, that was a real sickener! After that game, we met down in Bob O'Malley's pub on the Monday. P.J. Gillic was there, and O'Rourke was there, and Brian Stafford was there, Terry Ferguson was there, and they all said, 'Look, it's time to call it a day!' I said to them, 'We can't all go on this note,*

Dublin beating us by ten points!' But it was only myself and Colm Coyle who stayed on. That was their decision. There was never a right time to go. I was going to stay anyway. I was going to keep going with Meath until I wasn't wanted, or had a bad injury. To this day, I'd love to be still playing for Meath. Retirement, or quitting Meath, never entered my head, even though it did briefly in '87. I was still getting such a buzz out of it, such a kick.

P.J. GILLIC: *The break-up of the old team had come in 1992. I don't know what the hell happened us that day, for we had a load of goal chances, but if we had taken our points we would have won it. We should have beaten Dublin in '93 and '94 – they only beat us by a point or two – but there was no way we were going to win that game in 1995. That was a bloody disaster! It was a humiliating defeat. We had won the League in '94 and I suppose there were great things expected from us. We had a great win over Armagh in the final that year and you had the likes of John McDermott coming in. But the Leinster final in '95 was one of those games, though, that you felt we weren't going to win from early on.*

We were just building a new team. The likes of Trevor Giles, Graham Geraghty and Enda McManus were only settling into the team and, I suppose, it was a transition from the old to the new. There were quite a few of us in Bobby's that evening, on the Monday after the game. A lot of fellas had made the decision to pack it in too early, and that was probably a mistake.

A year or two before that I was starting to have a lot of injuries, problems with my knee, and groin trouble. I was after having two or three operations and I had more or less decided to take a year out and see if I could get myself right. I didn't make up my mind as to whether I would play again. I went in and I had the cartilage done on my knee before Christmas and I had made up my mind that I would take a year out to try and recover. And sure they went on to win the All Ireland that year!

I didn't find it particularly hard to take, watching the lads win that All-Ireland. I was at all the games and enjoyed them. I was up on top of the Hogan Stand. Brendan Cummins actually asked me to do a bit on the radio with him, on LMFM, for the drawn game and I was in the Hogan Stand for the second game as well. I had actually missed a large part of the League campaign in '94 – I had the knee operation around then – and was lucky to get back in for the League semi-final and final. But I felt by then that I was carrying injuries and wasn't able to train the way I wanted, so I had made the decision and told Sean.

In '97, I met Sean – it could have been at a funeral – and he asked me to have another go and, foolishly, I went back in, trained fairly hard over the winter and got myself back into a position where I was challenging for a place on the team. I played in the Kildare games that year and in the Leinster final. Looking back on it, I think that was a mistake. I was past my best, and trying to break into a team that had just won an All Ireland is kind of a stupid thing to do.

Sean is just amazing. I would have the height of respect for him. I never heard him saying a bad word about anybody. If he had anything to say, he'd say it to your face. He was very loyal, maybe too loyal, to a few of us. I remember saying to him after '95 that there were one or two of us that he had let off lightly in training, maybe to coax us through injuries, and that we just weren't fit enough when it came to the big game against Dublin.

Training had always been his strong point – going to swimming pools, dragging each other through the sand in Bettystown. We were never bored! There wasn't a night that went by when one of the lads wouldn't say, 'Jesus, he's stone mad!' He'd have brought out a new stretching exercise or something, and turned himself into a rubber band.

No, the success would never have happened without him. He brought a whole professional attitude to training, and the way we trained, being on time. Even if he was late plenty of times himself!

BOB O'MALLEY: *I was captain that year, in 1994, but I didn't feel that Sean was under any extra pressure just because Meath had failed to win a Leinster in the previous two years. I mean, being manager of the Meath team is a pressurised job, but I don't think he was under any more pressure than he was in other years. Sean is hugely ambitious, which is an aspect of his personality that people mightn't understand or realise, but above all else he has always had a good way with young lads. I would also have to say that he had a great belief in giving youth its chance. Sean never cared what club you came from or, indeed, what grade of football that club was. He always felt that if you had a chance of making it as a player he was prepared to give you the chance, no matter what grade you played. The other thing he had was great patience when dealing with people. He developed a personal relationship with players which, naturally enough, they were inclined to respond to positively. That was just one of his strengths as a manager.*

GERRY McENTEE: *Laois beat Meath in 1992, but that was always going to happen because that Meath team was finished. When we won the All-Ireland in 1996, that year was a bit like 1985, when a load of new players came onto the panel, except that this time they were all very young. There were only three seasoned campaigners on that team – Tommy Dowd, Martin O'Connell and Colm Coyle. I was sitting on the*

Hogan Stand for that game and Meath just never stopped plugging away against all the odds. As for the row? As far as I can remember the Mayo corner-forwards started it. I think the reason Liam McHale and Colm Coyle got picked out was because they were the last two seen fighting. It was a wonderful victory that day and the fact that they were so young, nobody gave them a chance. Everybody believed Mayo were going to win that All-Ireland, but that 1996 team had great talent and great mobility.

For man-management skills Sean was the best. He had great respect for people and no matter how busy he was, he had time for everybody. If any one of the team had a problem he would make time to help him out. He always seemed to understand the problems of domestic life and work. Some managers might say, 'I don't care, you have to be at training.' But Sean was not like that. He understood the difficulties. He knew the players well, what they worked at, what stresses were involved, and he took everything into account. He always understood if fellas had problems outside of football.

I remember the two of us sitting on the edge of a rock pool in Portmarnock, dabbling our feet in the water to try and heal some blisters I had developed on my feet from too much training. I remember the wonderful walks on the beach in Portmarnock on the All-Ireland final days. I can also say that I never once heard Sean Boylan encourage or condone any form of dirty play. Sean knew how to get players physically and mentally ready for matches. I don't know how he actually did that, but he knew if we had either trained too much or too little. Sean Boylan never sent a Meath team out that wasn't jumping out of its skin, physically anyhow. The only time I ever saw Meath go out flat as a team was in the 1990 All-Ireland final, and that was the players' own fault.

One negative aspect about Sean was that he didn't like telling players any bad news. There were a number of players on the panel, wonderful fellas who had given great service to the panel and even though they weren't always first choice on the team, they were still invaluable. When they were dropped off the panel they didn't find out as they should have. They deserved to be called and told the bad news directly.

But, nobody is perfect. I am absolutely sure I would not have two All-Ireland medals today if it were not for Sean Boylan being appointed Meath manager in 1982, and I am certain that Meath would not have won four All-Irelands in that period of time.

BRIAN STAFFORD: I played on until the Leinster final in 1995. I had to go off that day because I twisted my ankle, but we were well beaten and for me that was 'Goodnight Irene'. If I had known Meath were going to win the All-Ireland the following year, I might have stuck around. But I was the type that when I made my decision to retire, that was it. Looking back, the only time I was a little bit disappointed not to be involved was when they actually got to the final, but then, again, I would have had to put in the huge effort the lads had put in for the previous nine or so months. Sean did ask me back after a club game in Navan, but I said no, my decision was made.

I had an awful seat, above at the back of the Cusack in 1996 for the All-Ireland. Meath got lucky in the first game with Coyler's point that hopped over the bar. In the replay there was the row and Mayo probably felt they should have won that game too, but it was the fighting spirit again that helped Meath through to win. I was thrilled for them when they won, but obviously it wasn't the same for me as it was when I was playing. Then again, I was delighted for all the lads who had played and won. I didn't go down to the dressing room afterwards.

Once gone, always gone!

TOMMY DOWD: *The early '90s were very tough years because we were only being beaten by a couple of points in most games. Dublin were very strong, though. It swings over and back between teams over the years. It was Meath for a couple of years, and then Dublin for a couple of years. It was Dublin's turn to dominate, and that's what they did for '93, '94, and '95, before Meath took over again. It's like everything else. If you keep chipping away, maybe, eventually, you will have your day. But it's hard to ever see yourself winning anything after being defeated by a score like the 1995 Leinster final. It was so demoralising. But Meath is a proud county, proud of the footballing tradition that's there. They will always be there or thereabouts every year. Regardless of what kind of team they have out, they are still going to be hard to beat. It's hard to pinpoint what went wrong in '95. I think you just get one of those days, and everything went right for Dublin. Paul Clarke fisted the ball and it ended up in the roof of the net. It was more or less level up to midway through the second half – it was only in the last 10 or 15 minutes that Dublin pulled away. It was one of those days, I tell you. That's all you can put it down to. It wasn't that Meath were that bad a team, just that Dublin got their chances and took every one of them. And the way it happened, we hadn't a chance of coming back.*

I remember we were training up in Gormanstown a few months later when Boylan told me he was appointing me captain for 1996. I was delighted, but I could never foresee what was going to happen. We went out to play Carlow in the first round of the Leinster Championship, and all the talk was that Carlow were going to beat Meath. That's when you have to watch Meath, when people are putting them down. There were a couple of young lassies doing physio in 1996 with the team at the time, doing rubs, that kind of thing, and apparently some of the past players said that they even have women now on the team! Nobody gave us a chance. A lot of lads weren't happy over that. Some of the past players had made certain comments about the team, saying they would be playing golf rather than watching the game against Carlow, but you just had to use that talk as a motivating factor. When you're after being defeated by such a score the previous year, all you want to do is get back and show that you're not really that bad. We would have given anything at that stage to beat Dublin, whether it was a first round, a Leinster final, or whatever!

TREVOR GILES: *I had come into the team in about February of '94. Joe Cassells rang me. Joe and Mick Lyons were the selectors that year with Sean, and Joe asked me in. At the time I didn't feel that I was physically ready for it – Meath were such a big, strong, physical team at the time. I'd say we were on the phone for ten minutes before he convinced me that I was ready. Jody (Devine) made me feel very welcome straightaway. He'd be a nice fella anyway, and he wasn't that long in himself, probably a year before. From then, it was a case of putting the head down and putting in the work. You have to prove yourself to a lot of people.*

We played Laois in the Championship, and it was our third time playing them that year! We lost to them in the League, and we lost to them in the O'Byrne Cup. I played well. I got the 'Man of the Match' that day. We had won the National League the month previously. I had played seven or eight big games up to that, so I had a good grounding at that stage. It was a lot of success straightaway. I had been very successful at underage and with my own club, especially my first couple of years playing senior. And then coming straight into the Meath team and winning the League! It was a fairytale start. But it was also very hard going. Physically, it was a big step up from any of the other matches I had ever played. That was a very strong Dublin team at the time, a very experienced team. The Leinster final that year was the one game I found very hard – the speed of it, the toughness of it, on a wet, slippy surface. Every other game I was able to cope with well.

The following year in '95 we had a quiet League campaign and went into the Championship like that. We beat Offaly, Wicklow, Longford, and thought things were going well enough, thought we had a good mixture of youth and experience. And then, we're beaten by ten points! You were so used to a point or two between Meath and Dublin down the years that this was a complete aberration, a really clinical defeat. It looked like the end of Meath football for a long time. In Meath, people were so used to having the upper hand on Dublin, yet the younger lads like myself had never beaten them. So the jury was out. A lot of people had doubts about you because you hadn't done the business against Dublin.

I think there was opposition to Sean that year. It didn't amount to much, but it showed how bad it was. I was in UCD at the time and around Dublin a lot. So it was probably worse that way. 'Ten points' was the catchphrase – you heard that a lot around the place. And sure what could you say? You had no return at all. Even in Meath, you'd hear people saying, 'Ah, yeah, great underage fellas, but they haven't got what it takes! They haven't done the business where it matters!' As a team, we had huge doubts. That was the same time we were up running around the Hill of Tara. It's up and down there. There are some serious climbs, and we trained very hard. We felt there was a lot of good young talent and we'd a lot of experience, but the mix didn't work at all. It looked like a lot of those guys were going to leave the scene then, and that the team would break up. Things looked very bleak. But the following year, we didn't do too badly, got to the League quarter-final against Mayo in '96, and then were beaten down in Hyde Park after a fairly dismal performance. Now, I can tell you, that defeat didn't go down well in Meath at all. When you put it on top of everything else, things didn't look encouraging.

Mark O'Reilly came in after that. Up until then he hadn't been involved at all. Darren Fay was already there. He had played the whole League campaign, but Sean basically restructured the whole team. Brendan Reilly was put in at full-forward, Tommy Dowd was centre-forward, Graham Geraghty who had been a wing-back was now wing-forward, and I was the other wing-forward. Martin O'Connell moved to left full-back. Looking back, that probably was the turning point. We had suffered so much adversity, and with all the people knocking us, it was backs-to-the-wall stuff. At that stage, in 1996, Dublin had won the All-Ireland the previous September, had waltzed past Westmeath in the first round, stuttered a bit against Louth, but still went into the Leinster final with all eyes on them.

We were lucky to get Carlow in the first round and we got a great victory that day. Their form had looked good and with all the Eire Og success there was a genuine fear that we would be beaten. Colm (O'Rourke) had launched his book on the Tuesday night before the Carlow game, up at Kepak, and a few of us were invited up. We had just had a team meeting where the match team was picked so we were coming straight from training. A lot of the old guard were up there and, of course, they got wind of the team. And they didn't think too much of it! A couple of them were going to play golf on the Sunday when they heard it, rather than go to Croke Park. It was fairly personal stuff. That was what was being said. 'I think I'll go golfing on Sunday. You're not going to win with that team!' Even that was a huge spur to a lot of us –

fellas, who should have known better, saying that! We had just lost Colm as well. He was probably our best player in the '95 final, but he had retired. It added to the sense of desolation, and we were thinking, 'God, we're after losing our best player!' So we had to change our game a lot, restructure the team.

Winning that Leinster final in 1996, that would be my number one memory – of all the games. A lot of fellas proved themselves that day. Once you've beaten Dublin in a Leinster final – they were the All-Ireland champions at the time – that gained you a lot of respect around the county and you could hold your head high. And I played well enough. I got 'Man of the Match' that day. It was sort of similar to the breakthrough of '86 when they beat Dublin on a miserable wet day, in a low-scoring match. It was so unexpected.

But Dublin-Meath games can produce amazing results. There were 67,000 at the Leinster final in 2001, nearly the biggest crowd of the year. Compare that to an All Ireland final where you might have 20,000 supporters from each county and 30,000 neutrals who are just there with their arms folded! At a Meath-Dublin game, you have 30,000 on each side and the noise levels are so much louder.

To be honest, I can't say that I've ever had any trouble from the Hill. The goalkeepers do! I think Cormac Sullivan made a few pounds out of the last game with the coins that were thrown at him. It's a lot worse for someone like Ollie (Murphy), who's nearly standing underneath the Hill. Tommy Dowd was the same. I guess they tend to get a lot more grief. Colm Coyle was marking Jayo in the corner one year. If you're over there, underneath it, you tend to be a fair target, but I tend to be that bit further out the field. Back in '94 and '95, we used to tog out in the corner under the Hogan Stand. If you remember, back then, when you'd leave the dressing rooms, you had to go out the back of the stand

and there could be a thousand people outside the door. Walking out after a game, they'd be there waiting for you. If you happened to be on the losing side, you used to get a fair amount of stick. That used to be tough going. I remember playing for UCD against Dublin in '94 or '95 in a challenge match at Belfield. I think I was the only Meath fella playing. Bad idea! It was January, it was windy and raining, and there was some local Dublin lad refereeing the game. The UCD lads would help you a bit, but there was no protection at all. Jesus, one of the Dublin fellas nearly broke my jaw.

You'd be better friends with a Cork fella, that you know you might never play against again, than the Dublin players. I'd be fairly good mates though with Jason Sherlock. He would have been up at our flat at college a fair bit because he played soccer and I was living with a couple of lads who were on soccer scholarships. In '94 and '95, Jayo was a huge star back then. He was the top man.

Jason Sherlock was the most famous, and fêted, footballer in Ireland at the close of 1995. The diminutive corner-forward with the sensational pace and turning skills was on billboards all over the city, and the country! Jayo, within days of Dublin defeating Tyrone in the All-Ireland final, was even on the menu for the *Late, Late Show*. Yeah, the Dubs were All-Ireland champs again, finally, after waiting 12 years to get right back up on top of the Gaelic football tree. Sean Boylan, meanwhile, was close to being back where he had started almost a dozen years earlier when he brought Meath into his first Leinster final in 1984. Boylan and his young team had lost a massive amount of ground. As 1996 dawned, Trevor Giles had no good reason to believe that the Meath team was making its way to an All-Ireland title or that he, personally, was about to remove Jason Sherlock from centre stage and officially become the greatest footballer in Ireland.

The Genius

Chapter Eight:

1996

In the absence of Lyons, McEntee, Cassells, and now O'Rourke, the Meath team needed a new face. There were lots of contenders. A couple of ol' boys, a whole clatter of new lads, and then there was Trevor Giles, who had been handed the unenviable chore of following in the footsteps of Brian Stafford as the man standing over all Meath free-kicks. Amazingly, Giles would live with that incredible pressure, and also prosper as a play-maker throughout the middle third of the field. Off the field he was polite, inoffensive, charming to the point of being insufferable when asked his opinion of any opposing team but, most of all, Giles was a genuinely decent young man. Meath would not have found a better ambassador if the county had parted with one million pounds. How, then, in the following 12 months did Meath get branded as a tough, loutish bunch of footballers? The Meath team of 1996 looked like little squirts compared to the lumbering, giant-like team which Sean Boylan had sent out in 1986 to claim the first Leinster title of his career. What happened? Why did the team of '96 get tarred with the same brush as that which, a decade earlier, had done such a thorough job on the team of '86?

Gaelic football was not going through an age of innocence in the first half of the 1990s. The old game was as tough as ever, and with Ulster teams queuing up to get into Croke Park and win All-Ireland titles, only men of great resourcefulness and bravery were attempting to grab Sam! After Down had claimed the All-Ireland title in 1991, Donegal had followed up in an equally convincing manner by defeating Dublin in 1992. Twelve months later, it was Derry and Cork in the final game of the season, and the Ulster champions, once more, did not bother apologising for getting stuck into a fairly controversial game of football. Derry were crowned

All-Ireland champs, and then Eamonn Coleman and Co. handed the title back to Down in 1994, when Dublin were once again thwarted at the final hurdle. In 1995, Tyrone had failed to continue that brilliant winning sequence, when they failed by a single point to a Dublin team which fully deserved the biggest prize of all. Compared to these sort of football teams, there was certainly nothing threatening, or frightening, about the mostly young lads Sean Boylan sent out of his dressing room on 16 June, 1996. That month, people genuinely wondered aloud whether Meath would have the necessary skill-level or bulk of muscle to see off Carlow.

TREVOR GILES: *I had kicked frees with the Meath minors. I used to play in the half-backs, but then I was put in the forwards and they had no free-taker. Brian Stafford was called in to coach a couple of us. He ran through his practice routine and a few basic techniques. That was a big help. It was just a matter of keeping those few things in mind, and practising. I think when I came onto the team first, Stafford had a broken thumb, so I was given the job straightaway. I kicked them that year when we won the League, and in the Championship as well.*

The Laois games early on in my Meath career though were very tough going. There was always someone getting sent off – and it was more us than them! But they were games where you had to show to your team-mates that you could take a few hits. Your team-mates would know that you were a good footballer but whether you were strong enough to take the hits, or whether it would affect your game, that was the sort of thing you had to prove you could handle. That was accepted on the Meath team.

We played good football to win the Leinster title in '96, but when you

Ciaran Boylan, September 13, 2001

Mark O'Reilly, September 23, 2001

look at the amount of Tyrone guys going around with the 'headgear' on in the All-Ireland semi-final, then you'd have to say we deserved some of the criticism. What people forget, however, is that we played very well that day. We scored 2-15 against the Ulster champions of two years in a row. I felt that if that game against Tyrone had been the All-Ireland final and Mayo had been the semi-final, we would have got more credit because we played great football that day in the semi-final. There were a couple of incidents, but we didn't go out to do anything.

I think our semi-final against Tyrone did affect Mayo's preparations for the final. Everyone had been asking them how they were going to cope with Meath's physical approach? I think it definitely changed their approach to the whole occasion. The origins of the row in the replay came in the first match. Barry Callaghan tackled somebody just after the ball had gone wide in the first half. There was a bit of a skirmish and there were five or six Mayo lads in on top of him and, I think, only Tommy Dowd – his own clubmate – went in to defend him. That's how restrained we were the first day against Mayo. I would trace it all back to that. We were very restrained that day and Mayo, because of what everyone had been saying to them, were very keen to show that they wouldn't be pushed around. And they were big men! That sort of thing happened the first day when they had a lot of lads into a skirmish and we hadn't so I'd say the Meath fellas just said to themselves, if anything happened again, we'd have to defend our men.

I was out around midfield in the replay when the row began. It just started and you saw everyone congregating towards it. I just went with the flow and arrived. Jaysus, I didn't do a whole lot! Sure I wouldn't hurt anyone if I did throw a dig! But one of their defenders absolutely buried me, right on the chin. I had my eye somewhere else and didn't see it coming at all. Yeah, he hit me a good shot. Then I was on the ground and thought, 'I'd better get out of here quick!' It's not a good idea to be on the ground for something like that. I got up so and was probably swinging a bit, but I don't think I hurt anyone. I don't think it was particularly mad. You didn't feel your health was particularly in danger. And once the thing settled, that was the end of it. I don't think it was even mentioned at half-time. You didn't play the rest of the game going, 'Jaysus, that row looked terrible!' From a Mayo point of view, they felt McHale was a huge loss. I don't remember it having any affect on me. It was just down to the next ball, and you went for it! There was no 'afters', no retribution. You just played the rest of the game as normal. You weren't going around afraid of your life or trying to get a dig at someone.

The victory, however, was completely overshadowed by what happened in that first half. If there's a mass brawl among the players on the showpiece day, it is going to take a lot of the attention. We had never won an All-Ireland before, so we had no idea what it would have been like. In the two All-Irelands against Mayo, I was happy with my own performance. That's what you want to do growing up, not just play in an All-Ireland, but play well in one.

It's fair comment to say that what happened was a bad example. From the outside, that's what you would say. When you're in the middle of it though, you didn't feel your health was in danger. I'd prefer to be having a row out there on the football field than in a disco, where there would be lads with Doc Martens or bottles. I don't think we let ourselves down. The Meath supporters were thrilled we won an All-Ireland. It became a case of everyone else giving out about us, which strengthened the Meath supporters' respect for us, or appreciation of us. From that point of view, we probably went up in their estimation.

Nine players from the brilliant Eire Og club took their place on the Carlow starting 15, facing Meath in the first round of the championship. Eire Og were one of the greatest club teams in the country and, with former Laois hero Bobby Miller in charge, there was no reason to doubt that a severe test awaited Sean Boylan's young boys. In a flash, however, the game was over, Meath leading by 0-14 to 0-3 at half-time, and easing up in the third quarter before running out winners by a massive 0-24 to 0-6. The final point of a lazy, sunny afternoon came from Meath right corner-back Mark O'Reilly. In the Leinster semi-final, back at Croke Park, Laois never got to grips with the sensational running and scoring of Meath half-forwards, Graham Geraghty, Trevor Giles and Tommy Dowd, who accounted for 1-8 between them in a final scoreline of 2-14 to 1-9. The Meath full-forward line of Evan Kelly, Brendan Reilly and Barry Callaghan was not far behind, grabbing 1-6 in total. There was no doubt, Boylan's genius was at work – Geraghty and Reilly, able defenders, looked like they had been born for the new roles handed them up front. Reilly had perfectly set the tone of the game in the opening minutes, running onto a perfect pass from Tommy Dowd and giving Emmett Burke in the Laois goal no chance whatsoever with his shot. The Meath team also showed that it had a steady nerve, by hardly noticing Hughie Emerson's goal shortly after the restart.

GRAHAM GERAGHTY: *I came in just after the All-Ireland final of 1991 which we lost to Down. When I went in it was a daunting task. Meath were after going well in the Championship that year. They were beaten in the final, of course, but it was still a team of household names, who had been at the highest level for many years. When I came into the* team I was arriving into training sessions and matches, and sitting in the same dressing rooms as lads like Liam Harnan and Colm O'Rourke. It was a lot to take in for a young player. It was something that I had been waiting all my life to do. In my early days I would have been in competition with guys like Kevin Foley and Colm Coyle for the wing-back positions. I played all through the League of '91 at right half-back.

But we ended up playing Derry in a quarter-final, I think, and I was taken off for Kevin Foley. That was my Championship start gone. Still, I was sitting in the dug-out with Bobby O'Malley, Colm Coyle and Liam Hayes when we lost to Laois in 1992, so things didn't seem so bad!

In fairness, I wasn't really expecting to get a run against Laois. The first time I started in the Championship was against Dublin at Croke Park in '93 – and playing Dublin in Croker was the realisation of a dream. There was nothing in it at the end either, but Dublin just about won. One of the lows in my career was being beaten by Dublin in 1995. To be beaten by Dublin in any Leinster final was bad, but that year we lost by ten points. The last thing I remember from that game was Charlie Redmond floating a ball in over Mickey McQuillan's head. They just railroaded us after that. That was the end of the old guard. Colm O'Rourke and O'Malley and a few of the other lads left that year It was the end of the old Meath team. Of course, when we won the All-Ireland in 1996 no one expected us to do anything. All the talk was that Carlow would beat us in the opening game. Instead we beat them, then Laois, and then Dublin. Nobody had given us a chance before the Dublin game. After the previous year it was probably one of the sweetest victories we've ever had. At that stage, when you're a young player coming onto a team, you don't get too phased by all the big names. You're just happy to be there and you play your own game. Our new *lads had no inhibitions about playing and that was a great benefit to them. I was there a few years at that stage. So were Trevor Giles, John McDermott and, of course, Martin O'Connell. People were saying it was the worst Meath team in years, but in fairness there was an excellent core there. The guys who came in like Mark, Darren, Paddy, Barry and Donal just augmented that. Reading the papers at the time they'd have you believe that Meath were finished for a good number of years. Some were calling for Sean's head and saying this, that and the other. We just knuckled down and got on with it. We were delighted to prove everyone wrong. We didn't do particularly well in the League, but we got a good Championship run behind us. I remember before leaving home to play Carlow, it was said to me that we'd probably be beaten, and I turned around and said we'd win the All-Ireland! I got it dead right!*

DARREN FAY: *The big thing I remember from the earliest days of Sean Boylan's reign is the 1986 All-Ireland semi-final against Kerry. I remember Mick Lyons, Mickey McQuillan and Joe Cassells all colliding going for the same ball, and Ger Power snuck in to score an easy goal for Kerry. That was the real turning point in the game, but it marked the start of Meath as a real force once again in Ireland. Meath had won Leinster for the first time in 16 years in 1986 and Kerry were just on the way out. It was a natural progression for Meath to come through and fill that void. You get a lot of speculation and suggestion whether the teams of 1996 and '99 would have beaten those of '87 and '88, and it makes for great pub talk. Personally, I wouldn't like to say.*

I didn't always want to be a full-back. But Mick Lyons did become a role model for me, because I knew him quite well. He was good friends with my father and the two of them would have known each other through the Meath team and he was around the house a lot. Dad used to play behind Mick for Meath because he was goalkeeper and Mick was full-back, so I knew a lot about Mick. I never played full-back as a young lad. I always used to play centre-back or at midfield. I remember the first time I played full-back was when Sean threw me in there against Laois in 1995. Mick definitely was the main player that I would have been looking up to when I was a young lad, even if I didn't necessarily set out to follow him as a full-back.

I do a good bit of travelling during work, and whenever I'd be in another county talking about football they'd always mention the same four players from the 1980s. First up you'd have lads talking about Mick Lyons and comparing me to him. It's only natural, I suppose. But then I'd also hear a lot of people talking about three other lads, Bernie Flynn, Liam Hayes and Colm O'Rourke. It always seems to be the same names you hear. They were the stars, I suppose.

A great thing about Sean Boylan is his ability to see another side of a player. He converts backs into forwards, and vice-versa, so often when others simply wouldn't see it as an option. Take Brendan Reilly. To my mind, Brenny was always a half-back but Sean converted him into a great forward. Graham Geraghty is the same but, then again, he has that much talent that you could play him anywhere.

ENDA McMANUS: I was dropped for the two Leinster finals in 1994 and '95. Colm Coyle came back and got the nod ahead of me, so I missed out. Sean didn't give me any reasons. The defeat in 1995 was particularly hard to take because of the magnitude of the final scoreline. However, in hindsight it woke us up for the following year. I didn't join up with the panel until May of '96. I opted out in January to concentrate on the club scene. We were going hell-for-leather at training with Dunboyne so I concentrated all my efforts on that team. I told Sean *my intentions and, fair play to him, he didn't close the door on me. 'Just give me a shout whenever you are ready', he said. So one evening when the boys were training on the Hill of Tara I walked up to Sean and told him I would start the following Tuesday if that was OK. 'Yeah sure, we'll see you then', he replied.*

Sean Boylan showed no fear whatsoever in naming the late returning Enda McManus at centre-back for the forthcoming Leinster final against the reigning All-Ireland champions. Like the Leinster final of 1986, it was a miserable, rainy afternoon, and like the meeting of the two teams ten years earlier nobody complained at the end of a ferocious battle. Dublin took their defeat like Dublin and Meath footballers always do! The winning captain received a nasty facial injury during the course of the 70 minutes, but Tommy Dowd still managed to kick the final point of his side's 0-10 to 0-8 victory, before marching up the steps of the Hogan Stand to accept the trophy. Evan Kelly had scored the first point of the game after six minutes and Brendan Reilly was also on target two minutes later, but only Dowd, 23 minutes into the first half, managed another point for the challengers. Brian Stynes put Dublin two points up shortly after half-time but, soon enough, Trevor Giles, from a free-kick and from open play, had Meath level – Stafford's successor looked at ease with his great responsibility and was quickly making himself at home on the big occasion in Croker! Charlie Redmond and Giles swapped points, and Redmond put Dublin one up once again with a great score from a '45'. Eamonn Heery increased the advantage to two points once more. Dublin had the finishing line in their sights. There were only seven minutes remaining. Enough time, however, for Reilly,

Giles, Callaghan and Dowd to each shoot over a point and each prove himself a winner on the biggest stage in Gaelic football.

Meath had qualified for the All-Ireland semi-final for the first time in five years, and there they would have a date with Tyrone, the hottest team in the country and everybody's favourite to lift the Sam Maguire. It was a game which was destined to be memorable – an epic perhaps – if the new Meath team could lift themselves to the same level as the Ulster champions. Instead, the Meath team gave one of the greatest performances ever witnessed in Croke Park in modern day Gaelic football. It was a devastating display, fast, powerful, always furious on the ball and off the ball. It was 2-15 to 0-12 by the end, a nine-point rout. John McDermott and Jimmy McGuinness owned the middle third of the field in the company of Pascal Canavan and Jody Gormley, and with the supply of quality ball coming his way Graham Geraghty turned in a performance which was equally stylish and lethal. Geraghty scored one goal and four points. At half-time the teams had been level, but Gerard Cavlan was Tyrone's only scorer in the second half with three points. Meath continued to run the Tyrone defence ragged, and Geraghty set up Barry Callaghan for a second goal which condemned the Ulster champions to one of their most punishing defeats of all time. There was no doubt, Tyrone felt sorry for themselves at the end of the gruelling contest – as sorry as Meath had looked a decade earlier when they departed the field after losing to Kerry in the 1986 All-Ireland semi-final. On that afternoon, the Meath dressing room was jammed with the walking-wounded, after receiving a lesson in the physical demands of the game from the greatest football team of all time! Back then, secretly, Meath had been thankful to Mick O'Dwyer and Co. for the lesson. Tyrone, however, were in no mood to show their gratitude at the end of the 1996 All-Ireland semi-final. They had their best forward and bravest player, Peter Canavan still looking all shook up after a first half shoulder charge from John McDermott which was, approximately, five or six minutes late! Ciaran McBride and Brian Dooher also looked the worse for wear in the losers' dressing room.

JOHN McDERMOTT: *I've never been in a team dressing room, under Sean Boylan or any other manager, and heard him say, 'Right, go out and take the heads off these!' Never in a million years! If a manager sends you out to do that, he's not focused on the job. At the same time, can you imagine Sean Boylan saying to a fella, 'Mick, you went a bit hard for that ball now. The next time would you just calm down a bit.' No bloody way! It's a referee's job to discipline players. And a manager should defend his men to the last. If a player has faith in the manager and knows that he will defend him, that will be returned in kind on the field. None of the Meath players is stupid. Taking the head off somebody equates to getting sent off. Getting sent off lets down the team, lets down the job, lets down yourself and your family!*

Against Tyrone, in the All-Ireland semi-final in '96, Dooher had a bandage on his head that went out with the high bike! It looked like a feckin' turban on his head! I've never seen a bandage on a guy's head in Meath – at any level! You'd get a stitch in it if there was something wrong. And then, I remember the bandage came off, like it flew out of a car window!

I went flat out for the ball early in the game with Peter Canavan. What people forget is, I didn't shoulder him in the ankle – and that's where he hurt himself! Ask Peter Canavan, and he'll tell you himself! If he was in the reverse position, he'd feckin' take the head off me! If you look at the video of it, you'll see he holds his ankle. He doesn't hold his head, or his neck, or his arm, or his body!

DONAL CURTIS: *I was one of the Boylan Babes that came in before the 1996 Championship. A lot of lads were tried out at the end of '95. It was a new set-up to a certain extent with a lot of new faces. There wasn't too much pressure there really because as a new, young player nothing was expected of you. It was just down to having the raw, fresh enthusiasm, which we all had in bucketloads. Obviously people were saying that we still had to beat Dublin. They were always the acid test for a Meath team. The Leinster final of '96 was a great occasion for everyone. Early on a few balls came into the back-line, and I'll never forget Paddy Reynolds having no fear at all and just throwing his head in there to get to a tackle. That was the type of spirit in the team with the younger lads at the time. No fear!*

We were out on the field against Tyrone in the All-Ireland semi-final that year when it really kicked in for me how far we had come. Tyrone came out on the field after us. And the roar from the crowd would make the hair stand up on the back of your neck! Lots of lads were playing in their first semi-final and it was tense stuff. Mark O'Reilly kept Peter Canavan fairly quiet that day and he seemed to be the man to watch. The game will probably be remembered for the wrong reasons, however. At that stage Meath were getting a name for being a bit of a dirty team but it was blown out of proportion. I mean, if you think about it, we had Mark O'Reilly, Darren Fay, Paddy Reynolds and Barry Callaghan making their debuts in 1996. It's not as if they were going to be going around killing lads out there. Most them were only out of underage football. It was very unfair on those players. At that age they were still relatively inexperienced.

GRAHAM GERAGHTY: *The atmosphere at the Tyrone game in the All-Ireland semi-final of that year was just amazing. I was warming up with Donal Curtis out on the pitch when the Tyrone lads came out, and the noise was unreal. It was much louder than anything you'd ever get at an All-Ireland final. I'll never forget it. Donal was a couple of feet away from me and I couldn't hear anything he was saying. I think Tyrone expected to win that game. They had been blown up by the media, especially in the papers, to walk it. We just got on with what we had to do.*

Meath always had the reputation of being a dirty team, and that match did us no favours! But I think if you ask any of the Dublin or Cork lads who played Meath in the major games in the 1980s and 90s they wouldn't say that. They'd say Meath played hard football and got on with every game. We all went for a pint afterwards and had a chat. There were no lasting enemies made, but people still liked to talk Meath up as a dirty team.

MARTIN O'CONNELL: *There was a lot of talk about what happened in that Tyrone game and my part in it, but it was all easily explained. The first incident involving me was with Ciaran McBride underneath the Cusack Stand. The ball broke out and I went for it. I fell across him and my knee just clipped him. He'll probably say differently, and everybody in Tyrone will probably say differently, but I just clipped him by accident. It actually turned out that McBride picked the ball up. I was policing him when he fell, and I kinda fell over him. He actually picked the ball off the ground and the referee gave a free out to us.*

I didn't get booked for that incident, or the one with Brian Dooher. The one with Brian Dooher? Again the ball broke. It actually broke out to Peter Canavan and he scored a point off it. But when the ball broke, Brian Dooher fell in front of me or maybe I could have pushed him, but I was falling as well and my hand went down on his head and, trying to step across him, I caught him with my studs on the top of the head. I didn't stamp on him. I was just so intent on getting out after the ball.

I definitely didn't stamp on him! I'd never do that. Stamping is deliberately putting your boot down on a fella's head or leg. But this was just an accidental clip! It looked bad on the television, there's no doubt about that. But I was falling, I put my hand on his head to balance myself and I just threw my left leg across him and kind of clipped him on the top of the head.

The incident was discussed on Liveline on RTE the next day. I didn't actually hear it. I wouldn't have been listening to it in the van, but what happened was somebody rang me and told me to turn it on. So I listened to a bit of it. I thought it was bad form, what I heard. It upset me a bit, but it upset my family more. I took it with a grain of salt, kept playing away, training away, didn't pass any remarks. But my mother and father would have felt bad about it. I thought I got a bit of a raw deal with the press, but it didn't bother me until the GAA came out and said they were meeting, and there was talk that I might miss the final. I was worried then! To miss an All-Ireland final would have been a disaster because I knew I was coming to the end of my term. To play in another one after eight years was going to be great.

It didn't really affect my preparations for the final, I'd have to say. I just kept doing my own thing. Sean again was helping me out, and I got a few calls from Gerry McEntee and Colm O'Rourke and these boys, saying, 'Just keep the head. Pass no remarks, talk to nobody, and concentrate on getting yourself right for the All-Ireland final', which was *basically what I did. Papers rang me up about it and I just said that I didn't want to talk about it.*

When we went up to Tyrone to play in the League, three months after the All-Ireland, I took a lot of abuse. I got spat on by their supporters on the way in – that kind of thing. I remember coming in off the field with Adrian Cush and he said, 'Look Martin, pass no remarks on them'. I wanted to go up there for that match, because if I didn't I was showing that I had done something wrong, and did it on purpose.

FRANK FOLEY: *After the Meath-Tyrone semi-final there was an eruption of hysteria against Martin O'Connell, who had caused Brian Dooher to finish the game wearing what looked like Willie John McBride's headgear from his scrummaging heydays. On slow-motion camera Marty was seen to use Brian's head as a kind of starting block. Marty didn't realise that this had happened until he saw it on* The Sunday Game, *and he was upset and offended at the ensuing furore. But in training over the next few weeks many 'rises' were taken out of him by team-mates who enjoyed winding him up. At one team meeting to discuss where we had gone wrong in the Tyrone game Marty voiced an opinion that their running game hadn't suited our defence. 'A lot of the time', said Marty, 'I didn't know where my man was!' Donal Curtis caused huge amusement when he replied, 'He was on the ground, Martin!' After the laughter had died down, Marty, who wasn't noticeably amused, gave us all a little lecture along the lines that it was time to stop all such remarks, and the sooner this was done the better for all concerned. Sean Boylan saw his chance and said quietly, 'Right Marty! So what you're saying is, you want us to stamp it out!' End of meeting.*

That year was the start of an adventure for me, because Sean had asked me to join him as a selector. When we beat Carlow well in the first game, that woke a lot of people up. Then we beat Laois, but still you had the few people saying, 'Well, it's only Carlow and Laois.' Then we beat the Dubs in the Leinster final of '96. That was a really great win for such a young team. It was Darren Fay's first year and he was expecting to be marking big Joe McNally at full-forward, but they put Jason Sherlock in on him instead. Darren had a field day and won everything that came near him. He cleaned up.

I think everyone expected us to put up a good show but lose in the end. Of course losing by ten points the previous year was another great motivating factor for the Meath lads, aside from that. There were six or seven new guys brought in at the start of that year. There was talk about Colm O'Rourke coming back in between the All-Ireland final and the final replay of that year too, but in the actual camp there wasn't too much positive feedback about him returning. He played in a challenge game in Skryne and I think it was being billed as the final warm-up game for him before he came back. The fans would have loved to see him back, but there was no great desire on the part of the team or the management to throw him in for the final. The feeling was that this team had got us this far and they deserved to go out there, and win or lose the game themselves! They had earned that right and were entitled to do what they had to do themselves in the final. We ran away with it in the end.

The Tyrone game, however, was something else that year. I remember Peter Canavan being marked out as the danger man and he didn't do much. In fairness, he took a couple of rattles early on in the game from Darren Fay and Mark O'Reilly, and he was fairly shook after that. It was great after the win because going into the Mayo game there was all the craic of an All-Ireland final build-up and it was great to be involved in it. The second day was a wild, windy one and there was very little *good football. Everyone remembers the big row from that game more than anything else. We were sick listening to talk of 'dirty Meath' after that. It was only really in '99 when we won the All-Ireland again that we got rid of that type of talk – '99 was a clear-cut win and it totally redeemed us. In fairness to Colm Coyle in '96, he probably did connect with a few big thumps before he got sent off, but if the row hadn't lasted as long as it did, he would have had no part in it. If Liam McHale hadn't come in like the '7th Cavalry' I don't think Colm would have got involved at all. The ref had to be seen to be doing something and the boys were unlucky to be sent off, because it could have been any number of lads.*

BARRY CALLAGHAN: *I got a point near the end of the Leinster final that year. It was the second last point we scored and put us one up at 0-9 to 0-8. It was a wet day but a great day. In fact, it was probably one of the best games I was involved in with Meath. It was my first senior Leinster final. With the score at eight points apiece, the ball came down the field and John McDermott was running through the centre and he hand-passed it out to me and I couldn't really miss. It was a vital point to get at that stage, however. Graham Geraghty had a great game that day against Tyrone in the semi-final. I scored 1-3 myself and, in truth, we probably played our two best games that year in the Leinster final and All-Ireland semi-final. We didn't play as well in the final. For my goal, Graham was coming through in loads of space and he could have gone for a goal himself, but the goalie went to meet him and he hand-passed over to me at the far post, and I just flicked it in. It was a wide-open goal, and the goalkeeper wasn't even there, so it was a fairly simple finish. As I flicked it in I kind of hurt my ankle, but I had injured myself earlier in the game and didn't actually train much after that match* or before the final. I did a little but, basically, I didn't want to risk the hamstring and wanted to keep it right for the final. Fair play to Sean at the time, he gave me every chance to be ready for the Mayo game.

DARREN FAY: *There were five of us for whom 1996 was our first Championship year and Sean was, for us, the same as any fella that you'd see on the TV – a real star for us young lads. Most kids would look up to famous soccer players and that was how we viewed Sean – a real legend, I suppose. He strikes me as a man to be listened to and not to be spoken back to. He talks genuine sense and it's better to take it all in than spurn it. Before a game you would never hear Sean roaring at lads. He would always reckon that if lads weren't psyched up enough at that stage then they shouldn't be there at all, which is dead right.*
Going into that first game in the Championship everyone was expecting Carlow to cause an upset. Colm Hayden was banging in the goals for them before the Championship and he was to play at full-forward against us. From a personal point of view all I could do was go in there and try my best, but I was expecting a tough game from him. As it happened, Colm was coming into the game with a bit of an injury, so I fared OK in the end. We won by 0-24 to 0-6, so it was an easy enough game for me and, if I remember right, even Paddy Reynolds got a score, which doesn't happen often! It was a dream start for a lot of us, though we quickly found out that each game gets harder and harder in the Championship. The Dubs in the Leinster final – that was a whole different ball game! It was in front of a packed house and it was amazing to win that game. It was the first really great game that I was involved in as a Meath senior footballer.

MARK O'REILLY: *My first Championship game was against Carlow,* *and it was nerve-racking stuff in Croke Park. But when you're playing for Meath that's always there because a reputation has been built up from the team previous to the one you're in. We beat them well and because there was a number of new lads coming into the team, like myself and Paddy Renolds for example, it was great to get the win and that introduction. To be honest, we didn't know what way we were going to go really because it was a totally new team. But Sean Boylan had a certain aura about him after so many brilliant years as Meath manager – to get to play beneath him was brilliant. Even to get in for trial games was great! For any young lad it's a great experience. Everybody starts to talk about you when you get in there in the Championship.*

We played Laois in the next round. Dublin was the big game for us in the Leinster final that year. It was the big one for us because we knew that our team was being compared to the old team who first won the Leinster title in 1986 after 16 years of missing out. It was hard-hitting stuff and everything you'd expect from a Meath-Dublin game. I remember, in the last minute, the ball rolling across the goal-line and we escaped by the skin of our teeth It was a massive thing to do, to beat the Dubs in what was the first outing for many players in the team. I was marking Charlie Redmond that day and he was a very tough opponent. He was one of the players that Dublin always looked to for inspiration so it was going to be difficult to keep him quiet. To be marking him in my first game was a daunting experience. When I came out onto the pitch and first stood side by side with him, it put everything into perspective, of where I was, and how far I'd come, how far we'd all come that year. Sean, however, was a great believer in telling a lad that he had earned the right to be there and not to feel intimidated. That's what he said to us before we went out that day. I think we all took that on board. I got my first ball that day early on and immediately the nerves settled down. It was a great challenge after that and I wasn't really daunted. I was prepared for anything.

The All-Ireland semi-final was one of the most incredible games I've played in as a Meath player. The atmosphere was something else. Croke Park was absolutely full to capacity. Meath supporters were well outnumbered that day – I'll never forget the roar when we came out onto the pitch. We didn't say much coming out onto the pitch but all the lads were thinking the same thing, 'Bloody Hell!' I don't think it'll ever be matched. Even in an All-Ireland final I don't think you'd see such support for a team as Tyrone got that day, and for us to come out into that was very difficult. We went down a couple of points very early on. Before we knew it things were getting on top of us. But as usual we managed to get back into it and it turned out to be a great day for us, which silenced a lot of the Tyrone fans! It's been described as a hard-hitting game but I wouldn't really agree. It was more that there was intensity in each tackle. There was nothing really rough about it. True, it was hard at times but it was all fair stuff. There was no quarter asked and none given by either side. It was the speed of the game as much as anything that made it even more important to put in the big tackles, but there was nothing illegal about any of it.

TOMMY DOWD: *No matter who Meath are playing – and maybe we're paranoid – but we feel that everybody is shouting for the opposing team. I suppose we never got the credit we deserved from anyone else outside our own supporters. We were very disappointed with all the talk from Tyrone and Mayo players in '96, no doubt about it. We were very disappointed with that. You never would have heard those kind of comments from any Dublin player. Mayo players were trying to say they were provoked into doing what they did. This was still going on well after* the All-Ireland was done and dusted. It was all to do with the row, that their best player had been sent off, and apparently our worst player had been sent off – Colm Coyle. They forgot that Coyler was the man who got us there after scoring the equaliser the first day in the All-Ireland!

Tyrone were criticising Martin O'Connell and, as long as I know Martin O'Connell, he was the most dedicated player I ever played beside. There wasn't a bad bone in his body. He'd come to training and his boots would be shining – you'd see yourself in them – and he'd always be first to show up. There was never, ever any malice in Martin O'Connell. I remember going up to play Tyrone in a League game a few months after it and the abuse they threw at Martin was unbelievable. It was probably a game in which Boylan shouldn't have played him, with the amount of abuse that he got.

When the row started against Mayo in the All-Ireland replay, I was up the other end of the field. All I remember is thinking, 'There's a bit of a row. The referee will be in, and it will all be sorted out.' But it just went on and on. You were waiting for it to stop but it went on for about 30 seconds – which is a long time out there. So I ran down to the other end, but by the time I got there it was all sorted. It was a pity it ever happened. You have so many people viewing the All-Ireland and you have so many spectators there that it doesn't look good. In saying that, I don't think there was a decent punch thrown!

For me, as captain, it didn't take from winning the All-Ireland at all. We were just thrilled to win it. For all those lads who were after coming on the panel, it was their first All Ireland, so it didn't matter to us what happened, as long as we won. Maybe Mayo thought, that we thought we were hard men. We just wanted to get on with the job. If you look at that team, the average age was 22 or 23. So who were the thugs? These 'thugs' were only young lads. These so-called hard men were only *youngsters.*

Colm Coyle's last-gasp kick from over 60 yards out hopped over the bar to give Meath a second bite at the 1996 All-Ireland final. While that kick was worth well over one million pounds to the GAA, it rendered a great Mayo performance over the previous 70 minutes altogether worthless. The Connacht champions, suddenly looking at a scoreline of 1-9 to 0-12, would have to outplay Meath all over again. They had allowed a second-half lead of six points to disappear, and if Monaghan referee Pat McEnaney had allowed any more than 20 seconds of injury time then Mayo would surely have paid an even heavier price for their appalling lack of conviction in the last quarter of a contest they had dominated for so long. Liam McHale, in particular, had reigned supreme in the middle of the field and it was not until the introduction of Colm Brady, after 47 minutes, that Meath began to get the upper hand on the Irish basketball international. Maurice Sheridan, and James Horan who would turn out to be the most inspirational player on the field over the two games, totted up seven points between them – two less than Trevor Giles (six) and Brendan Reilly. It was 0-7 to 0-4 at the interval, and Mayo looked within touching distance of winning their first All-Ireland title since 1951 when, ten minutes into the second half, Paddy Reynolds failed to clear the ball and Ray Dempsey delighted in finding a Meath defence at sixes and sevens before slipping the ball past Conor Martin. Incredibly, with their tails up and their large following roaring them on, Mayo stopped in their tracks. They only managed one point for the remainder of the game. Giles and Reilly pointed at the other end. There were 15 minutes remaining.

Loyal to the end, September 2, 2001

Graham Geraghty, June 23, 2002

Giles landed his fifth point. Mayo substitute P.J. Loftus replied at the other end. McDermott shot one over for Meath, Giles got another, and then Reilly again. There was one point in it. Nobody would have put money on Colm Coyle, who had a quiet, relatively peaceful All-Ireland final in the Meath half-back line, to level the game.

Two weeks later came the replay and the 'row'. The All-Ireland final replay was a strange and wonderful game from Mayo's point of view. They lost their most inspirational player when McHale was sent off early in the first half, but they managed to continue on from their accomplished performance in the drawn game and again dictate matters to Meath for lengthy periods. With a big wind at their backs, Mayo should have led by a sizeable margin at half-time, but a Trevor Giles penalty kick on the stroke of 35 minutes reduced their interval advantage to a disappointing four points. Meath had reduced that margin to just a solitary point within five minutes of the resumption but, courageously, the Connacht champs held onto their lead until ten minutes from the very end when Tommy Dowd showed remarkable opportunism by slipping to the ground and shooting home Meath's second goal, after he had received a quick free-kick from Geraghty. James Horan, once more, was in magnificent form scoring five of the most exquisite points ever seen on All-Ireland day. Mayo did so much right during the 70 minutes, and came so, so close!

Mayo had every reason to be immensely proud of themselves over the All-Ireland fortnight. But, so too had Meath, who had left their greatest performance of the year behind them in the semi-final, and still dug deep, and dug again and again, before awarding their manager with his third All-Ireland title. And, nobody got through as much work as the winning captain, Tommy Dowd, who scored one goal and three points, was fouled for the first-half penalty, and never stopped encouraging his younger team-mates to chase down Mayo's long and worrying lead. Dowd and Giles scored 2-7 between them, with Barry Callaghan and Brendan Reilly getting one point apiece, though Reilly's would turn out to be the coolest and most valuable score of the whole game.

BRENDAN REILLY: *The All-Ireland final replay was the worst game we played all year. And it'll always be remembered for the big mêlée. I was the only Meath man on the pitch to miss the row! There were three on the pitch that managed to keep out of it, the Mayo keeper and his full-back and myself. It was just too far down the pitch to go running the whole way. I was half-injured at the time, so I just didn't bother running. It was unlucky for Colm Coyle and Liam McHale getting sent off, because the two boys that started the row just lay down on the ground. They got the dirty end of the stick.*

People used to label Meath a dirty team but I think it was only an excuse to be against us. It was the 'everyone hates a winner' mentality – Clare hurlers suffered the same kind of thing when they won All-Ireland titles in 1995 and '97. By the end of 1997 everyone just wanted to see them gone! The media were a bit guilty too. I think there was a lot of anti-Meath stuff coming out. We were being touted as a bit of a rough lot but, in truth, we were always fair and honest. You know, Mick Lyons, as hard and all as he was, I don't think he ever put in a bad blow on a player. Like all the Meath lads under Sean, Mick could mix it with the best of them, but he was fair.

In one way, the 1996 final was the high point of my career, yet I had a poor game and was disappointed a bit. I scored the winner off my left boot right at the death. I was just thinking, 'I'm going that poor that if I get the ball I'll have a go. Something has to go right for me!' It fell nicely, and I just lobbed it over. It worked out well in the end.

I actually thought we were going better in 1997. Before the Leinster final against Offaly which we lost, we had played three games against Kildare. A few of the lads had picked up suspensions from the last of those three games, including Darren Fay. I remember something like, if the game had been played a day later, the Sunday and not the Saturday, Darren would have been eligible to play. I think we lost a couple of games like that in the next year or so, small things that hit us hard in different ways. Offaly hit us on a bad day in '97 and scored three vital goals. I finished up in '98. If it wasn't for injury I probably would have hacked on for another while – I needed a groin operation after 1996. I always had a bit of trouble with it and the pain seemed to come out in my back. For 12 months solid, before I gave up, I had a pain in my back and I just said, 'Enough is enough.' It seemed to fall right for Meath after I left in 1999. I thought we were just as good in '97 and '98 but because of suspensions, injuries, and a bit of bad luck, it just didn't happen. My last game was the Leinster final of '98 against Kildare and I was sent off. It was one of their half-forwards that I collided with. I remember looking back at the video of the game and the tackle did look very dirty, but it wasn't intentional. I saw him coming late at me. He ducked, and in an instant I dipped my shoulder and caught him bang on the head. I went up afterwards to shake his hand and apologise. He wasn't having any of it, though. I could see that he knew I was walking towards him because he started rolling his eyes to heaven before I even got over to him. I didn't bother with him then. That was enough for me!

MARK O'REILLY: Mayo overran us in the first game, and we managed to live off scraps and just about get the draw. It was thanks to Coyler right at the end with his point that bounced over the bar that we got the replay. We just couldn't get ahead of them at all that day. It was only right at the end that we drew level. We all gave Colm the nod after that and kind of said, 'Nice one, you got us out of jail.' The second day was a strange day. It was dominated by the mêlée. It was freakish – I don't know what to say about it! We never thought anything like that was going to happen. The referee sent off Liam McHale and Colm Coyle but no matter what he did he was going to be seen to be doing wrong. I think he had to do something. That's why he picked one from each team and sent them off. I think those particular players were unfortunate because you could have picked any number of players to punish. The whole thing, in fairness, was blown out of all proportion and I think a lot of players came out worse than they really should have.

James Horan was great during both games. Everything he kicked seemed to go over the bar. He scored four or five points from play. You get that in All-Ireland finals. There's always a couple of players that stand up and are counted – against Galway, in 2001, it was Padraig Joyce. That year it was James Horan. Thankfully for us, Tommy Dowd played one of those games the second day too. We managed to get the scores at the right time and we got the win. If it had gone on for another ten minutes who knows what would have happened? Tommy Dowd got 'that' goal in the second game when he kicked the ball into the net while he was on the ground. They went back up the field and scored another point straight after though. It was only when Brenny Reilly got the point with a few minutes to go that we managed to hold out. There was no better man to take control than Brenny. If you wanted one man to take control and have a shot, it was him.

JOHN McDERMOTT: *We were lucky as cut cats the first day against Mayo. Pure lucky! With the Tyrone thing, Mayo came in with nothing to lose. We were the best team supposedly, blah blah blah. And the next thing, all hell breaks loose. A replay is a disaster, for a start. What happened was Fay got done, and I grabbed the guy who did him. I grabbed him and the next thing lads started coming at me from all angles. I got the head nearly wrenched off me so I held my peace for a bit. Then I grabbed one fella and said, 'I'd hold on now, see how things develop.' Funny enough, I didn't know what was happening behind me. The next thing is, I looked around and saw a flash of someone going by me. It was McHale coming in! Lucky enough, Fay was beside me and kind of diverted him away. He was coming in full tilt after running 30 or 40 yards. That's what annoyed me afterwards, this thing that he wasn't involved! If he wasn't involved, he should have stayed where he was – not run 30 yards. But Fay diverted him away. So I says, 'Right, he came for me. I'll have a bit of that!' So off I went after him. And I got him. But he put his head down. I had him in a head-lock when Coyler came in and – Bam! _ hit him. Then hit him again a couple of times. The worst belt I got was Coyle's hand hitting the back of my hand. You know when you get a bang on the back of your hand, it kills you. And I said to myself, 'Jaysus. Coyler's after hitting me here.'*

Coyler was going around putting his oar in a couple of situations. He got bored with mine, then ran off somewhere else. McEnaney was sending myself and McHale off. That was it! He'll tell you that freely. He went to the umpire and the umpire said, 'Coyle has to go! He's after decking about three fellas!' And McEnaney says, 'I want to send McDermott and McHale off.' He'll tell you that freely. So I was blessed. And the worst of it then was, you're that psyched up to play on McHale and, suddenly, he's gone! It threw everybody. Sure it threw everybody in the stand, never mind the players!

It was just one of those things. They didn't stand back, and we didn't stand back! Nobody died. I have no regrets in the world. Probably the most ridiculous thing about it was a woman ringing up Pat Kenny a day or two later saying the players should be fined. Sure, how the hell could you fine a player when he's not being paid? That's how ridiculous it was. It's not a thing we're proud of, but it's not a thing we're ashamed of either. It happened and, if the truth be told, if Mayo won the game, there would have been a lot less said about it. All the same, people will remember that All-Ireland a lot longer than they will remember some Mickey Mouse ones. The football was cat, in both games, absolutely atrocious! Mayo blew it. They had us dead and buried both days. People would have the perception that you didn't win it fairly, that there was the row, and you didn't win it with good football. You had the likes of Pat Spillane saying it was the worst team he ever saw!

You want to win the thing. It's a battle of wills as much as a physical battle. If you asked Mick Lyons, 'Would you like beating Dublin or decapitating five or six of them?' he'd say, 'I want to beat them.'

Meath had a lot of big men in the 1980s and '90s! You'd see McEntee, Hayes, Lyons, Harnan, O'Rourke – they were all well over six foot, and well put together. They looked big. The team after them was minute! There's a picture of the mêlée against Mayo. It was taken from the Hogan Stand and you can see half the Hill behind it – and everybody on the Hill has their jaw open! They just couldn't believe what was happening.

Every team that would come up against us then, they'd be thinking, 'We have to take them on physcially.' And that's the last thing you want. You don't want to be going out every time saying, 'This lad is going to be bubbling for action.' But other teams were coming out and saying,

'Yeah, we've got to take the heads off these lads!'

ENDA McMANUS: *The buzz was unreal in the dressing room. The thing about that team was that, although we had been written off at the start of the year, there were a lot of players who had come to expect to be participating in Leinster and All-Ireland finals. A lot of the lads had played on successful minor and Under-21 teams. You could nearly say that we had been in this kind of position before, just not at senior level. That is something not many people talked about. We were not new to finals. The dressing room was the same, but when we went out onto the pitch the atmosphere was unreal. I played centre-back and was marking Colm McManamon that day. He was a tough man to track down. He must have covered every blade of grass on the pitch, without even getting the ball! I followed him and also tried to sit in front of Darren Fay, and keep it tight. Coyle's point right at the death was so lucky. Many a time that would not have hopped over the bar.*
I remember being the fifth or sixth man getting into the row under Hill 16. I think I caught John Casey on my way in and, suddenly, everybody else was throwing punches all around me. Martin O'Connell and myself had to try and break it up then. At that stage it was just mental. They were running from all over the field to get involved. I was actually amazed how badly Meath got presented after that row. Everybody blamed Meath and there was a lot of bad press about our team. There was another team in that row and they didn't get half the rap Meath received afterwards.

DARREN FAY: We were beating all the teams that were expected to beat us in 1996. The referee went out with the intention of sending off one player from each team in the All-Ireland final replay. In the end it was *a bit of a lottery and I suppose you could say that Colm Coyle and Liam McHale were unlucky that their numbers came up. When lads like myself started off in our first year there was never a sign that we were going to go on and achieve anything. Until we'd actually won the All-Ireland in 1996 we were just young lads who'd broken into a team. Personally, I don't think you can actually call a player 'great' until he has finished his career anyway.*

When Colm O'Rourke and Bobby O'Malley left in 1995 after the Leinster final defeat to Dublin, people in Meath probably said, 'Well, that's the last of the old lads. We won't have the same success for another 20 years!' I think we've given them some good times since though! When I came in I didn't think about winning anything. It was always a huge ambition just to play for Meath. When you're growing up you just want to play for Meath. You don't say to yourself, 'I want to win with Meath.' So just pulling on the jersey was enough for me. Sean instilled something in the new lads, that they didn't feel any pressure. He just left us feeling delighted that we were playing at all. There was no pressure on us at all. Though, from a personal point of view, that didn't last very long – there was massive pressure in 1997. When you know what has to be done and when you're at the top, I suppose it's easy to let things slide and keep going down.

BARRY CALLAGHAN: *Obviously, you would be a bit nervous before an All-Ireland final, and if you weren't nervous there would be something wrong with you. Generally when you get out on the field though, you are OK. The dressing room is the worst. The night before the final I stayed in. I didn't go out because a lot of lads would come over and be asking you about the game, and the last thing you want to be doing is talking about it because you are trying to get your head right. As* *ever in the dressing room, all the lads would be preparing in different ways. Some fellas would be talking and others would be quiet. The likes of Conor Martin and Cormac Murphy would be the lads having a bit of craic beforehand, with an odd comment here and there. Other players, like Darren Fay, John McDermott and Trevor Giles would be very quiet before a game.*

I wasn't involved in the fight in the replay. I didn't think it was going to last as long as it did. Dermot Flanagan was marking me and he didn't get involved either. I suppose we were up the far end of the pitch and the fight was down under the Hill. We both kind of half-ran down the field, but when we got there it was pretty much over, which was probably just as well really – better off not getting involved because there were enough fellas caught up anyway. I remember Brendan Reilly's point at the end. It was a great point. I also remember thinking that Mayo were not taking their chances. I was down the other end of the field and every time they went forward they had chance after chance, but they never seemed to punish us.

MARTIN O'CONNELL: *In the drawn game against Mayo, this eejit came down out of the stand at the end and stood about five or six yards from me and called me all the names under the sun. Obviously from Tyrone, and giving me everything! I could see him going off then and I was mad to get after him. Luckily, with the crowds, I didn't! He never said who he was but I got a letter in the post from one Tyrone supporter calling me this and that soon afterwards, and no name put to it.*

The row in the replay happened in front of the goal and I was on the goal-line at the time. All hell broke loose. I was running after lads trying to push them away, trying to cool them down. I never got a box, and I never gave one, but it looked like it went on for so long when you saw it on the television. It was special to win that All-Ireland, because it was with a whole new bunch of lads. A lot of fellas had given it up after '95 but, like I said before, I thought Meath would win another All-Ireland. However, I didn't think I'd be a part of it.

GRAHAM GERAGHTY: *The row in the final against Mayo, looking back on it, probably appeared a bit worse than it actually was. I think if you had a good look at it again, not too many lads actually got hit. There were lads throwing punches and kicks and the game will always be remembered for that, but no one actually got hurt. It was just something that got a bit out of control but did nobody any real harm. We were very fortunate the first day that Colm Coyle equalised when he hopped a long kick over the bar. Even the second day we were struggling at one point in the second half. Mayo had their chance to equalise near the end but they didn't take it. Thankfully Brendan Reilly stuck one over and pretty much won it for us.*

In 1990 I won a minor All-Ireland medal, and in 1993 an Under-21 medal, but to win the senior in '96 capped it all off. It was against all the odds that we had done it too. There's not too many lads going around with All-Ireland medals. There was probably a sense that we had stepped out of the shadow of the team of 1987 and '88 too. Up until 1996 we were a good team but we hadn't won anything. We had won the League in '94, but still with part of the old team. Then, 1996 was the first win for our team – Boylan's Babes. I remember going into the dressing room and you couldn't move after beating Mayo. Parents, supporters, everyone that was involved in the team – you name it, they were in there. It was a great feeling. And it's strange, comparing that to five years later. In 2001, after Galway, the dressing-room was silent. Everyone was just looking at each other, wondering what had happened.

COLM BRADY: *By 1996, I almost had myself on the scrap heap. I think I was resigned to it. From a personal point of view, I was suffering too many setbacks and it was actually becoming a health issue for me. My family doctor was Jack Finn, who was the team doctor, and he sat me down and said, 'I know what this knee has been through. As your family doctor, I can't recommend that you continue to play football!' I was spending all of my time over with Ann Bourton. I was being rubbed this way and that way, and all I was experiencing was this intense frustration. Looking back now, I don't think I got to exploit my full potential as a player. I'd say I only got 70 per cent out of it. The potential was there when I was starting to form the partnership with Liam Hayes. How good I felt! How fit and strong, once the first couple of setbacks were experienced! That was being steadily eroded, my confidence was being eroded, it was taking longer to recover, and there were more operations.*

I remember talking to Boylan after having another set back in 1995. I was back on crutches, and I remember explaining to him that from a personal point of view, for all the effort I had been putting in and with getting so little back, I had to call a halt. I mean, I was four or five times a week at physio – on top of training, and trying to hold my job down – and I just felt that from a personal point of view it was weighing too heavily on me. It was affecting too many other areas of my life. Everything in my life was geared around rehabilitation, trying to get right. Everything had been tried. I just felt that that was it, I'd take a break. It's amazing! In '96 I watched Meath playing Carlow in Croke Park with my girlfriend at the time – my wife now – a beautiful, sunny day. It was my first time trying to get used to the idea, officially, that I mightn't play for Meath again, and, 'How does it feel now?' All that sort of thing. And then, after that, I went on holidays with a crowd from

Wexford, namely a bowzy called Sean Collier, who was best man at my wedding, and who is now training the Wexford hurling team. We used to train together in college in Waterford and there would have been loads of articles written at the time about my fitness. People would have remarked on the fact that I was training with a boxer – a kick-boxer! – blowing it up! We went on holidays and we had the greatest craic. I used to give out about these people who went on sun holidays, drinking all night and sleeping all day – said I'd never do it – but that holiday, I did just that. We went to Santa Ponza and had a ball. I got home mouldy, tired and wrecked, and a phone call came from Liam Creavin, that there was a challenge in Pairc Tailteann and Sean wanted me to come in, just to take part in the challenge, make up the numbers. Now, I was in no condition to play. I hadn't trained. I hadn't done anything, and I went in and I was marking Trevor Giles. He was playing centre-forward and I was centre-back, and Boylan asked me after that match to come back in. I remember Giles, when I came back in a few days later, saying, 'Jaysus Brady! I don't remember being that bad on Sunday!' I felt very uncomfortable about returning like that, but I said I would give it a go. The love for playing football was just unreal. The whole thought of not being able to play was just too much to deal with, particularly when, age-wise, you should be able to play. At the time too, I was working for the Leinster GAA Council, so I was immersed in it. I was uncomfortable coming in because I knew how it felt, having done all the winter training previously, and a new fella would arrive in! I remembered that, and that's why I was uncomfortable. I'd always like to be there on merit. I always liked to do all the work, to be there, not to skimp or cut corners. The other side of it was, the team – that younger, newer team – were so uncomplicated. They were an absolute pleasure to be involved with. They were a breath of fresh air. They were so easy to get on with – no baggage, no egos, no anything – and from that point of view, my fears were quickly allayed.

I didn't play one game prior to being introduced in the Tyrone match. It was the one year Sean never played any challenge matches, not even games among ourselves. We never even had a 15 versus 15 scenario, and that was my only fear. We played Tyrone and I was introduced and Jesus, it felt great. Unbelievable! It confirmed how much I had missed the whole thing. I felt good, really strong, because I had done a lot of weight training. So physically, I was in good shape and I felt that I had matured. I was coming in with a different frame of mind too. I hadn't trained, I had gone on this mad piss-up for the week, something that I would never do. Any other time we were training, I would have a ban on myself drinking. I just wouldn't do it. But that week was the best thing ever. I was relaxed. I was enjoying it, and the way I looked at it, whatever happened, happened. To this day, the fact that I got playing in the All-Ireland final was just so rewarding. In some ways, people would say, 'Well, it made up for all the previous hardships.' But no way did it – not even close! That's what I would love to let people know – it never could make up for the frustrations, because there were too many.

We were being beaten. Mayo were on top, and I was told to warm up. I remember standing beside Sean Boylan – he had his hand on my arm, giving me a few quick directions – and Mayo scored a goal. So it was looking pretty gloomy. You were watching this game unfold from the sideline and there were things that you were pulling your hair out about. It looked like very simple things were going wrong, a lot of possession being given away, misdirected passes, rushing on the ball. So, going in that first day I felt I could contribute. When things are going badly, it's good to go in as a substitute because if you can contribute anything at all that starts a comeback. You can be accredited with a lot more than you're due. I remember it was frenetic. Mayo were good that year, very strong, very composed, very methodical about their play. They didn't panic, didn't rush, but there was enough time there to scrape the draw. Colm Coyle was having a stinker that day. A stinker! Every ball he got he dropped, or slipped – just things that happen when you're having a bad day. He was coming out soloing with the ball, slipped and dropped it. Even when McDermott gave him the pass – a simple pass to him – he dropped it. But then he got it, turned around, and just belted it! I'd say he was belting it out of sheer frustration. And it's a well known fact that the ball travelled 300 yards!

Playing on that team was so different to the team of the '80s. There would have been the hard image associated with Meath back then, but one man who didn't fit that image was Liam Hayes. I would feel an intense loyalty to Liam. I do feel he assisted me as much as he could, brought me along. He really did. Brian Stafford would have been another one, and O'Rourke. On the other side there would have been a few who would have been difficult to get on with, who always wanted the ball always put on their chest, or would want the ball a particular way. I remember having a chat with Mattie Kerrigan, who was our Under-21 coach at the time, and Mattie was questioning me as to what was wrong, why was I playing so differently with the senior team. I was bickering all the time, bitching and giving out stink. Midfield seemed to be getting the flak all the time and I was pissed off, fed up with it. Bernie Flynn in particular was on my case, bitching about the ball arriving this way and that way, not arriving on his chest. When things were at their lowest ebb, and you drive in the ball – lucky to have got it at all – there were times I felt that Bernie was running away from his man when he knew he wasn't going to get it, and it made you look worse. As a young player, it wasn't encouraging. He was established. He could get the scores! Kerrigan's advice was, 'The next time that happens, deal with it.' And it happened. It was against Antrim or somebody, and I told Bernie what to do. He could feck off, and he could do this and he could do that, and that ended it. He didn't realise what he was doing.

In the All-Ireland final replay, the direction I was given initially was to stay in, because it was expected that I would come out. If Sean thought people would expect one thing, he'd often do the opposite. He told me to stay in initially but as the match wore on, I ended up coming out, hovering around the middle to add an extra body. I was employed to chase back, hassle, harry, get an extra body behind. The likes of McManamon and those guys were notorious for losing the ball, so the aim was to pick up the breaks and counter. Enda McManus was marking James Horan and he scored three or four points. He had a big influence at that stage, and near the end of that game Sean came on and gave me directions to mark him. So I actually finished up playing centre half back.

One of the funniest things I ever saw happened in the row at the beginning of the game. Paddy Reynolds came in mad to kill, and he tripped and fell, and McHale or somebody came running in, and had to jump over him. Only Paddy fell, it might have turned out a lot differently. I came round the back of that row and from every single photograph that was taken, I can see where I was by the bandage on my knee, but there's nothing that can incriminate me at all. Everybody was coming in so fast that most people missed each other. I could see the referee was trying to focus on something, or somebody, to make a decision for afterwards, and he was looking at the two boys. So I dragged McDermott away because he would have been a huge loss. I didn't get to trim anybody. No.

To win was unreal! At that particular time when the whistle went and *you knew, 'We're champions. We've won this', first of all, all the raw energy dissipates from you. I fell to my knees – Jody Devine was running at me at the time – and as I went down on my knees, he fell on top of me. You go from elation, to exhaustion, to, 'It's all been worth it.' And then you think of the lads, your family. Particularly for me, the family was a big thing. I had just lost my grandparents. My grandmother was a huge source of inspiration to me all through my career, and when you come in off the pitch to meet the family, I remember that was one of the strongest emotions, thinking of the people who weren't there, because they would have been the ones who consoled me when things were bad. They were always there for me – only this time they weren't there to physically see it. You just wish they could have been there for the time you made it.*

The only other time I've experienced such support was on my wedding day – the absolute feeling of goodwill towards you. You're bombarded with it! You can only feel good, you can only feel elated, you can only feel on top of the world. And then you go through a period when you reflect on the whole thing, what it means in the bigger scheme of things. You're still being carried on a wave of excitement. The game is over and then you're back to the hotel, there's a meal, you're getting ready to party that night, then there's the meal with the other team the next day, and before you know it you're on the bus on the way home. So it's all very much scheduled, and you're being carried along on it. You're probably drained actually. You're tired and you're knackered, coming off your high, but the support is just incredible. There's nothing I could say went close to being in a Meath jersey. I felt then that I was flying again, that I'd be going on to play football for another five or six years.

How finely the thing was balanced! Our first game back after the All-Ireland was against Cavan in the League and I was playing wing-back that day. I got a ball and kicked it, and the knee tore again. It wasn't a collision, it wasn't a bang, it wasn't a twist, I just kicked the ball and it went. It was that finely balanced.

I remember the presentation out in my club, in Simonstown, when Sean Boylan came out. I penned a poem, sort of going through the Championship, describing the matches against Carlow, and Dublin, and Tyrone. At the time, you had the whole Martin O'Connell thing, the bandages on the head! There was this 'mad wan', who rang in to the Marian Finucane Show about it – and when I mentioned her in the poem, well, when I read this out in the club and mentioned her, the place went wild. It was Meath versus the world! Think about it. Prior to playing Tyrone, Meath were going to be wiped off the pitch. The articles in the papers were describing Meath as being small and weak compared to previous teams. Tyrone were big and physical, powerful men. And then, after that Tyrone match the nature of the articles suddenly turned on their head. Meath were suddenly this big, ferocious team. But Mark O'Reilly is not big, Donal Curtis is not big, Trevor Giles is by no means the biggest guy in the world. There were only a handful of big men on the team.

Chapter Nine:

1997
1998

The day after Meath had taken possession of the Sam Maguire Cup, Sean Boylan might just have been excused for taking a day off! But as the 1996 All-Ireland champions journeyed home that evening, the most successful team manager in the county's history could not deny himself the opportunity of catching one of his future stars unawares.

NIGEL NESTOR: *I had been on the Meath panel for the O'Byrne Cup campaign in 1995, but not for the Championship. Then, after the All-Ireland final in 1996 there was an incident and, to be honest, I don't know if Sean remembers this or not. The team was in Kepak, in Clonee, celebrating the win on the Monday evening and I was there as a fan. I was shaking hands with all the boys and that sort of thing, and Sean Boylan came up and he said, 'You'll be there next year!' And he said it a few times to me and I just kept shaking his hand and nodding, because I had about eight pints on me at the time! I was standing there in my*

Meath jersey with a few pints on board and little did I know that he was genuine. I was just like a supporter that day and I wasn't thinking about playing. I'm not sure if Sean knew I had a few drinks on me at the time. It sticks in my head and not many people know about it. I'm not even sure if I told my family. Barry Sheridan, Fergal Lynch, Michael Newman and a few mates of mine were around at the time and they always slag me about it. But even then, I didn't know I was on the panel until I got a call from one of the selectors and was asked to come along for a League game against Cork, and that was how it started really.

I had been playing midfield for my club and even when I was brought onto the panel at first I think I was looked on as a midfielder, but I twisted my ankle in a club game five or six weeks before the Championship in 1997. I made it back just in time for the Dublin game, in the first round, and although I had played midfield during the League, they decided to try me out in the backs, and lucky enough it worked out well.

I made my Championship debut against Dublin that day. I remember we stormed into the lead and were in front by a couple of points at half-time. I will never forget walking towards the dressing rooms at half-time feeling great. Here I was, playing on the Meath team that had won the All-Ireland in 1996, and we were beating Dublin in the Championship, and I was thinking to myself, 'Oh yeah, this is grand!' Sean just told us to keep the concentration and keep it going the way we had in the first-half. We were kind of expecting them to come at us in waves, but if we had kept going the way we were they wouldn't have been capable. They did come flying at us, but we still ran out three-point winners. I was marking Paul Clarke that day and he got taken off in the first half. It was a good debut, and it looked good on my part that Paul got substituted. The crowds were able to come onto the field back then and

I remember Dublin got a penalty, with time nearly up. We were ahead by three points, so if they scored it would have been a draw. Paul Bealin took the penalty and it smashed off the crossbar and I caught the ball. The referee blew the final whistle immediately and I put the ball under my shirt so nobody could get their hands on it. I ended up keeping the thing. I still have that ball at home signed by all the lads.

I played in the first of the three games against Kildare. I had an injury, but played on until half-time. I went down on my elbow and put it out of place. So, at the break, I was given an injection but it wasn't good enough. Therefore, I wasn't fit for the replay and Paddy Reynolds took my place. The second game was Jody Devine's match!

We had a bad build-up to the Leinster final against Offaly because Martin O'Connell got injured that morning and Ned Kearney was brought in at the last minute. We had already lost Darren Fay and Mark O'Reilly, so the whole full-back line was brand new. It really didn't suit because at the time their full-forward line was one of the best in the country. We thought we would get back into it in the second half, but it just wouldn't happen for us and the more we tried the worse it got really. I felt gutted walking off the pitch. To be part of the Meath team that had come so far in this Championship, and who were the current All-Ireland champions, and then to lose by so much was hard to take.

The next year, in '98, I played midfield with John McDermott and we destroyed Kildare in the Leinster final. However, we seemed only to get to a certain point up front and couldn't get any further. It was frustrating because we just couldn't score. They really packed their defence. We didn't look like winners, but it still didn't feel like we were going to lose. Then they got that late goal from Brian Murphy. After the games in 1997 it was sweet revenge for them.

Nigel Nestor was, indeed, the future of the Meath team. Sean Boylan was among the first of the country's football managers to realise that the game was changing, and that footballers who doubled as athletes, and athletes who doubled as footballers, would form a substantial part of the Meath team which would see out the decade and enter a new millennium. Against Tyrone, in the 1996 All-Ireland semi-final, Meath had shown that they could run one of the fittest and most ambitious football teams in the entire country off its feet! The old game was continuing to change at a furious pace, and Nigel Nestor may not have known it at the time as he continued drinking that night in 1996 after Sean Boylan's short, private promise, but he was made to measure for the team's future needs. Nestor would play in defence, midfield, and in the forwards over the next couple of years, though against Dublin on 15 June 1997, he was chosen at right half-back. It was a day for the reigning Leinster and All-Ireland champs to prove that there was nothing lucky about their win 12 months earlier. It was also a day for every young man on the Meath team to prove that he had, beyond any remaining doubt, left his boyhood far behind him. Dublin, still, had most of the faces from the team which had claimed the 1995 All-Ireland title. They were out for revenge. Many of their household names were also singly intent upon showing that they had the kick of a ball still left in them!

It was relatively easy for Meath in the end. Too many of the Dublin footballers who had given their all against Meath throughout the '90s were all out of gas! Nevertheless, as the game entered injury time, Darren Fay was whistled up for a dangerous block on Mick Galvin in front of the Meath goal, and Paul Bealin had the opportunity of leaving the scoreline 1-13 each. His shot rebounded off the under side of the crossbar. Meath's luck was definitely in but, in truth, they had proven beyond doubt over the previous 70 minutes that their 1996 Leinster final victory was the genuine article. Of the six Dublin forwards who started the game, only Jim Galvin managed to get his name on the scoresheet. The Meath defence was that good, the Meath midfield that dominant. Dublin had raced into a 0-3 to 0-1 lead after ten minutes but, suddenly, the young champs stirred themselves and completely dominated the next 24 minutes of the game, scoring 1-9 in reply to one sad point from their opponents. McDermott and McGuinness, from the middle of the field, had each kicked a point apiece to start the ball rolling towards the Dublin goalmouth. When Ollie Murphy palmed the ball past John O'Leary shortly before half-time, the game was effectively over, and a rout was on! A humiliation did not follow, however, for Mickey Whelan's team. Instead, it was simply a good sound beating, despite Keith Barr's sensational goal for Dublin in the second half, and Bealin's almost inch-perfect penalty kick. Donal Curtis was on the opposite side of the Meath half-back line to Nestor that afternoon, with Enda McManus between them in the No. 6 shirt.

DONAL CURTIS: *I knew Sean before I joined up with Meath because he was involved with Rathkenny when we won a Junior championship. I was still a bit in awe of him – I was listening to his every word. He was great. He let myself and the new lads do our own thing to a certain extent, and if he needed to pull any of us up on things then he'd have no problem doing that either. The whole homecoming celebration in '96 was a great occasion. In '87 and '88 I would have been one of the people on the Fair Green in Navan cheering Sean and the lads back. Now it was* me and the current players people were coming to see. My first start in the Championship was against Dublin in '97, the day they missed the penalty with the last kick of the game and, thankfully, we pulled through. We played very well but let them into it in the second half when we should have been closing up on them.

We got a lot of criticism in 1997, however, after the loss to Offaly in the Leinster final. Yet we had guys playing in positions that they hadn't played before – Ned Kearney, for example, who made his first start in the full-back line because of all the suspensions we had from the last of the Kildare games. That needed to be taken into consideration, but I don't think it really was. I was the one who missed the block at the end against Offaly that year. I could feel the ball going in under my body. I still think we could have had them that day, but they showed an awful lot of resolve, to be fair, and kept going right til the end.

In 1998, after Kildare beat us, I thought that they could go on and win the All-Ireland. I was in Canada watching the final that year and I really couldn't believe that Galway only got going in the second half. They allowed Kildare to play their own game far too much in the first half.

DARREN FAY: After the 1996 All-Ireland final replay against Mayo a lot of us were suspended because of the row. We didn't have any winter training and the League was starting in October of that year. Becasue of the suspension I didn't start back until early in 1997. I wasn't fit at all going into the Championship. I had trained up to that but I had put on a bit of weight too and I wasn't feeling great at all. I think a lot of us went into 1997 a bit naive. Too many of us were remembering the great times of '96, but we weren't thinking exactly what it was we were doing that got us that far in the first place. You have to enjoy yourself over the *winter because if you bogged yourself down in football for 12 months you'd be worn down in three or four years. You have to enjoy yourself, but you also have to know when to get back down to serious business too. I think that in '97, from a personal point of view, I didn't realise how hard I had trained to get an All-Ireland medal the previous year – subconsciously, of course. I learnt very quickly after that. The Dubs in 1997 was a great match. When I look back at that game, we hit points over from the sideline, and every sort of thing was going over for us. We were more than a bit lucky. Everything went right for us. Paul Bealin missed a penalty chance right at the end of that game, but from our point of view everything went right. We were quite fortunate and there was a lot of luck involved. We weren't ready for Kildare in the next round at all. I don't think we had given them enough respect. We drew with them in the first game. Niall Buckley was on fire that year. And then, by the time we reached the Leinster final, the whole full-back line was in the stand for the Offaly game. Martin got injured and I was suspended after being sent off in the second Kildare game. They totally overran us, and that was the end of that.*

MARK O'REILLY: *We played the Dubs in the first round and, in comparison to 1996, we overran them, but they came back at us with a rush of scores. That did worry us a bit. It was another of those games where the atmosphere was just electric. I'll always remember Tommy Dowd in 1997 giving the Dublin fans a 'salute', if you know what I mean, after he scored a point. It didn't go down too well, I can tell you! I think they were calling Tommy some sort of a rude name, which I wouldn't like to repeat here, and he decided to seek retribution himself. We all had a good laugh. I'll never forget that. It's funny when you're on the pitch how you tend to hear voices and everything that is said to you*

Darren Fay, June 23, 2002

Trevor Giles, June 23, 2002

– good and bad. You don't have time to react even if sometimes you would like to. Sean always tells us to keep focused and concentrate. The games against Kildare were exhausting. We just about got through them in the end. But being beaten by Offaly in the Leinster final after all that work was a real sickener. Myself and Darren Fay were missing that day because we had been sent off in the final Kildare game. It would be different nowadays because we had both got two yellow cards which, back then, meant you were suspended for the next game. It was a real sickener to be standing there watching a game that I should have been playing in. Looking back at the yellow cards it was a very wet day against Kildare on the third day, and if you don't time your tackles correctly then you're always liable to see red from the referee. At the time you never agree with being sent off, but you just have to accept it and get on with it.

The game against Kildare in 1998 was a game we could have won. We ended up trying to stick with them. Trevor Giles got injured with about 10 or 15 minutes to go, and he was a massive loss to us. Kildare, in fairness to them, didn't miss much that day. We coped well with them in the backs but it was mainly from frees and such that they had the beating of us. It was close enough right until the end, when Brian Murphy got the goal that did the damage. He was the difference, I suppose.

It took Meath from 6 July to 3 August to get Kildare out of their way, but the team did pay a heavy price at the end of that month-long Leinster semi-final. It was 0-12 to 1-9 at the end of the first of the three games it took to decide who would advance to meet Offaly in the decider, and Niall Buckley just failed to end the contest there and then when, with the last kick of the game, his '45' landed just beneath the Meath crossbar where it was fielded and cleared by John McDermott. Kildare had also got off to a flying start, when full-forward Martin Lynch blasted to the Meath net in less than 60 seconds! No doubt about it, the defending champions played well within themselves, and a fortnight later they found that Kildare's confidence had soared. Again Meath looked in trouble on several occasions and it took the ultimate coolness of the 1996 'Footballer of the Year', Trevor Giles, to haul the team out of what was becoming a fair-sized hole! Even with Giles close to his very best – he scored from a penalty kick, and missed a penalty kick – and totting up a total of two goals and eight points, Meath were six points behind the Lilywhites when the first period of extra time finished. Substitute Jody Devine made one of the greatest individual entrances in Croke Park by kicking four beautiful points, as Meath rattled off seven scores on the trot and, in the end, Kildare needed one of their own substitutes to save the day for them – Paul McCormack punched the ball over the bar for the levelling score, making it Meath 2-20 and Kildare 3-17. Kildare had led 1-7 to 0-7 at half-time thanks to a Tom Harris goal on 21 minutes, but points from Tommy Dowd, Brendan Reilly and Giles brought Meath right back into it early in the second period. For those who thought that the tension and trauma of Dublin and Meath in '91 could never be repeated, it was time to get down to some serious 'pinching' right through the second 35 minutes. Brian Murphy scored Kildare's second goal, Giles blasted home his first penalty, Graham Geraghty got his marching orders for a foul on Glen Ryan, Kildare led by three as the final minutes raced by and, still, the game was only getting interesting! A foul on Dowd left Giles with a second penalty kick, but his effort was well saved by Christy Byrne. From the resulting clearance and sideline ball lobbed in by Ollie Murphy, Giles was first to the flick and directed the ball into the net to give his earlier disappointment an extremely short shelf-life. Kildare proceeded to score 1-3 without reply in the first period of extra time, but Jody Devine, in the most spectacular fashion imaginable, then rode into town!

Devine didn't earn a place on the starting 15 for the second replay, back in Croker a week later, however. Giles was much quieter in the third game, also, and only managed two points for himself. But Ollie Murphy grabbed his opportunity and became a match-winner, as all hell broke out around him – Longford referee Pat O'Toole sent four players to the line, and put six other names in his little book. Meath, third time of asking, dominated the game right from the start and their opponents suffered the most devastating blow imaginable when their brilliant full-back Davy Dalton was red-carded after only 16 minutes after an awkward challenge on Brendan Reilly. Seven minutes later, Murphy kicked his third point of the afternoon and Meath were 0-7 to 0-1 in front. It was 0-9 to 0-5 in favour of the champions at half-time, but by then Mark O'Reilly and Brian Murphy had also been dismissed from the field for second bookable offences. On the restart Eddie McCormack blasted a penalty kick over the bar, after Padraig Graven had been fouled, and with that high shot Kildare's hope of claiming their most famous victory under Mick O'Dwyer's guidance was at an end. Meath's hope of marching into the Leinster final in confident mood was also upended by the final whistle, when Darren Fay joined O'Reilly in the dug-out after getting into a mix-up with Lynch off the ball. It was 1-12 to 1-10 at the end, but Meath's gutsy defence of their Leinster and All-Ireland titles was also just about over. A fortnight later, a jaded, under-strength

Meath failed by eight points to Tommy Lyons's fired-up Offaly, 3-17 to 1-15, with Vinny Claffey, Roy Malone and Peter Brady taking absolute advantage of a makeshift full-back line. The Offaly trio scored three goals and eight points between them. At the other end, Brendan Reilly found it was his turn to be Meath's scoring hero, shooting seven points, one more than the combined total of a relatively subdued pairing of Giles and Murphy. The Carnaross player had not quite settled himself firmly into Sean Boylan's plans at this time, and the Meath boss was making Murphy serve a long apprenticeship before giving him the nod, at the very end of the decade, to display his uncanny instinct for vital scores

OLLIE MURPHY: *I had come on for the last minute or so of the 1996 All-Ireland final. It was great to be part of the panel at the time, and it felt brilliant to be champions. The next year, in the third game against Kildare, I remember scoring our goal shortly after Darren Fay had been sent off. The ball just came down and I turned, ran towards the goals, and shot. Thankfully, it hit the back of the net. But I was dropped for 1998. I suppose I just wasn't playing well. Ray 'Smoothie' Magee and Stephen Dillon had come in and were doing well, so I was dropped. I came on as a sub in the second half against Kildare in the Leinster final, and I think John Finn was marking me, but unfortunately they got the goal towards the end and won.*

GRAHAM GERAGHTY: *The three in a row with Kildare was the lasting memory of 1997. I was sent off in one of those games and we had a few lads missing for the Offaly match. We just couldn't settle on the day against Offaly, but I think that whenever we went out in '97 and in '98, whether it was bad luck, suspension or injuries, we never seemed to* *have our best 15 ready to play. I think if we had had 15 lads going out each day, who were fit and in form, then we'd expect to have done a bit better. It was hard in those years, and there were lads getting fed up. At the start of 1999 we had a meeting and we all sat down and said where we wanted to go and what we wanted to do to achieve it. Our main objective in 1999 was to win a Leinster Championship. That meeting was kind of a one-off – it didn't really happen any other year. But we meant what came out of it and Sean got the ball rolling early on that year with a few challenge matches. We played a lot of games that year and it stood to us.*

The first round of the 1998 Leinster Championship proved that Meath, undoubtedly, were the top team in Leinster the previous season. With Fay and O'Reilly back in the full-back line, and with the team fresh and healthy, Offaly were polished off at Croke Park. Revenge was as sweet as could be! Meath had exactly one dozen points to spare over the team which had ko'd them in the previous year's provincial final, and this time around the famed full-forward line from the Faithful County managed just one point, from Roy Malone, against Fay and Co. Barry Callaghan, in the No. 6 shirt for the first time, was rarely stretched, and Nigel Nestor at last got to show off his athletic abilities in full by teaming up with John McDermott in the middle of the field. All three of the Meath goals were created by Graham Geraghty in the second half, the first being slotted home by Raymond Magee, Stephen Dillon beat Padraig Kelly for the second, and new team captain Brendan Reilly scored the third before retiring injured. But if Sean Boylan indeed had the best team in Leinster, it sure didn't look like the label was all that tightly secured on the final Sunday in June when Louth pushed their neighbours all the way before losing by the slimmest of margins, 0-15 to 1-11, in the Leinster semi-final. Gerry Curran scored the opening point of the game after just 18 seconds, and Louth relaxed into a fluid and lively brand of football which was a delight to watch, and which really was worthy of a draw. A controversial point from Geraghty, 10 minutes into the second period denied the Wee County a replay – the umpire signalled the kick wide, but Wexford referee Brian White overruled his official. A superb Stefan White goal had Louth ahead by double scores, 1-5 to 0-4, at half-time and Aaron Hoey stretched that advantage within 60 seconds of the restart. Three points in a two-minute mini-blitz by Tommy Dowd signalled the 'Royal' recovery and a fifth point from the same player eight minutes from the end should have been enough to see off Paddy Clarke's spirited boys in red. His team never stopped believing in itself, however, and White and Colin Kelly left one point between the teams. At the final whistle, Meath were victorious and exhausted, and the sight of the injured Reilly bringing his tired team back to the dressing room should have sounded alarm bells throughout the county.

Meath had some unfinished business to see to against Offaly in the first round of the Championship, and Kildare were on the exact same mission in the Leinster final. Mick O'Dwyer was about to experience one of the most rewarding days of his long and brilliant career, and eight years after first giving Kildare the benefit of his unchallenged wisdom there was going to be a decent chunk of silverware on the table by the end of the summer. Micko's 27-year old son Karl kicked two points in a fully merited 1-12 to 0-10 win over a 14 man Meath team. Captain Brendan Reilly was sent off after 50 minutes, and six minutes later Trevor Giles joined him on the sideline after suffering a horrific knee injury. After landing badly, Giles played on for 13 minutes, but being a physiotherapist he had a good idea that he was in some serious trouble and, eventually, he took himself out of the action.

TREVOR GILES: *The three games in 1997 were probably the making of Kildare. Before that they were being ridiculed by people about not being able to battle, about throwing in the towel. The following year they came back and beat us in the Leinster final and were favourites going into the All-Ireland. So I think it helped to make them as a team. They're great things to win. The second game was super. There were a few American friends of my father's over and they just couldn't believe the game. It was a great victory. For the Leinster final that year we had only 18 players. We had only three players on the bench, which is amazing. Graham was suspended, Mark and Darren were suspended, Martin O'Connell woke up the morning of the game and couldn't play with a back injury. Jody was after kicking four points, prior to that against Kildare, and he was only a substitute! Evan Kelly was also on the bench, and Cormac Sullivan was the other one. He was the sub-goalie but he had an outfield No. 16 jersey on him in case he had to actually come on in midfield or full-forward. It's quite funny looking back on it. There was only a week or two between the last Kildare game and the Leinster final. We hadn't time to get anyone else in to fill the gap.*

Against Kildare in '98, I just jumped, maybe jumped a bit too high, came down off balance and the leg just snapped underneath me. It was very sore for a few minutes, but once I put some ice on it and moved it a little bit it actually didn't feel too bad. So I sort of hobbled about. I tried to go for a couple of balls then, and it just gave way from under me. Funnily enough, the ball just came to me at one stage. Somebody came at me then and I just hand-passed it away. If everybody had left me alone I wouldn't have been able to go anywhere. At that stage Ollie Murphy was on the subs bench. I was thinking, 'Jaysus, Ollie would be far more dangerous than me in my present state so I'd better get myself off the field here.' I went over to the sideline and told them I was struggling. I'd say Sean was giving me a chance to see if I could run it off. It's very hard to diagnose these things and it just looked like a bang on the knee.

I wasn't too impressed with the referee John Bannon though. I knew I was in trouble but he was going, 'C'mon, get up and get on with it.' He was under pressure to keep the game going and he didn't want a big stoppage for a few minutes and the crowd maybe getting on his back. I was saying, 'Give me a minute.' Right away, I thought it was the cruciate! From that point of view I knew I was in trouble. I thought my career could have been over even then, and I didn't appreciate his lack of sympathy. When the thing snaps, that is when most of the pain is. When the thing completely tears, there isn't that much pain because, basically, there's nothing there. Once the initial five minutes passed, it wasn't that bad. The physio Ann Bourton put a heavy strapping on it, iced it, and I was back on. I went with the lads to Bob O'Malley's pub after the match, to have a few drinks. I think I was on crutches. It was a Bank Holiday weekend. I was on to Pat O'Neill, the former Dublin manager, and in fairness to him he agreed to see me the following morning. I went up to him about 11 o'clock and he diagnosed it.

Looking back on it, it was plain sailing. I got the operation done pretty quickly and I had a fair idea of the rehabilitation process. I got back playing after six or seven months but I'd say it took a full year before it felt like a proper knee. But that's just time and natural healing. Certainly, there were times, three or four months afterwards, where you'd wonder would it ever be right. There is a lot of worry until you actually play a match, and get a few balls, get a few bangs! You go to an inter-county match and wonder have you lost a couple of yards speed or would the free-taking put extra pressure on it. You have all that worry until you play again.

ENDA McMANUS: *I was playing wing-back in that Leinster final, marking Dermot Earley, and I had kept him relatively quiet. Apart from two or three kicks of the ball he got, I thought I had played pretty well. However, Colm O'Rourke gave him 'Man of the Match' afterwards on RTE and I was like, 'Oh no, Colm!' It is not an award you want the player you are marking to receive. I couldn't believe the way we lost, because we were far better a them on the day, but what happened in the last five minutes was unreal. Brian Murphy scored a late goal and we were out of the Championship. Anyway, after the final whistle I shook hands with some of the Kildare players and then walked over towards the empty dug-out and just sat down. Obviously we had to stay out on the pitch as the Kildare team collected their silverware, so I looked on from the dug-out. I sat there alone for a while and then my girlfriend, who was in the Cusack Stand behind the dug-outs, came in and sat beside me to offer a bit of consolation. The two of us just sat there while the Kildare team celebrated. It was tough and I'm not really sure why I headed for the dug-out in the first place, but I just needed to sit down. A photograph of me and my girlfriend, now my wife, sitting there appeared in the newspapers later that week. It was a strange place to be at the end of a game.*

DARREN FAY: *Louth should have beaten us in the Leinster semi-final in Croke Park in '98. It was just as well they didn't, because it would have* *been a massive loss for us. Tommy Dowd put in a 'Man of the Match' performance for us and it's just as well too because we'd never have heard the end of that one if they'd beaten us. Kildare finally beat us in 1998, and fair play to them. They went on to play Galway in the All-Ireland final and I thought they had a class team. We were going through a tough period then. It took us from '96 to '99 to get the hunger back, and to realise the hard work we needed to put in to get anywhere close again.*

BARRY CALLAGHAN: *The injury I picked up towards the end of 1996 stayed with me and I didn't play in the '97 championship. I played a small bit of club football but that was it, because the hamstring and my back were both at me. No matter what I did, it wouldn't heal. Sean did a bit of treatment with me but not that much. Eventually, I just stopped getting it treated because it wasn't getting any better. That was a disappointing year because a lot of the lads were injured. Maybe if we had all been fit we might have gone further. I played centre-back the next year in the Championship. The selectors had tried me out in that position in a challenge match and I did OK so that's where I started in the championship. I don't know who made the decision to play me there initially, but it was probably Sean's suggestion. Generally, you wouldn't be telling him where you wanted to play because you'd just be happy enough to get a jersey.*
I was on Declan Kerrigan in the Leinster final and he was hard to mark. He was a good footballer. Himself and Keith Barr were two of the best opponents I played against – sometimes you don't actually realise how good some players are until you mark them. We had just drawn level with a couple of minutes left when the ball came downfield. I remember Darren Fay and Donal Curtis going for the one ball and leaving a space in the centre. Martin Lynch won the ball and he put it across into the

Tommy Dowd, September 29, 1996

Nigel Nestor, June 15, 1997

centre. Murphy was free, with only the goalkeeper to beat, and he scored a killer goal. A lot of things went wrong that day, with Trevor getting injured and Brendan Reilly getting sent off. That really was a disappointing day because we thought we would beat Kildare.

Cormac Sullivan had been sitting in the Meath dug-out, watching Sean Boylan at work, waiting his turn, and agonising as much as anyone else at the great effort expended, and the missed opportunities, in 1997 and '98. His day was about to come. And, remarkably, within a year, the big keeper would be viewed as the best in the land. Indeed, he would officially become Ireland's No. 1 when he toured Australia with Colm O'Rourke's International Compromise Rules team.

CORMAC SULLIVAN: *I remember being on holiday in Lanzarote in 1996, after the All-Ireland final, with the Meath panel. Colm Coyle and Colm Brady sat down either side of me in a pub one night and they chewed the arse off me about my intentions for the Meath team. It was like you were courting a girl and the father was giving you a right going over before you brought her out on a first date! They wanted to see if I was just there for the glamour of it, I suppose. They laid down the gauntlet to me to prove myself and I said to myself, 'That's it, I'll show them!' There's always a lot of lads coming and going from the team, and I suppose they wanted to see if I had the staying power. It was a test to see what I was made of. In hindsight, it was probably good that two older lads sat me down and told me what's what. This was a bit different though, in that they just ridiculed me for over an hour. But it showed the huge pride they had in the team, that they weren't prepared to hand over the reins without knowing it was in good hands, so to speak. You earn* that right, when you're a Meath player for so long, to tell a lad what's what if needs be.

My first memories of the Meath team were from the 1986 All-Ireland semi-final against Kerry. The lasting memory I have from that match is Joe Cassells, Mick Lyons and Mickey McQuillan running into each other, and Ger Power having an open goal. Mickey McQuillan was in goal and, because he was from the same club as me, I felt particularly sorry for him. It was a terrible thing to happen to a goalkeeper, and I'm very fortunate that nothing like that has happened to me because it can easily happen. That was a very good Kerry team and Meath put up a reasonable performance. I don't know if anyone expected Meath to actually win, but they gave themselves a good chance. It was an up and coming Meath team and Kerry were really coming to an end at that stage. There was great hype around the area and, of course, the team went on to win the next two All-Irelands. For any young fella like myself, that was a great introduction to football, to grow up and watch what was happening in the game around us. But the moment I really began to support Meath big time was in 1991. It was hard to pick a favourite player but, that year, I got Bobby O'Malley's jersey off him. It was one he had worn years earlier, but he gave it to me. After that, he was probably the one I always remembered and had a special inkling for. Even though Mickey McQuillan was from my own club, I wouldn't say that I dreamed of being a goalkeeper like him. I wasn't that interested in playing in goal at that stage. I wouldn't have been studying him or anything, but he was a great servant to Meath football. I actually play midfield for my club at the moment. From a midfielder's point of view I would say that the Hayes-McEntee pairing at that time was the best Meath have had under Sean Boylan. I don't think there are many pairings that could surpass them. John McDermott is the only one that has consistently played to the level that they did. In many ways, John was a lot like Liam Hayes in that he was great at fielding a ball, carrying it and taking his score. When I came in to the dressing room, a lot of the older players in the team were just coming to the end of their careers. Colm O'Rourke had just left the scene at the time and there were a lot of fresh faces coming in. I first came in for the '96 League and played in a few League and challenge matches. It was great experience and there were still a few older players there to guide us through – Tommy Dowd and Martin O'Connell had both been around for a while. I was sitting on my arse for the whole of the Championship though. I was No. 25, the third choice goalkeeper behind Ronan Finnegan and Conor Martin, who was in goal. I didn't feel any pressure at all because really I knew it was a long shot that I'd be playing. I was able to enjoy the whole buzz of it all, however, which is difficult when you know you'll be playing.

I would have been there at the games as a fan anyway. It was a long time since Meath got so far – eight years in fact, so I was a fan as well as being a player. It was a pretty young team that was there in '96. Sean told us at the time that although we were young the chance might never come again. He told us not to be waiting for the chance to play in another All-Ireland because we were already in one and it may be our last. It was good advice, but for a player who was outside the starting team it was a bit worrying for a while. You know, I started to believe that the chance might never come again. Thankfully that wasn't the case.

Finally, 1999, was my first championship year and I was ready because I'd been sitting around for long enough beforehand waiting for my chance. The highlight of it was beating Dublin in the Leinster final. The intensity of it was something you don't grasp as a fan. I had been there for Leinster finals before, but standing in front of a packed Hill 16 as a *player is something else altogether. If I remember rightly, it was a roasting hot day as well, which made it tough. We did well to beat them. You just try to block out the people but obviously it's more difficult for a keeper to do that standing right in front of the crowd. Sometimes you get lads roaring abuse at you but you have to just ignore it for 10 or 15 minutes, and they'll usually stop, or direct it at someone else! I remember going back to collect my cap after the game that year and a pound coin landed beside me in the goals. A fan threw it and it just missed me. I realised there was nothing I could do about it so I just picked it up, kissed it and took it away with me. That's my lucky coin now. I still have it in my house.*

Chapter Ten:

1999

Hank Traynor started his first full Championship game for Meath on the day of the 1998 Leinster final. It was a bad day to officially begin life as a Meath footballer. For Hank Traynor, that day was also the start of a time in his life which would include previously unimagined highs, and lows which could easily have forced a lesser man, or a man with fewer true friends, to walk away from the Meath dressing room for a long, long time. He had come into the Meath squad during the winter of 1997, reluctantly. He had been invited into training two years earlier by the Meath selector, Eamonn O'Brien, but Hank wasn't having any of it. He said, 'No.'

HANK TRAYNOR: *I had been approached and asked to join up with the panel. At the time I was working in Navan in the Home Décor store and Eamonn had called in a couple of times. He wanted to know if I would come along and, to be honest, I said no because I was more interested in having a good time and going out for a few pints with my friends. But, I was probably a little bit scared also of going into a* dressing room with a lot of big names present – Tommy Dowd, John McDermott – and all these guys were still on the team and I was a little anxious at first. I didn't really know how to react but, thankfully, they kept at me and persevered until I said yes. The first time I entered the dressing room, I just looked for a fella that was maybe looking back at me and smiling or something. When I walked in I'm sure most of the lads were thinking, 'Who on earth is this guy?' I just headed for a clear space. Who I ended up sitting beside, I'm not really sure – it's all a haze because I was petrified, but the lads and Sean were great and helped me feel at home.

I got my first Championship start in the Leinster semi-final against Louth in 1998. I came on at half-time and scored a point. I was absolutely delighted to get a score on my debut. It was a tight game and we only won by a single point. The Leinster final in 1998 was tough because they got a late goal. I started wing-back that day, but it was disappointing. Everybody was down after the game. Nobody really talked in the dressing room. We just sat there.

I remember before the Championship in 1999, I was keen on going to America to spend a couple of months, or a year maybe, over there. I wanted to have a bit of craic and maybe even play a bit of football. I hadn't really told a lot of people, but somehow Sean got word about it and one night before a training session in February or March he called me out of the dressing room we were all changing in and brought me into the empty one next door. He just asked me to come in for a second and then he started telling me he had heard I might be going to America. He told me he didn't want me to go but wouldn't stop me either. The way he was talking to me it sounded like he wanted me to stick it out and not throw all the hard work away. 'Just do what is best. Do what you think is the right thing', he said. That chat with Sean persuaded me not to go *and, lucky enough, I didn't because we went on to win the All-Ireland. I scored a point in the Leinster final, when we beat Dublin earlier that year. Ollie gave me a great pass, and I collected it and put it over the bar – it was a handy enough score. Ollie had a great game that day. He scored a great goal. We walked out easy winners. Armagh were fancied to beat us in the All-Ireland semi-final, but we played well and came out on top. I didn't have a great day, though. I remember I was marking Diarmuid Marsden for a while and he was giving me the run-around a little bit and actually got a goal off me. It came about 15 minutes in when a ball was played in from under the Cusack Stand side of the pitch. I was following Marsden, but he got away and collected the ball. He was running in towards the goal with Cormac 'Spud' Murphy in front of him. I was chasing after him but, suddenly, he just let fly with a thunderbolt shot, which left Cormac Sullivan with no chance. It ended up in the bottom corner of the net. I remember as he hit it, Cormac Murphy jumped like a goalkeeper to try and stop the ball, but Marsden's shot was too powerful. It was the first goal we had conceded during the Championship. And it was my man! When we went in at half-time we regrouped and Sean made a few changes. Spud Murphy went to mark Marsden and I took his man. To be honest, I was grateful. Spud shut up Marsden then and kept him relatively quiet, and I settled down a bit and we ran out winners.*

It was my first All-Ireland final. It was scary in the dressing room beforehand. Even the build-up in the weeks prior were tough because you had the media ringing you up and everybody around the county wishing you the best and wanting to know how the team were preparing. The one thing that sticks out in my mind is that you become almost tutored in dealing with the media. In the weeks before the final I was saying the same things over and over again. 'Cork are a good team and it is going to be really tough, and they have a lot of good players', and so on and so on. We listened to Sean too. He is brilliant with the media and we all tried to say the sensible thing without blurting too much information out.

Anyway, on the day of the game I ran out on the pitch and it was a daunting atmosphere, but I was thrilled I was part of it all. I was marking Micheal Cronin and I didn't give him a thing all afternoon. I got booked midway through the first half for a late shoulder on him. He hand-passed the ball forward but my momentum carried me on and we collided. But, apart from that, I played well. Barry Callaghan came on for me with about ten minutes left and I watched the clock wind down to the final whistle. Trevor Giles gave a brilliant ball in for our goal. He was under the Hogan Stand around midfield and launched a huge pass towards the Cork goal. It reached the small square and Graham Geraghty slapped it down to Ollie Murphy, who just slotted it past the goalkeeper. The dressing-room afterwards was just mayhem. Everybody was delirious and there was hugging and kissing and jumping around behind that door.

I was injured for our first defence of Sam, against Offaly in the first round, and I didn't even tog out. My ankle was at me, so I watched the game from the Cusack Stand. We were bad. Offaly deserved the win. All in all, 2000 was a very bad year because my girlfriend, Lorraine was very sick with cancer at the time. She was in the Cusack Stand sitting behind me. She died shortly after that game. That day the game didn't bother me too much – sometimes football has to be put into perspective. I was annoyed that we had lost, but I had a lot more important things on my mind. Sean was very supportive when Lorraine died. He was very good to me and he would phone up to see if I was OK. I guess he kind of nursed me when I needed it most. The day of the funeral I got up and *said a few words in the church but, I kind of broke down as I was up there, and I was getting very emotional. So I just came down and sat on my seat and I remember Sean coming over to me. He was sitting on the far side of the Church and he just came over, sat beside me and put his arm around me. Sean is a good guy, a real good guy.*

Nigel Crawford was handed a Meath Championship jersey for the first time on 6 June 1999. The tall, 19-year old from Sean Boylan's own neck of the woods in Dunboyne was thrown in against Wicklow's giant pairing of Darren Coffey and Fergus Daly in the first round of the Leinster Championship. He had no John McDermott with him, as the Skryneman went down the day before the game with a bout of flu.

NIGEL CRAWFORD: *Sean approached me when I was just out of the minors, and I played a couple of challenge games, but I wasn't brought in on the panel. He had helped me out with my game in my earlier years and advised me on how I could improve. If he sees something which you can improve on in your game, he will tell you, but will not force you to go out and do it. He will leave it up to you.*

I am, generally, not too nervous before a football game and that helps, because Sean doesn't let the whole occasion get to the players either. He doesn't shelter you away from it, but he doesn't let you get caught up in any needless hype. That's the way it was before the Wicklow game that year, and it was the same way before the All-Ireland final. Enda McManus, who plays with my club in Dunboyne, missed the coach to the game that morning. I don't think any of the players were aware of it on the journey to Croke Park. I certainly didn't have a clue! Everybody was just so focused and concentrating on their own thing that they were not worried about anybody else. I really didn't realise what had happened at all until shortly before the throw-in, when I saw him coming in through the door. It was funny, though.

It was a wet day. A Joe Kavanagh goal put Cork ahead for the first time in the game, and I also remember Trevor missing the penalty. It was a great finish by Kavanagh. He started the move going and played a one-two, which put him through on goal, but he was still a good bit out. I dived in front of him to block the ball but he just blasted it into the net. At the very end I remember looking up at the clock and we were three points ahead. I was thinking, yes, we were going to win the All-Ireland! A lot of managers, I think, have one face for the media, another face for the players, another face for the family, and so on – in other words, a different face for different people – but with Sean what you see is what you get! I have had a huge amount of people come up to me and ask, 'What is Sean like? He seems like a really nice man.' I just tell them that he is a nice man and that none of his smiles are fake. That is the way he is, very genuine. The way he treats and respects all the players sets him apart. He picks out lads that other people wouldn't bother with, and makes a footballer out of fellas whether they want to be one or not.

Richie Kealy did not start any game for Meath in 1999. Like Hank Traynor, he was someone who was getting a call from Sean Boylan a little bit 'late' in his football life. Four times that summer, including the All-Ireland final, Boylan sent Kealy into the action. And, just like Traynor and Crawford, Kealy found that the Meath manager fully believed that he would succeed as an important addition in Meath's All-Ireland winning season.

RICHIE KEALY: *In 1996 I would have been playing with a lot of the*

Meath Under-21 lads, who were breaking onto the senior team that year. The All-Ireland win really was a big surprise because the same Under-21 lads formed the backbone of the team. It was progression beyond, I suppose, most people's wildest dreams. People wondered would Meath be happy with their Leinster win in '96, and if they'd maybe done enough to satisfy themselves. But they destroyed Tyrone in the All-Ireland semi-final. I was at most of the games that year, and that one too. The atmosphere in the Tyrone game was something else. Tyrone were coming up to win an All-Ireland, and they had the majority of the fans at Croke Park. I think they thought that these young Meath lads weren't going to stand in their way. Brenny Reilly's winning point was a brilliant one against Mayo in the (All-Ireland final) replay. It was a huge point for him, and everyone! It just showed the type of player he was, and the character of the man.

I would have been in knocking around the panel the next year. In 1997, before the Leinster final against Offaly, myself and Dermot, my brother, were brought in a week before the game. We had a trial on the Tuesday and the Thursday, but we didn't make it. I came in for the League in 1998 but, again, I didn't make the Championship. There's a world of difference between the League and the Championship! The build-up is totally different. In 1999 I made my Championship debut at last, and it was a great year. We went into every game mentally and physically in brilliant shape. There was no game where it looked like we'd be beaten. We were under a bit of pressure in the Armagh game, the All-Ireland semi-final, when they scored two first-half goals. But when we came under a bit of pressure we responded very well and went about our task very professionally. After '96, there had been a lot of talk that Meath were a dirty team. I was sick of listening to it, to be honest. The win in 1999 got rid of that 'dirty' tag because we won every game fair and square, and there could be no more of that talk.

Beating Dublin in the 1999 Leinster final was the highlight of my career. I came off the bench in the final early enough in the game. To be honest, I was surprised that I came on. Enda McManus got injured after about a quarter of an hour and I got the call. You'd be nervous, of course, but I was ready for it and it was great to go on so early in the game. It was my first year and my first Leinster title. There were a lot of top players on the bench that day, and I still got in there! I was put in at corner-forward. I just kept thinking to myself I was on for three-quarters of a Leinster final that Meath were going to win!

Talk about a turn-around in 2000. It was so disappointing. In my first full start for Meath, against Offaly, we were beaten. I was playing at wing-back. It was some change-around from the previous year. The preparation coming into the game just wasn't right that year. We were in the National League final against Derry just weeks previously and it went to a replay. A lot of players were coming into the Offaly game in the wrong frame of mind and probably a bit tired. If there had been a back-door system in operation that year it would have given us a great wake-up call. What can you say about Sean? He's given 20 years of service to Meath, and was there when I was a young lad. When you first come into the Meath squad you're still seeing him as though you were that young lad. It's total awe.

When Meath played Wicklow in the first round of the Leinster Championship in Croke Park in 1999, Hank Traynor was centre-back, and Nigel Crawford partnered Jimmy McGuinness, a late replacement for John McDermott, in the middle of the field. Richie Kealy was introduced during the game in place of Donal Curtis. The match was no contest. Trevor Giles was not back to full fitness, but he had made a complete recovery from the cruciate ligament injury he had suffered in the previous year's Leinster final and he led the attack, contributing a modest toll of only two points. Meath played against a stiff breeze in the opening half but retired 1-5 to 0-4 ahead at the interval. The team also returned to its dressing room with only 14 players as Hank Traynor was sent off by Tipperary's Paddy Russell for a second bookable offence in the 33rd minute as he tried to stop his direct opponent, Kevin O'Brien. It was 2-10 to 0-6 at the finish, with no Wicklow player managing to score more than one point. In the Leinster semi-final, Meath had seven points to spare over Offaly (1-13 to 0-9) but, like the previous season, the story of the game was the complete dominance of the Meath full-back line over Offaly's hot-shot full-forward trio of Vinny Claffey, Roy Malone and Peter Brady. The trio managed one more point than they had scored in 1998, stretching their combined tally to two points – it was another great day at the offices of O'Reilly, Fay and Murphy Ltd! Once the game had ended, Tommy Lyons made it clear that he was retiring as Offaly team boss. He was happy to leave his personal battle with Sean Boylan as it stood, two games to one, to Boylan!

The Leinster final belonged to Ollie Murphy. Meath's 1-14 to 0-12 victory over Dublin on 1 August was the day in which Ollie Murphy proved that he had the nerve to take the biggest stage in Gaelic football, and virtually command that entire stage on his own! He had been waiting many years for his big day, almost half a decade, but scoring one goal and five points from play made him, officially, one of the greatest finishers in the game. Over the next two years, he would hold the title of the No. 1 finisher. Dublin corner-back Peader Andrews was the man who, for 60 minutes, had the unenviable task of being closer to Murphy than anyone else in Croke Park – but Andrews could never quite get close enough! Murphy and Giles scored 1-10 of Meath's winning total of 1-14. There were only two points in it with 50 minutes of the final completed, same difference as existed between the teams at half-time. But when Giles zeroed in on Murphy with one of his magnificent 50 yards passes, the game was really over by the 59th minute. Murphy had found space behind his man and gave Davy Byrne in the Dublin goal absolutely no chance. The one single difference between the teams on the day was that Dublin could not manage to threaten the Meath posts from play, and too many of Declan Darcy's six points were from free-kicks. Meath had Ollie Murphy!

And Meath needed him, more than ever before. Tommy Dowd had an operation on his back two days before the Leinster final, and without his scoring power and his trusty, commanding presence in the opposing half of the field, life was sure to be increasingly difficult for Giles and Geraghty. After starting off the year in spectacular form, Dowd already felt he was out of the team picture for good.

OLLIE MURPHY: *That game seems like a lifetime ago now. Trevor just launched the ball in for the goal, and it landed straight in front of me and I just grabbed it, took it forward a little and stuck it in the back of the net. Peader Andrews was not playing well that day, but he was pretty new on the scene also. The celebration after scoring the goal was not planned. It was just spur of the moment. I scored the goal shooting into the Hill and, then, just put my arm up to celebrate. I had a knee injury, which I picked up against Armagh in the semi-final, so I was quite worried* *leading up to the All-Ireland final itself. I was getting a bit of physio from Sean at the time and also over in Maynooth as well. Anne Bourton was also there, so I was hoping that I would be fit. I really didn't think I was going to make it back in time though, and was quite worried about it. Then, on the Saturday week before the match, Sean came over and brought me aside and told me not to be worrying, that I was going to be playing. The team was not being announced until the Tuesday or so but he still told me a few days beforehand that I would be playing. It was a good move on his part because it got my head sorted out and I could concentrate on the game then. He didn't have to come and tell me but he did and that has remained with me a lot because I would have been on tenterhooks if I didn't know if I was playing or not.*

I was delighted to make it for the game eventually and I scored a goal, so I was happy! I remember Trevor Giles gave another long ball in and Graham Geraghty knocked it down for me. My man had jumped up for it, but I got it and probably could have gone for a point but said to myself, 'No, I'll go for a goal' and hit it low past the goalkeeper's right-hand side, and it went in.

MARK O'REILLY: *Ollie was the man with the goal in the Leinster final against Dublin in '99. It took him a while to reach his potential, but any of the backs in Meath will tell you how hard he is to mark. Even back in '96, most of us agreed that Ollie was the most talented man on the panel, but, for whatever reason, he didn't seem to be producing the goods. It's amazing what a couple of good games can do for a footballer and, right now, Ollie would be seen as one of the leaders on the Meath team. In 1999 and 2001 he was our main man! He got the vital scores, and we'd be lost without him, to be honest. I've marked him a good bit in training. We play in opposite positions and, for me, I always use Ollie* as a good marker to see exactly where my game is at — if I can mark him on a pitch, I can mark anyone!

TOMMY DOWD: I felt in '99 that I was having one of my best years ever. I never thought I was going as well. I felt great, felt very fit. I played the first round against Offaly, scored three or four points, but after it my back went into spasm and didn't come out of it for a long time. I think it was from a knock! I had a bit of back trouble going into the game from an incident in a club match, and it was something that never cleared up. After the game I just couldn't walk. I had an operation then on the Friday before the Leinster final where they repaired a disc in my back. The disc was hitting a nerve and driving the pain down my back. They let me out for the game though, on the Sunday morning. It was very frustrating to miss out on the big games that year, but once you have back trouble, that's it! You'll never be the same again. You'll try and convince yourself that you'll be back to where you were but, in fairness to Boylan, he knew that I wouldn't! There were times after it happened, when you felt you should be playing, that you should be getting a run, but I think Sean would be more worried about your health in the long term rather than throwing you in there and causing another injury.

I never quite felt much a part of the team again after the operation. Unless you're playing, it's not the same at all — being a sub to me just didn't mean anything. There's nothing to compare to playing against Dublin in a Leinster final, despite the abuse you get from their supporters! I remember several occasions when 50 pence pieces were landing at my feet from Hill 16. They'd be giving you serious abuse, calling you a sheep shagger and all this kind of thing, from start to finish, calling you other things, chanting at you. But you enjoy all that! Mick Lyons would always have loved the chanting from Hill 16, and I think *the Dubs really loved Lyons at the back of it all. He was such a strong, hardy man that they had a lot of respect for him at the end of the day. They would have loved Lyons to be playing for Dublin. I remember talking to a couple of Dublin supporters one time and I remember them saying, 'The only thing wrong, is that Mick Lyons was born in the wrong fuckin' Summerhill.'*

I had known Sean Boylan a long time. I remember I had an injury before a Dunderry game, before I got involved with Meath, and he promised to have a look at it. They were training in Bellinter at the time and one of the Dunderry lads brought me over there. And whatever he did, he got me right. That was the first time I was ever in close contact with him. I remember seeing the lads going to Bellinter, and saying to myself, 'God, it would be great to be part of that whole thing.'

Boylan has time for everyone. There is no one that he wouldn't talk to. He'd talk to the dogs on the street. He's a very, very friendly man. People outside the Meath supporters mightn't think a whole lot of him, even though Meath would always give it their heart and soul. They liked to think that he was sending us out with certain tactics.

He never once told a player to go out and take a lad out of it. Never, ever! He knew how to treat lads. He knew how to treat different players in different ways. He was always the same. He was the same from start to finish with me. When you were going out, you were doing the job for him – as well as yourself and the team. That's because he put his heart and soul into it. He had a lot of time for the players, who were his main concern at the end of the day.

It was great, but you know when your time is up, you know when you've had your day. The fact that Boylan has soldiered with you for so long, he finds it hard to tell you that that's it! That's his biggest weakness, but I suppose you can't blame him for that. Anyway, I think it reaches a stage when you know in your own heart and soul that you won't be up to that standard again. When I was a sub for the Offaly game in 2000, when we were beaten, I knew it. I thought I'd be given a start in that game and when I didn't start, that was the time to call it a day.

Where Sean came up with his training ideas, I don't know! The craziest thing was when we went on holiday one particular year, in the Canaries, in January after winning the National League the year before – P.J. Gillic was with us. And Sean had us crawling up sand-dunes on our hands and knees. There we were, crawling up sand dunes in the Canaries! We had sand in our hair, sand in our eyes, sand in every feckin' thing. I remember so well, P.J. saying, 'This man has now definitely lost the plot!'

Meath have always had a plan. But it was never any secret, because other teams knew what it was! Just leave two lads inside who can score! And that is still the case. There's no mystery but still Meath can make it work. It was a case of getting the ball into the full-forward line as quickly as possible. His style of coaching would have been all off his own bat. He wouldn't have been copying anyone else.

Mattie Kerrigan, whom I trained with for Leinster, he would be more of a man for tactics. I think Sean would be more worried about getting the best out of a fella. You can have all the tactics you want, but come a Leinster final, or All-Ireland, it mightn't work anyway. He has made very good players out of very mediocre players. He has made great players out of very mediocre players, and still continues to do so. He'd never run down a player in front of anyone. You could make ten mistakes, and he might tell you to up your game a bit. I don't know where the drive and motivation comes from with him. Now that I'm finished, I wonder where I got the time to even go training. And he's got a bunch of his own young kids at home to go with it! I'd say he's the only manager in Ireland that doesn't get paid for it. You hear of other guys on anything from 10 to 20 grand per year. If anything, Sean Boylan would be well out of pocket. If we went training down the country, for example, and there were a few players who didn't want to go to the hotel after the game, he'd throw them 50 quid to get fish and chips on the way home. That often happened. And that would be out of his own pocket! Then, it could be five in the morning before he'd be finished talking, going round shaking hands with people. This would be at dinner dances, everywhere! Myself and Geraldine often wonder where he gets the energy. He'd be up and he'd be singing and he'd be playing the harmonica. And he doesn't take a drink. It would never be the drink talking.

Midway through the All-Ireland semi-final against Armagh, Ollie Murphy was stretchered off the field. At half-time, Armagh were leading by 2-4 to 0-8, thanks to spectacular goals from Diarmuid Marsden and half-back Kieran Hughes. The first 35 minutes had shown Meath to be guilty of watching Armagh! But when the teams reappeared, the Ulster champions suddenly found themselves in a game of football and they genuinely seemed surprised at this turn of events! They scored one point, from Paddy McKeever, in the second half and kicked five bad wides between the 45th and 49th minutes. And when full-back Ger Reid was sent off for a second bookable offence in the 54th minute, Meath had a straight road ahead leading directly to the All-Ireland final and Cork. The Leinster champions took the lead, for only the second time in the game, with ten minutes remaining, through points from Raymond Magee, Giles and Evan Kelly. Another string of points from Donal Curtis, Giles and Kelly completed an impressive comeback, leaving the final scoreline 0-15 to 2-5. Meath had played pretty well all right for three-quarters of the game. Armagh had been quite brilliant in the first-half. But, in the second-half, they played like a team which was more concerned with how they were going to get back home before nightfall.

In the All-Ireland final, Tommy Dowd made a very brief appearance at the finish and was able to say his farewell to the loyal Meath supporters in the place he loved best – and not from the dug-out. Meath won, 1-11 to 1-8, thanks to the athleticism of the team captain Graham Geraghty, and the strong, direct running from deep by Evan Kelly – and both men chipped into the pot with three excellent points apiece. In the wet, slippery conditions Cork never looked all that comfortable. They had their chance early in the second half, when Giles failed from the penalty spot to increase his team's three-point interval lead. Kevin O'Dwyer saved the shot, and shortly after Joe Kavanagh raced through to score a fantastic goal at the opposite end of the field. Cork captain Philip Clifford had scored one of his five points of the day a little earlier, and the Munster champs found themselves in the lead for the first time in the game. In the last 30 minutes, however, Meath outscored Cork by six points to two. Giles, who found it tough to escape the shackles of Eoin Sexton, put his side into the lead with a brilliant '45' and in the closing minutes Giles and Geraghty each tagged on an extra point.

TREVOR GILES: *If we were to win another All-Ireland, then we had to do it the way we did in 1999. We beat Wicklow by ten points, beat Offaly by about eight, Dublin by six or seven, Armagh by four, Cork by three – it was very comprehensive stuff. The only downside of it was that* we lost Tommy Dowd after the Offaly game. Tommy was after kicking five points that day but didn't really play for the rest of the year after being injured. To go on and beat Dublin in the Leinster final without Tommy – and win well – that was something! That year we had Tommy, Ollie and Graham in the full-forward line. That's three great targets when you're trying to hit a ball in. That was us at our best. There was also very little controversy that year. We played good football, won seven Allstars! There were no complaints from anyone. Everyone recognised that Meath were the best team that year. It was a big moment for me as well. I had torn the cruciate ligament the year before, so to get back playing at the highest level and have a good season was a big thing.

Joe Kavanagh got a great goal right after I missed the penalty. You're saying to yourself, 'Jesus, this is my fault if we lose today!' That runs through your head. At the same time, you just try and put the head down and do your best. I didn't have a particularly good final, but in the last 15 minutes I picked up a lot of breaks and kicked a few frees, so I was happy I finished strongly.

In every All-Ireland we played in, I've had to take a penalty, 1996, '99 and 2001. The thing about taking a penalty is that it's worse if you choke on it. The thing about that one, in '99, was that I hit it with conviction, hit it well, but tailed it wide. If you'd just scuffed it you'd have serious regrets, but I just picked my corner and went for it. I would have had that corner in my mind for a good few weeks – that's what you'd be practising in training.

ENDA McMANUS: I had damaged a disc in my back during the Leinster final, and I was only 50-50 for any games for the rest of the year. We beat Dublin comprehensively, but I was always worried in case I would *miss the All-Ireland final. As it turned out, I nearly missed the most important game of the year for an entirely different reason!*

I missed the team bus to the All-Ireland final because I was watching a Formula One race in the hotel. I was all set to go down and meet up with the lads, when Heinz Harald Frentzen and David Coulthard pitted simultaneously. Frentzen was in a Jordan and was leading, with Coulthard in the McLaren placed second. Anyway, Frentzen emerged out of the pits fractionally ahead, but as he approached the first corner his car suddenly stopped. I couldn't go and miss what was happening so I stayed for a bit longer to see how things would turn out. I just got stuck looking at it. When I eventually left, and was walking down the hallway, I could see the girl at the front desk, but none of the lads! So my walk down the hall turned into a gallop and I legged it down to the desk. I got to the girl and she told me that the team had gone. I said, 'No they have not. Don't be silly. But they were. I walked out the front door of the hotel and there was not a sinner about! I was all alone. The bus, the lads, even Sean had gone to the biggest game of the year without me. I ran back in and went up to the front desk again and there was a taxi driver standing around. I went up to him and said, 'You are taking me to Croke Park. I really need you to bring me!' He was aston-ished, but obliged. So I hopped in the car and as we were going by Pearse Street Garda Station he ran in and got a patrol van to give us an escort to the game. So we got to Croke Park and I threw the taxi driver a £20 note for his hassle and proceeded to run the length of the Cusack Stand to get to the dressing-room. When I eventually got there, all the boys were already togged out and were going into the training room to warm up. I arrive and Sean takes a look at me, but doesn't say a word! 'I'm warmed up already Sean', I said, and he just kind of laughed and told me to get changed.

I was marking Joe Kavanagh that day and I had the better of him for much of the game. I had him in my back pocket, but he still managed to score a goal. Podsie O'Mahony got the ball and Nigel Crawford was in behind me, and I told Nigel to watch Kavanagh. Nigel was taking him so I went out to confront O'Mahony, but as I approached him he gave a pass over my head, just beyond me to Joe. He then sold Nigel an absolute peach of a dummy and stuck the ball in the top corner of the net. But, apart from that, he did nothing for the whole game. The feeling of winning the second All-Ireland was actually much better than 1996. The first time you win the Sam Maguire it is completely lost on you. You don't appreciate it first time round. But 1999 was bloody great.

GRAHAM GERAGHTY: *We played Cork earlier in '99 and it was a really low-scoring, poor game. When we got to the final it was like two different teams – it was nip and tuck most of the way through. With about 15 minutes to go we were fairly comfortable. Cork had not been putting too much pressure on us. The fact that we had won every game fairly convincingly in 1999 was great for Meath. There were no rows or hassle throughout the whole year. It was the best way to win it and I think all that stuff about Meath being a dirty team died down after that. I suppose when you're winning, everyone wants to knock you! A lot of that would have come from the 1987 and '88 teams, and the tough games they were involved in – everyone was expecting a row during the games in those years. That cliché stuck and we had to live with it. A lot of refereeing decisions also went against us. I think a lot of referees were making decisions in games based on the past reputations of Meath teams. It's hard to blame referees because they have a hard job to do, but we just wanted fair play, no special exceptions or anything like that, just fair play.*

DARREN FAY: *Only for our midfield work, Dublin would have beaten us in the Leinster final because anytime they got the ball in, I was under pressure from Ian Robertson, who was playing at full-forward that day. He didn't get a whole lot of ball in because of how well our midfield pairing of Nigel Crawford and John McDermott were doing, but when it did come in, I was finding it difficult. He always seemed to be 10 or 15 yards away from me. I was always half-blocking his shots, or he was just getting bad balls in. I suppose we were lucky enough to get away with the win in the end. Ollie Murphy got the all-important goal that day for us. We played Armagh in the semi-final, and it was a strange second half! Armagh backed off, big time! They got a lot of criticism after that for getting everyone behind the ball. They played it like it was a soccer match. Except that Graham Geraghty had the beating of Ger Reid, I don't think we would have done as well as we did. Reid was eventually sent off for persistent fouling. I have always maintained that if Armagh had just played their normal game of pushing forward with the ball, then we would have been beaten. As it happened, they retreated and we got back into it.*

We were hot favourites going into the Cork game. You never like to go in as hot favourites. It's a hard tag to live with. We didn't play particularly well and I don't think we won too many fans for our style of play, but it didn't matter to us. We won it in the end and that's all that really counted. That was good enough for us.

NIGEL NESTOR: *I think we spent some time in Trinity that morning – one of the main men up in Trinity is a big supporter – and he let us use the grounds for a bit of a kick-around. I was playing half-forward and Ciaran O'Sullivan was marking me, but I was given a specific role to carry out by Sean. I actually got a pretty serious injury at the start of* the year. I tore my kidney in four places and that kind of knocked me back a little. I missed the Wicklow match and only played about five minutes of the Offaly game. Then, when I returned to full fitness, I couldn't get back to midfield because Nigel Crawford was playing well. In the final Sean had asked me to play as a third midfielder to stop O'Sullivan from going up the field. Sean has said to me that my versatility was useful. I mean, I am not a Trevor Giles and I never will be. That day my role was very specific. I had to play almost as a defender more than a forward. I wasn't seeing much on the field but it didn't bother me. I just wanted to play in a green jersey in an All-Ireland final.

I remember running around the pitch with the Sam Maguire, trying to spot my family in the crowd. After winning the All-Ireland it was a very proud moment. I met nearly all of my family on the way around. They were all in different locations in the ground and it was great to find them.

BARRY CALLAGHAN: I was a sub all year, and the only time I played in the Championship was actually in the final against Cork. Hank Traynor picked up an injury and I went on for him. I had been injured earlier in the year and only really came back to fitness about a month before the final. At times you would maybe think about dropping off the panel because of all the injuries. It is hard enough to play at that level of football when you are fully fit, never mind when you are half or three-quarters fit, so it was tough because I did get a lot of injuries. There were times when you would ask yourself was it worth it, because you couldn't do the training, and then having to try and get back to the same level as the lads. Even if you were injured or not you had to be there for the training sessions because Sean would want everybody present and to be accounted for. But, definitely, when you get to play in an All-Ireland final you realise it was worth sticking it out.

I actually got a lot of ball when I came on in the final. It just seemed to come to me the whole time. I wasn't on long, as I only came on during the last 10 minutes, but still saw a lot of the ball. I remember Ollie Murphy actually ran into me at one stage and gave me a dead leg. He accidentally gave me a knee in the leg. I think we enjoyed 1999 more so than '96 because we didn't really realise what we had achieved in '96. I mean, that was the first year I played in the championship for Meath, and I go out and win an All-Ireland! Therefore, you probably take it for granted and think that success comes easy, but in 1999 we realised how hard we would have to work and we really earned Sam that year.

CORMAC SULLIVAN: In the semi-final Armagh had come out and looked great early on. They scored a couple of goals and they kept coming at us. But they kicked so many wides! At one stage I was actually tired from picking up the ball, kicking it out and watching it come back in again. It was mad stuff, very monotonous! We ground them down though and that was no mean feat because they were a very physical team. They were an excellent team aswell and it was a great win. It was a battling win. They didn't score more than a couple of points in the second half. The final was a massive match from our point of view against Cork. It wasn't the greatest of games but that didn't matter to us because we held out for the win. I remember Richie Kealy coming in and steadying things up, and Trevor Giles was great that day too. He's such a reliable free-taker and players like that are worth their weight in gold. He handles the pressure brilliantly and we would all have great faith in him.

TREVOR GILES: One of our training spins before that final was the trip to Holyhead! Meath had gone to Scotland in '91 for a big booze-up, so when we heard we were leaving for the weekend, we thought, 'Great, we're getting a trip here!' We thought we'd be flying somewhere. So we met up in Kepak about five or six in the morning on the Saturday, got the bus then to Dun Laoghaire where the ferry was waiting. We had all our Meath tracksuits on us, and I remember that there were all these Man City supporters on the ferry, going over to see Man City playing, which I couldn't believe! So we got as far as Holyhead where we went to this training pitch. Well, if Roy Keane had seen it! It was on a council estate, just a green field with a couple of soccer goals on it. And then with Holyhead being almost on the sea, you had the pitch going one way and the wind blowing the other! We couldn't use the soccer goals so we had a couple of branches of trees for goalposts. When you took a shot and beat the 'keeper, the ball would run for 100 yards. So that's where we did our training a week before the All Ireland!

I could never complain about anything Sean did – he's been very good to me. From the first game I played, I was never dropped! I should have been taken off in the second-half of the '94 Leinster final, but I wasn't. We weren't playing that well as a team and the full three subs were used. I deserved to be taken off but wasn't, and that was probably the closest I've come to it. Jody Devine is always telling us that he's going to bring out a book because Jody has been warmed up so many times, and about to come in for different lads, and then hasn't! So he reckons he has the inside story on who was meant to be taken off down the years.

I'd say the first dealings I had with Sean was around '93. Meath played Mayo down in my parish in Skryne. It was the opening of the club pitch, they had new dressing-rooms down there and, of course, the showers didn't work, and it a desperate wet night!

Jack O'Shea was manager of Mayo at the time and because the game was in Skryne, I had access to the dressing-rooms. I was mooching about and, suddenly, Sean introduced me to Jack O'Shea and told him I was going to be a great footballer! I'd never met Sean before - or Jacko - so this was great stuff. That was my first dealing with Sean. For a fella I hadn't met before, it was a good start. He was in my good books straightaway.

Chapter Eleven:

2000
2001
2002

If Sean Boylan was looking out for the perfect exit and ever wanted to retire as Meath football manager, then the days and weeks after the 1999 All-Ireland final would have served that purpose very nicely indeed. But, the months passed. He had four All-Ireland titles to his name, and a whole clatter of National league and Leinster Championship victories. He wasn't only the longest serving manager of the last 20 years, he was, undisputably, also the greatest. John O'Mahony and Paidi O'Se would both have claimed Sam twice by the time Boylan began his 20th summer in charge of Meath. In that same period of time, Pete McGrath and Billy Morgan – two of his older adversaries from the '80s and early '90s – also twice brought Down and Cork teams the whole way to late September glory. The only man who came close to matching strides with Sean Boylan over those 20 years was Mick O'Dwyer, who saw his Kerry team win three in a row in 1984, '85 and '86, and who then set out on a decade-long crusade with Kildare but came up agonisingly short in 1998 when the Lilywhites had second doubts in the second half of the All-Ireland final against Galway. Boylan had four All-Irelands after 17 summers. And after 20 summers, his number was still stuck on four, despite the incredible courage of the Meath team of 2001. What has Sean Boylan been searching for over the last 20 summers? If that is a question which has often been in the heads of Meath football fans, and Gaelic football supporters throughout the country, then it is also a question which Boylan's boys over the last two decades have also tossed around between themselves. By and large, they conclude that their manager has never had any private plan. They agree that Sean is happy just to get through one night of training! That's unfair, of course, but the boss has always been more than happy to let them think exactly that!

Meath's defence of Boylan's fourth All-Ireland was destined to be short-lived. In 2000, the Meath team played only one competitive game of football – in their 0-13 to 0-9 first round defeat by Offaly in Croke Park. It was only the second time in 20 years that Meath football folk had only one game to talk about for months on end – the county's last fast exit from the Championship had been back in 1992, when Laois came to Navan and won by a single point. During the long, quiet summer of 2000, Sean Boylan wasn't saying boo!

TERRY FERGUSON: *To this day, you could go up to Boylan's house and stick on the kettle! It's kinda like a hostel for retired footballers and current footballers. That's Boylan's house for you. Sean is very easy to get on with. He is a very personal and friendly kinda fella. Sean had his* *moments too. He stormed out on a few occasions. I maintain a manager is only as good as his players. You could have 'Our Lord' looking after a football team but it doesn't mean they are going to win anything. But in Sean's case he was the catalyst. He took a lot of brave decisions, bringing in lads like myself, more or less greenbacks. I was playing intermediate football, P.J. Gillic was playing junior stuff, but he still picked us. He took a risk and nobody wanted to let him down. Sean is not just a manager, he is a friend. He is a hard worker and has great enthusiasm. It is his enthusiasm that has kept him going. As far as quitting is concerned, Sean will know himself when it's time to give up. When I went up to manage Fermanagh I ran them ragged just like Sean had done to us. They thought I was mad coming up there to make them train so hard. But we thought Sean was mad training us the way he did, and look what it got us. The memories we have, we have because of him.*

Once again, the Offaly full-forward line had failed to inflict too much damage on Meath. But Colm Quinn and Finbarr Cullen, who were named on the half-forward line, notched up nine points between them. Quinn was exceptional, with a personal tally of seven points after his afternoon's work, and after the teams turned around level at half-time (0-5 apiece) he continued to tear at the heart of the Meath defence. Without the suspended Graham Geraghty in the full-forward position – Mr Utility, Donal Curtis started the game with No. 14 on his back – Meath never really threatened for the goal they needed to spark a winning rally. Ollie Murphy was a lonely figure up front with the 1999 All-Ireland winning captain, and he was held scoreless for the afternoon by Cathal Daly. Offaly had also lined out without their suspended midfielder Ciaran McManus, but they chased down the victory in the closing minutes and four unanswered points from Vinny Claffey, Cullen, Karl Slattery and Quinn earned an impressive and fully merited win.

Twelve months later, in June of 2001, Meath again looked destined to make an instant disappearance and it was all due to the grace of God and the wonder of Ollie Murphy that the team managed to defeat Westmeath in the first round of the Championship. Ger Heavin scored an opening goal for Luke Dempsey's men inside the opening 60 seconds, and Heavin continued to exploit a roomy Meath defence before finishing up with a personal tally which also included five points. Westmeath's first ever Championship victory over their neighbours looked fairly certain all through, despite a Geraghty goal in the second half. Midfielder Anthony Moyles was sent off after the break, and the same fate befell Westmeath full-back David Mitchell near the end. But, at the very end, Murphy found room where none existed and scored the vital goal which earned an extremely fortuitous 2-12 to 1-14 win. Meath and Westmeath would meet again, on two occasions, in the All-Ireland quarter-finals, when Dempsey again talked his men into a brave and gutsy battle, but with Murphy's confidence and trickery reaching higher and higher levels, the most memorable Sunday in the history of Westmeath football was always going to be as far away as ever! In the Leinster semi-final, new Meath captain Trevor Giles continued on from where he had left off against Westmeath and scored 1-5 of the winning total of 1-16 to 1-11. Giles had now scored one goal and 11 points in two games. Meanwhile, Geraghty and Murphy were keeping a close eye on one another, as both scored 1-2 against Westmeath and added four points each in the handy enough victory over the defending Leinster champions. Padraig Brennan struck three points early in the second period to edge Kildare ahead, but Meath stormed over the finishing line. Dublin were certainly the hungrier team in the Leinster final, but a tiny slice of luck in the opening minutes of the game allowed Sean Boylan to savour his sixth Leinster final victory over the Dubs. Davy Byrne in the Dublin goalmouth failed to hold a high lob from Ollie Murphy right at the start and Geraghty was in like a flash to bundle the ball to the net. It was controversial, but it was allowed, and it was the difference between the teams at the finish as Meath won 2-11 to 0-14. Meath did have good luck, but they also had a surprise package in Evan Kelly, who kicked three magnificent points from play in the first half of the greatest football game of his Meath career. Richie Kealy's 55th minute goal made it quite clear that this was not going to be Dublin's day, no matter how hard they or how much Tommy Carr deserved his first Meath scalp as Dublin team boss.

For a second time, Westmeath looked far too good for their high and mighty neighbours when the teams met in the All-Ireland quarter-final on the first Sunday in August, and for a second time it was Ollie Murphy who robbed Luke Dempsey's gutsy team. After receiving a pass from Geraghty in the dying seconds, Murphy negotiated an inch of additional space for himself before belting the ball into the roof of the Westmeath net with his left foot. Westmeath had raced into a nine points lead in the first half, with Paul Conway and Michael Ennis shooting goals past Cormac Sullivan. Ollie Murphy scored his opening goal of the game in the 22nd minute, but right on the half-time whistle Dessie Dolan made it a hat-trick of goals for Westmeath. Their advantage was still healthy at seven points at the interval, 3-7 to 1-6, but in the second period Westmeath did not score from play, and two points was never going to be sufficient to kill off Meath's tenacious spirit. One week later, Meath showed their sticky opponents how it should be done! Graham Geraghty scored the opening goal of the game in the seventh minute and although Boylan saw his numbers reduced to 14 when Hank Traynor was sent off in the 16th minute for a second bookable offence, Meath played like a team who knew in their hearts that they were going to win the game. Points from Joe Fallon and Paul Conway had Westmeath in front in the second period, but a Ray Magee goal settled the three-game issue and left it 2-10 to 0-11 in Meath's favour.

CORMAC SULLIVAN: *It was a great relief to beat Westmeath in the first game and in the end it was a free from Trevor, late enough, that kind of sealed it for us. In the second game they obviously knew what to expect and they really put it up to us. We were fortunate to get the draw with a late goal from Ollie Murphy. He has a great habit of getting crucial goals at very important times. They got three goals against us and the third came right before half-time. It was a real sickener because Dessie Dolan's shot went in over my head. I wanted to put the ball down and get on with the game to try and counter-attack quickly, and get our spirits up, but the ref blew the whistle for half-time and it was, like, you were helpless!*

We had learned our lesson for the third day. The big thing about this Meath team is that we have great experience. Even as far back as the replay against Mayo in 1996 we had shown that we had great spirit when a game went the distance. We've been in a lot of tight situations but we've never panicked that we wouldn't be able to pull something off. We finished off Westmeath handy enough. Nigel Crawford had been playing all the way through the League but was dropped for the opening Westmeath game in the Championship. He came on for the last 10 or 15 minutes of the first game. It did him the world of good in the long term and it gave him the kick up the backside he needed. It was the selectors' decision and, from their point of view, I think they got it spot on. Nigel carried on that form for the rest of the year and I don't think he really had a bad game. He was unlucky not to be nominated for an Allstar.

RICHIE KEALY: *Against Dublin in the Leinster final, I got my first score of the Championship in the first half. But the real highlight was scoring the goal at the Canal End late on that more or less sealed it for us. I had just missed a handy chance in front of the goal, when I should have scored. But I didn't let it put me off. In training we had worked on this move, and we pulled it off perfectly. I passed it to Nigel Nestor and he gave it back to me, and I just let fly. Thank God it wasn't in front of the Hill, because the Dubs would have went mad! It was a great feeling though, and the place erupted nevertheless.*

DONAL CURTIS: *In 2000 we were missing Graham Geraghty for the match against Offaly, as well as Nigel Nestor and Hank Traynor. I'm not saying that the lads who came in didn't do well. It's hard to know what went wrong. We had played the League final replay against Derry, and lost, near enough to that match which didn't help us. From '96 onwards we came into every game with the same players, Darren Fay, Trevor, Graham, Ollie Murphy and John Mac. I think if we'd had another game that year we would have bucked ourselves up a lot. We were always going to be a hard team to beat, but we just lost it!*

I came on as a sub in the first game against Westmeath in 2001. There were a good few changes that day – Nigel Nestor and Anthony Moyles started at midfield. One of the hardest things Sean has to do as manager is to drop lads. Whether it's to take a lad off or actually drop them, it's always difficult because he's known most of the players for years and he knows what it means to them. I'd be fairly easygoing about being dropped. I'd be down but I wouldn't take it as a personal insult or anything. But I know other lads who wouldn't take it so well.

Like, any time you play them, the Dubs in the Leinster final of 2001 was a big one for us. They were aiming to make up for their defeat to Kildare in the final the year before, but at that stage we were starting to make progress ourselves. John Mac was back for us, and that was a massive boost! There was a lot of talk that Nigel Crawford played better when John wasn't there, but no one was complaining when John came back. The pair of them are similar in that the two of them are up and down the field, they've got great engines, and they're mad to be catching balls. When we drew with Westmeath again in the All-Ireland quarter-final, I was taken off with about ten minutes to go. It was a freaky enough goal by Dessie Dolan that looped in over Cormac Sullivan that day that most people will remember, but we showed an awful lot of resolve to come back from that and eventually go through.

BARRY CALLAGHAN: *I played corner-forward against Offaly in 2000, and it was a bad day for all of us. We had played Derry in a League final replay shortly before and it definitely took our edge away. We didn't have the chance to get in some of the hard training that we would generally do before the Championship. I'd say that worried Sean also, but he never said it! I feel if we had beaten Offaly he would have got us back doing a lot of hard training and that would have set us up*

Sean Boylan, September 23, 2001

Sean Boylan, July 21, 2002

nicely for the rest of the Championship. But unfortunately, they beat us well on the day.

I was on the panel early in 2001 but I wasn't picked on the squad for a game, and kind of left it at that. Sean rang me on the Thursday night the team was announced and said they had to pick 25 or 26 of a panel out of about 30, 33, 34 or so lads. So he rang me and told me that they could only tog out a certain number of players and that I wouldn't be togging out. I told him I wasn't going in to do the training and then sit on the stand! And that was more or less it! I didn't fall out with him or anything. At least he contacted me before it was announced. He is there to make decisions and they have to be made, so you just have to accept them. He told me straight and I told him that I wasn't prepared to do it if that was the case, and even after that he asked me would I stay on. And I said, 'I'd think about it', but I had been injured anyway so there was no point in risking it further. I have been talking to him since on and off, so we never fell out because of it.

I think Sean's best attribute is that he gets the best out of players. He is able to motivate everybody. He is also able to get a team to play together as a unit. He is a very pleasant man to everyone, but when something has to be said, he will say it at times, if that's what has to be done. Over the past 20 years I would say he has definitely been the best inter-county manager in the country. Most good managers win an All-Ireland or two with one group of players, but Sean has won four All-Ireland titles with two completely different bunches of players. The '87 and '88 teams were made up of great players, and then to bring another team along in the mid and late '90s is something extraordinary. One of the amazing things about Sean, is that in the dressing room before a game there will be no shouting or talking. In fact, he would put lads into meditation almost before games. There wouldn't be a word in the dressing room. *Everything would be very quiet. He would talk away, then say a few words, and then everybody would shake hands with each other and he would wish everyone the best of luck. He was really great at that, getting the players just right.*

DARREN FAY: *I don't know what went wrong against Offaly. We were probably back to the situation of having the hangover from an All-Ireland final, like we had in '97 and '98. Nothing went right for us that day. We played Kerry in the League semi-final in Thurles in 2000, and we were about ten points down with just a bit to go. They were just toying with us and it got to the point where they were just playing trick passes down the middle of the park. They were that much in control! Then Graham and Barry Callaghan came on and we scored two goals which helped us win the game. We won it, but none of us knew how. It was a ridiculous scoreline in the end. We got into the League final but, in fairness, we had no real hard training done. We ended up playing Derry in the League final, and in a replay, which took it out of us badly. That left only two weeks before the Championship against Offaly. We put in a week of hard training and then relaxed for the second week. Coming into the Offaly game we weren't in the right form, but you can't blame the preparations too much either.*

The next year, we played terrible against Westmeath in the first game. Only for Ollie Murphy again we would have lost. He came up with a late goal in Croke Park which just got us through. We found it very hard against Dublin in the Leinster final. When we won the Leinster, we didn't want Westmeath again, but somehow we just knew we were going to get them in the quarter-finals. On the second day against Westmeath, Ollie got yet another late goal for us. Brilliant! On the third day we said to ourselves that the only reason Westmeath were doing so well against us was because they were scoring too many goals. We said to ourselves, 'Right, no more goals and we'll see where that takes us.' So we shut them out at the back in the third game, and it won us the game. That was a big, big game for us.

OLLIE MURPHY: *Westmeath came at us early and scored a goal in the first minute. Luckily we came back though. For my goal, one of their players was bouncing the ball, trying to clear it upfield, and I just robbed it off him and scored. I scored two goals in the second game against them, but I'll never forget the second one in particular. It was a great comeback, and then the goal came near the very end. There was a crowd of players around me and I kind of got pushed, but the shove gave me momentum and although I kept falling and falling, I managed to hit it with my left foot. And it hit the back of the net!*

HANK TRAYNOR: *There was a lot of switching going on around the field during those Westmeath games. They were ding-dong battles, but I got sent off for two stupid fouls on Dessie Dolan in one of the drawn games. I remember sitting on the sideline absolutely gutted because, as the game went on, we looked like we were going to lose. I had my head between my legs and was thinking that it was all going to be my fault. I was sent off after only about 12 minutes so I felt terrible looking out at the lads. I was sick watching it. When I came off the pitch Sean came over to me and said, 'You were unlucky, Hank. It was a bad decision.' He didn't give me a roasting or anything. He realised that I shouldn't have been sent off.*

MARK O'REILLY: *In the full-back line we all keep to ourselves. Myself and Darren, anyway, would just get on with our own games. But, for* most of the team, we would have struck up a relationship over the years and we know the score now. It's not too often that one of us would bark at the other. Most of our Championship games tend to be in Croke Park anyway, so you don't hear too much of what anyone is saying. You could be shouting at a lad ten yards away and he wouldn't hear you.

We only lasted the one game against Offaly in 2000. It was hard to explain. We just didn't perform. Looking back on that game, if the back-door system had been in place in 2000, then I think we would have come out of it really strong. It was the boot up the backside we needed but we never got the chance after that. The next year was an adventure from start to finish. We began against Westmeath, who were a fairly fresh team with some excellent players – going forward they were very strong. I was marking Ger Heavin in all three games. In the first game I got a bit of a roasting in Croke Park and I got taken off. It was about the first game I'd ever been taken off in, and it was a real kick up the backside for me. I'm not 100% sure who came on for me and, to be honest, it was a game I'd rather forget. We played them in the All-Ireland quarter-final and again in a replay. I was a lot better those two days. I seemed to have the eye on the ball a bit better. Once bitten, twice shy and all of that.

ENDA McMANUS: I had come in as a sub against Offaly with about 15 minutes to go, but it was no good. We were beaten, knocked out of the Championship in the first round! I had made my Championship debut against Laois in 1992 when Meath lost in the opening round, and after losing to Offaly in the first round of 2000, it seemed an appropriate time to hang up the boots. When the game was over I just said to Sean, 'This is a serious enough injury I have, and there is no point in risking my health any longer.' He just turned around and said, 'Well, if that's the *way you are feeling Enda then so be it, but sure we'll probably have a chat later on in the year.' We did, and I came back.*

I started the first game against Westmeath but came off with about ten minutes to go. I got a knock on the back of the head. They got the early goals and raced seven points clear, and we came back and beat them. Three times in 2001 Westmeath could have beaten us, but they didn't, or couldn't!

I was relegated to the stand after the second Westmeath game. I was actually sitting up with David Beggy and the two of us were going absolutely mental when we beat Westmeath in the All-Ireland quarter-final. But as for the semi-final against Kerry, I think it was one of the worst things that could have happened to Meath. Nothing was happening with Kerry that day. At one stage I looked down at the line and saw Paidi O'Se just strolling off the sideline and going to sit in the dug-out. Very rarely does he sit in a dug-out. But he just sat down and looked at the game from there because there was nothing else he could do. I think Galway were just too good in the final for Meath in the end. Whatever luck we had in 2001 was all used up against Kerry, because nothing seemed to go right after that. Ollie had to come off, Nigel got sent off, and Trevor missed the penalty! So many things happened out there, that we knew it just wasn't going to be our year. I had my gear with me that day. In fact, I had it down in the dressing room for most of the games that year just in case I got the shout from Sean. In some ways, it was a fitting way to end my career with Meath, because it mirrored the way it had all begun. I turned up with my boots for that challenge game ten years earlier more in hope than anything else, and here I was in 2001 doing exactly the same thing, bringing my gear in the event that I might be needed. Just in case!

Sean is one of the best man-managers in the business. He would call me over occasionally during a game and tell me to take more risks, or advise me on some other part of my game but, then again, when I was starting out with the Meath team I wasn't short of any tutors. I had Mick Lyons, Terry Ferguson and Bob O'Malley all helping me out with little tips here and there, and I learned from the best in the business. I think Meath would have struggled to achieve the amount of success they have enjoyed in the last 20 years if Sean Boylan had not been in charge. The players were there, but it took a man like Sean, a different man, to get them together. He literally went to every division of football in Meath and took players from junior clubs and intermediate clubs – he even turned a rugby player, Jinksy' – into one of the most exciting footballers in the game. He took players from obscurity and built an All-Ireland winning team, not once, but four times.

With Galway already in the 2001 All-Ireland final, having accounted for Derry by three points, 1-14 to 1-11, the stage was cleared for Meath and Kerry to get to grips with one another for the first time in Croke Park, in late summer, since 1986! Sean Boylan had travelled a long way since his team was on the receiving end of a lesson in Championship football from the greatest team which has ever played the game. But 15 years had passed, there was no mention in the Meath camp of a revenge mission – most of the young lads around Boylan had never even seen a video recording of that memorable meeting, and cared less! The only common factor with the game from 1986 was that Kerry were coming into town as All-Ireland champions, and Sean Boylan was still on the Meath sideline. Nobody was prepared for the most extraordinarily one-sided game of football seen in over a decade at Croker. After the first ten minutes, by which time Kerry had already settled into an impressive rhythm, there was absolutely no sign of the ruin and great embarrassment awaiting them. But the defending champions went a full 20 minutes of the first half without scoring a single point – and their only second-half score in a calamitous 15 points' defeat, 2-14 to 0-5, came from substitute Declan Quill! Maurice Fitsgerald had damaged his back before the game, but despite favouring his star attacker for a 15-minute role late in games, Kerry boss Paidi O Se had him on the field before half-time! John McDermott scored the opening goal just before the interval to make it a sensible-looking 1-6 to 0-4 scoreboard at the interval. It was after that, that things went crazy. Ten Meath players got in on the scoring act, with Ollie Murphy topping the Meath charts on the day with four points and substitute John Cullinane running onto the field late and scoring the second goal with his first kick of the ball.

Nobody was to know that it would take Meath as long to recover from that famous victory, as it would Paidi O Se and Kerry! John O'Mahony's Galway, despite being on a par with Meath and Kerry for the previous five years were, somehow, rated as rank outsiders for the All-Ireland final. Meath, lovers of the under dog role, were in trouble long before the game even started. And, when Michael Collins from Cork did get proceedings under way on 23 September 2001, Galway quickly began to play like a team which felt no pressure in the world! How different it was for Meath, with Trevor Giles scoring one point all day, same as Ollie Murphy! Graham Geraghty did not manage to get his name on the scoresheet at all. Like his Meath counterparts, Galway full-forward Padraig Joyce did not look like he was in the middle of the greatest game of his life – up until half-time that is! In the second period, Joyce scored nine points, five of them coming from open play. He left the Meath full-back line in little pieces by the end of the 70 minutes. The defence was not at all helped by the speedy runs downfield of Galway's 'Man of the Match' Declan Meehan. The elderly pair on the winning team, midfielder Kevin Walsh and centre-back Tomas Mannion, also chose the same day to give their greatest performances in Croke Park. There was very little Sean Boylan could do about the onslaught! Where to begin? That was the toughest question Boylan faced. Ollie Murphy had suffered a broken finger after 41 minutes and was replaced by Paddy Reynolds, and ten minutes later Nigel Nestor got dismissed for a second bookable offence. And tenminutes later still, Trevor Giles shot wide from the penalty spot when given the opportunity of reducing the margin to a reasonable two points. It all went wrong in the second half. The teams were level, 0-6 each, at half-time, with full-forward Joyce responsible for just one of his team's scores! It was only for the final 35 minutes that Joyce entered the game of his dreams.

NIGEL NESTOR: *I got booked 15 minutes into the first half of the All-Ireland final, and then in the second half I picked up a second yellow for a clumsy tackle on Paul Clancy. I was disappointed to be sent off, especially as I genuinely went to shoulder Mannion in the first half when I got booked. I felt I should have had a free moments beforehand, when a couple of Galway players ended up on top of me, and maybe some people think I reacted to that. But I just went to give him a shoulder and I thought he made a meal of it. Then when I got the second yellow I tried to plead my case with the referee, but I knew as soon as I looked over at him after making the tackle that he was reaching for the card. I knew at that stage it was curtains! It is a horrible feeling. Clancy actually put his hand on my shoulder as I walked off. I think he realised he was after* *getting me sent off in an All-Ireland final but, then again, it was a clumsy tackle so I got booked. I just walked over to the dug-out, and didn't talk to Sean or anybody! I sat on the ground and, to be honest, I was more disappointed for the team than for myself, because I felt that I was after letting them down.*

NIGEL CRAWFORD: *It was a very strange occasion, that game against Kerry! Towards the end I was actually waiting and hoping it would finish because the longer the game went on the more it dragged out. And Kerry always looked beaten! The only thing that was going to happen was that Kerry were going to start feeling really down, and almost humiliated. I mean, it's great to beat teams but you don't really want to humiliate them. There is always the realisation that the longer it went on the worse it was for them. The crowd were cheering every pass and there was a kind of party atmosphere, so we knew that Kerry were going to remember this, and revenge would be on their minds for another day. As much as you try and ignore the crowd, there are certain sighs and cheers that you can't help but hear, and that was the case when the Meath fans started cheering every pass. The players didn't want to get caught up in that, and we certainly weren't making passes just to get a cheer.*

I didn't read any of the newspapers or listen to any of the media prior to the All-Ireland final, so there was certainly no complacency or over-confidence involved going into it. I do remember people coming up to me and saying it was going to be a tough game, but the last thing they would say would be that we should win it though. I thought we were in a great situation at half-time. We hadn't played well, yet we were still in the game. I thought that when we went out in the second half something would happen and there would be a spark, but unfortunately not! We lost Nigel and Ollie, Trevor missed the penalty, and there were a couple of bad decisions against us. Galway seized the initiative and we started to feel like Kerry had felt a few weeks previously.

Straight after the match we went for a few drinks and tried to forget about it, if we could, but it was a terrible feeling. I will never forget walking into the function room of the Burlington afterwards, where we received a fantastic reception. I couldn't believe it, and was just gutted that we had lost. It began to hit home then. We just walked in and got an amazing reception from the families and supporters.

RICHIE KEALY: *The Kerry game was a great win for us, but it wasn't the real Kerry. They fell apart and they were missing a couple of lads themselves. Why that happened, I don't know. It certainly wasn't great preparation for us going into an All-Ireland final. There was nothing we could do about it. For ourselves, we could have done with a good tough semi-final. Having said that, up until about ten minutes into the second half the game wasn't out of our reach. A couple of little things changed that game. Ollie went off injured and he was a huge loss, a psychological blow considering everything he'd done to claw back games earlier in the year, and we missed some bad chances. Throw Padraig Joyce's brilliant form into that and you can see how things were going against us. On another day, it could have been another winner, but people never remember it like that. There was very little said in the dresing room afterwards. Everyone got their gear together, got changed and left as quickly as possible. We had to go through the whole after-match routine of dinner and all that. It's great if you win, you love every minute of it. But it's different when you lose. It's the last place you want to be, but you have to take it.*

OLLIE MURPHY: *Kerry was probably one of Meath's greatest con-*

quests. I guess it was kind of a freak game but everything was going well for us coming up to the match. I mean, we were after beating Westmeath and training was going well, everybody was fit, so it all came together right on the day - but it is perhaps unfortunate that it came so right because there was the downturn in the final. Prior to the match it was all, 'Meath this and Meath that' in all the newspapers, so the media were building us up a lot. I broke my finger in the second half of the game. There was a couple of players around me and when I went down to pick up the ball one of the Galway lads pulled on it, and I got a kick on the hand. I'm not really sure what happened, but they actually ended up getting a free out! I knew straightaway that something was not right. I didn't know it was broken though, so I ran over to the sideline to get it tied up a little but by the time I got over my hand had all swollen up so I had to come off. At the time they were a couple of points ahead, and then Nigel Nestor got sent off, so things went against us. It was just a disaster. Afterwards, in the dressing room, it felt like the last few months had been all for nothing, but when you relaxed and thought about it a few weeks later you realised that it had been a great year.

JOHN McDERMOTT: We were on a hiding to nothing. Kerry weren't right that day. It wasn't that we were good, they just weren't right. The wheels came off the wagon. They are a good Kerry team, good footballers. The likes of Dara O Se and Mike Francis Russell don't become bad footballers overnight. We have a knack of beating Kerry. They were 14 points up on us in the League semi-final and we came back and beat them. It's like Derry over us – Boylan has never beaten Derry. In the All-Ireland final, Galway were the better team. It would have been worse if we were beaten by a point. We were just outplayed, outgunned, out-thought – we weren't right for it! Bar locking yourself in a sound-proof room for three weeks before it, and erasing the Kerry game from your mind, there was nothing we could do about it. We might have had a chance then. Galway were waiting in the long grass. They couldn't have written the script better. It was just a disaster.

DONAL CURTIS: It was incredible against Kerry. I thought we played very well but I'm sure the Kerry boys would admit they just gave up! We played very, very well in my opinion. Afterwards, I came into the dressing room and looked at one of the lads and said, 'We'll pay for that some day!' I never thought the pay-back would come so soon, though. You couldn't have scripted it. I don't think in our minds we took anything for granted before the Galway game. Things just went wrong for us on the day. If you went around to most of the players, I think they'd all say the same thing, that we had great respect for Galway and their free-scoring forwards. We were still in it at half-time, you know. We were hoping that we would improve, but everything just went against us. It was amazing that when Ollie went off, not one of the players on the team realised it for about ten minutes. If there was a big thing made of it, that might have lifted the lads, but play was gone down the other end of the field, and he just went off. If the game had been held up and Ollie had been down on the ground, then lads would have been rallying around shouting, 'Come on, let's do it for Ollie!' I was thinking that when we won the penalty maybe we might get a draw and knock out a replay. But it was not our day. In fairness to Trevor, the pressure on him was awesome. I've talked to him about it a couple of times since and he's always said he was happy with how he struck the ball. If you're happy with the strike then you can't really have any regrets – it's just fate on the day.

It was fairly depressing after the game. We had a good day the *following day though. The crowds came out for us even though we had been beaten. Beforehand, I just kept thinking I don't want to be here doing this. But when I actually saw the crowds and all the kids, it was a real lift. In truth, I don't think the loss really sank in for another two weeks or so.*

GRAHAM GERAGHTY: *We were all looking forward to the semi-final but what happened against Kerry, beating them so easily, went badly against us in the All-Ireland final against Galway. A lot of lads were very cocky going into the final and Galway just railroaded us. After beating Kerry by so much we were red-hot favourites. I thought in my heart that lads just looked over-confident. Don't get me wrong, confidence can be a good thing. But I think in this case, it didn't work in our favour at all. That's one of the hardest things for a manager to do, to bring lads down off a high and get them thinking straight again. I think Sean thought he had done it right but, in fairness, I don't think the lads were ready mentally. They let the game get to them. Like Dublin in 1995, losing to Galway was very close to being one of my lowest moments in football. It was a big blow to be beaten in an All-Ireland final. Then again, you have to lose some to win some. Thankfully, I was lucky enough to win two out of three finals. I can't really have any complaints – it was probably better that Galway won by so much in 2001. By the end, we knew we weren't in with a chance. It wasn't as if we had just lost it by a point or two. A lot of things went against us in that game. Ollie was there one minute, and the next minute he was gone! Lads didn't know til the game was nearly over that he had actually been substituted. We just didn't rally that day at all. We lost Nigel and then Trevor missed the penalty, which all happened in the space of ten minutes or so. Padraig Joyce and Declan Meehan were on fire* *too, which hardly helped.*

DARREN FAY: *The Kerry game was something that happens once every 50 years, if that! It was one of those days where everything just clicked for us. Kerry seemed to be running around at sixes and sevens. They couldn't get a grip on things at all and we seemed to be strolling around the park for a finish-up. It could have been down to their two big games against Dublin in the quarter-finals in Thurles, but I think they did very well to get so far anyway. That may sound strange, but for a team that has put so much in the year before, to nearly reach another All-Ireland final was a fair achievement. I don't think Meath were that much better than Kerry. It's just that their heads dropped early on and we ended up winning by a cricket score. At half-time we were only leading by a few points and we really wanted to just keep going. When we went into the dressing room we couldn't hear the brilliant atmosphere anymore. It was as if we were going out for the start of the game again, so the nerves started to build up on us again. It worked out OK in the end. We totally overran them in the second half. After the game it was like scenes from an All-Ireland final – purely because it was the great Kerry that we had just beaten so well. We knew what the neutrals were saying as well, 'We're glad you stuffed Kerry because they've done it to practically every other county in the 1970s and 1980s!' The funny thing about 2001 was that, as soon as we returned to training on the Thursday night after we had beaten Kerry, someone or a group of people from the media were at every one of our training sessions until the final. There'd always be a media night before an All-Ireland final, but it seemed as if after the way we beat Kerry there was more interest in us. It was as if the media were saying, 'Well, there's no way Meath can be beaten, so we'll cover them as much as possible.' The media got carried away a bit and, as far as* they were concerned, the All-Ireland was done and dusted for 2001, before the final had even started.

Sean kept telling us not to believe in any of that. He kept telling us that it was rubbish, but subconsciously it must have got in on us a bit. We were surely thinking that all we had to do was go out and win, and that was a very dangerous way to be thinking. We paid the price. It'll hurt for a long time to come. Padraig Joyce went mad in 2001, and kept up his great form all the way until the final. The whole of our full-back line was in disarray in the final, to be honest. Everything mitigated against us. Ollie had a hand injury, and then Nigel got sent off too and it seemed nothing was going right for us. Still, if you were to boil it down to any one thing, then I think you could say it was the form of Padraig Joyce and Declan Meehan. Even on the bench they had so much talent, but those two players were above everything else that day. We try and keep a low profile going into the start of any new year. When we do that we seem to do well. Every year there's a lot of press and commentators saying, 'This is the last year for Meath!' – no matter what type of form we're in. I don't know why they don't say it about other counties as much.

MARK O'REILLY: None of us really performed in 2001, in fairness. By the time we knew it we were in the final, and I'm not exactly sure how we managed that. Still, we should have done better against Galway, but we never settled and we knew from early on that things weren't right at all. It was disappointing that we didn't perform, particularly on such a big stage in such a big game. Having said that, I think it was a one-off. Even at half-time we thought we were still in it. We believed we hadn't played nearly to our potential in the first half. One of the lads said to me in the dressing room, 'It can hardly get any worse!' I agreed that we had *to do better, but unfortunately it got worse, a lot worse. We were expecting Ollie Murphy to come up trumps and stick over a few points, like he'd been doing all through the Championship. But it wasn't his fault. He was carrying an injury and the rest of us didn't perform anyway. Padraig Joyce came out after the break and struck over a quick point which really kicked us in the teeth. It was a crucial point in a lot of ways. We needed to get a couple of scores ourselves to steady things up but it just got worse and worse after that. We had said at half-time that we needed a couple of quick scores to rattle them.*

John McDermott had ended a short-lived retirement in order to make one last, great effort with Meath in the summer of 2001. He gave his all right to the very end of the hefty defeat by Galway in the All-Ireland final, and almost handed his team the keys to another famous recovery by being fouled for the late penalty kick which his Skryne clubmate, Trevor Giles, blasted narrowly wide ten minutes from the end of the game. McDermott retired for good immediately after the defeat, and made it abundantly clear that he would not be answering his front door to any more knocks from hopeful Meath footballers or officials in the future. With his retirement, and a similar announcement by Graham Geraghty nine months later after Meath's 2002 Championship ambitions stuttered to a halt against Donegal in the All-Ireland qualifiers in July, Sean Boylan had been left in absolutely no doubt that a whole new Meath team had to be built – all over again. The twin departure of McDermott and Geraghty equalled the loss of three or four top quality players in most other counties. Sean Boylan found himself back where he was in 1985, and in 1992, and again in 1997 – there now appears to be two or three years of hard, mostly unrewarding work ahead of the Meath manager! With Dublin winning the Leinster title for the first time in seven years under the bright, breezy and fiercely ambitious management of Tommy Lyons, Boylan is going to have to be every bit as energetic and imaginative as he has been for almost all of the previous 20 years. Meath people wonder can he do it. And that includes old Meath footballers, and young Meath footballers – they too find themselves talking and speculating about Sean Boylan's future! Nobody believes he will retire, but everybody accepts that he will have to walk away from the Meath team some day. The departure of McDermott and Geraghty, like so many great footballers before them, must make him stop and think, and reminisce, but Boylan has been through so many emotional farewells and quick goodbyes by different footballers, and he has always turned around to give his full and undivided attention to the lads still standing behind him. This time?

The summer of 2002 remained very much in the shadow of the previous year's Championship, and there was little excitement and craic, or savage disappointment, for Sean Boylan and the people of Meath. Westmeath and Laois proved all too easy in the Leinster Championship, and Dublin proved too keen, too speedy, too good in the provincial final, thanks in the main to a spanking new full-forward line, and the inspirational presence of two-goal hero Ray Cosgrove. The best fun Meath football fans had all summer turned out to be a memorable Saturday evening in Navan, when Louth looked to have put one over on their illustrious neighbours and had already started their celebrations, seconds before Meath executed the fastest and most lethal recovery job in Sean Boylan's 20 years. Late, last gasp goals from Richie Kealy and Graham Geraghty meant that Meath enjoyed that brave victory just six days after losing to Dublin in the Leinster final, but time was also up on the team anyhow. The qualifiers would not prove a road to recovery and glory for Meath, as the new back-door system did for Galway 12 months earlier. On 21 July, back in Croke Park again, Meath looked like a team which had still not fully recovered from the triumph or trauma of the previous September. The Meath full-back line was in a spot of bother again, with Brendan Devenney and Adrian Sweeney scoring nine points between them in a 1-13 to 0-14 victory. It had been 1-9 to 0-7 in favour of the Ulstermen after 47 minutes and, whatever about the team's nerve, there was no doubt whatsoever that a fire remained in the belly of the Meath football team. Nigel Crawford powered into the game, Nigel Nestor began winning more and more ball after being released from his defensive role, and Ollie Murphy, too, found some freedom. Trevor Giles had relocated to centre-back for the second half and, all told, the 'new' looking Meath team could, and should perhaps, have won the game when Donal Curtis flicked the ball inches wide of the goal deep into injury time.

DONAL CURTIS: *I was expecting bigger things from Westmeath in 2002, but they were poor. We played well on the day admittedly. We didn't really know how we'd do after the year before – we'd had a decent League run, but you never know how well you're going before the Championship. Without a doubt, lads always up their game for the start of the Championship. There was a lot of talk that it was a game out of Croke Park and maybe we wouldn't perform in Portlaoise. For a lot of lads it was great to get out of Croke Park, though. There was no pressure. The Dublin game was my worst occasion on a football field.*

It just didn't happen at all. I was taken off after 30 minutes. The goals, when they came, really hit us at a bad time. I really believed that we were coming to win the game before they got their second goal. It was ironic because Dublin had never done that before in the previous years. They came up with the goals just when they needed them. Ollie Murphy was struggling all through the year. Basically, we went from having a 'Footballer of the Year' to not really having him at all. That was a massive blow. He was great when he came on against Louth, though. Playing Louth six days after the Dublin game didn't give us much time to get over the huge disappointment of losing a Leinster title. It really was a big blow. It was a matter of regrouping as quickly as possible and Louth were given a good chance against us. We opened up very well, and then got a really late goal, but it doesn't matter when you get the goals, once they come. Against Dublin we just stopped when Ray Cosgrove got his second! We were better against Louth. Trevor had a nightmare against Louth. He'll be the first to say it was one of his worst games ever, yet he ended up passing to Ollie to set up the last goal. Everyone was flying right up until the whistle.

GRAHAM GERAGHTY: *In 2002 there seemed to be a bit of trouble in the Westmeath camp. I had talked to a few Westmeath supporters and they told me that things weren't right. They just never performed against us on the day, and we won easily. But we really didn't know where we were either! It was like when we played Laois. It was the worst performance from a Laois team in a long, long time – we were totally on top and that gave us a false sense of security. Against Dublin, I suppose the first goal was a mistake between Darren and Cormac – one lad waiting for the other to come for it. The second goal was an opportunist goal. Cosgrove followed the flight of the ball perfectly. Lads were* *saying Ray fouled Cormac, but I couldn't argue too much. I seem to remember Colm O'Rourke doing something similar on John O'Leary years earlier.*

I was down at a wedding in Wexford before the Louth game and came back up for the match. At one stage, I was saying to myself that this game is over. But Ollie gave a ball across to me right at the death and I suppose the rest is history after that. It's a game I don't think Meath supporters will ever forget – to beat Louth was a big win for Meath fans. When the ball came across I was just happy enough to get it. To be honest, I never thought about going for a point, even though that was all we needed. People said it was great composure and great instinct, but if it didn't go in you'd be the worst in the world! I went straight back down to Wexford for my friend's wedding after that by helicopter and it was a great buzz. The whole day! There was a lot of laughing and talking done about the game that night.

Against Laois, in Portlaoise, they never put up a fight. I was expecting a lot more from them. To be fair, they had been a bogey team for us years before, in 1985 and 1992. And if they had beaten us this year I believe it would have been the end of Sean. Thankfully it wasn't. I believe Sean will stay on for at least another year, but you never know. It's his call, and it's up to him.

In football, you're always remembered by your last game, which in 2002 for me was the loss to Donegal. It was a sad way to go, but I said early on in the year that I would finish up regardless of what happened in the Championship. At the moment I have no plans to go back on that.

CORMAC SULLIVAN: *Any time the real pressure has come on Sean, he's managed to put out a new team and not just survive, but do really well. It's amazing. It happened before the run in 1986, and the same* *thing again ten years later after a desperate year in 1995. There was a lot of pressure coming on Sean in 1996, but he went on to win the All-Ireland that year. I think he was given a year's grace at the end of 1995 but, credit to him, he came up with the goods and wasn't afraid to put his faith in the younger players. I don't think at this stage he'll be told to go. He'll go when he decides to, and he'll stay for as long as he wants. He's earned that right. It's hard to know who'd take the job if he left this minute. Colm O'Rourke, I suppose, would be an obvious choice or maybe Mattie Kerrigan, until he took up the manager's job in Cavan. Unless the new manager does well in his first year, he will be immediately compared to Sean. He's a legend at this stage. It'll be very hard to replace him – and the possibility is that no manager will be able to replace him. I don't think the success he's had will ever be done again. I don't think anyone could give 20 years to Meath football from now on because of the demands of the modern game.*

DARREN FAY: *I've always said that I hope Sean stays for as long as I stay – I wouldn't like to see anyone else in there! After 1995 he was under the cosh a bit. It's only natural. Every county in Ireland would be thinking that once you've had a bad year you have to think about things, and who's there, and what kind of a job they're doing. Sean stuck with it though, and I don't think the people of Meath can ever pay him back for what he's done for the county before then, or since.*

Sean is not just a players' manager on the football field. If there are any problems you have outside football, you can go to him as well. He puts his attention to whatever is wrong and, more often than not, he will fix it – and he gets the players' respect for that. He does an awful lot for the players off the pitch. I know for a fact he's sorted players out for jobs so they can better themselves. He's done a lot of things like that, which would have nothing to do with football. He provides the potions too, of course. He wouldn't be the same man if he wasn't providing them! We never know what's in them, but you drink them anyway. Maybe after training, or a match, you'd be thirsty and you wouldn't even taste them going down, which is just as well!

NIGEL CRAWFORD: *Dublin were overdue a victory against us and they got it that day, unfortunately. I remember scoring a point midway through the second half and thinking we were getting back into the game. Nigel Nestor passed to me and I just kicked it over from the Cusack Stand side of the pitch, shooting into the Hill. I really felt then that we were going to make a bit of a rally, and we were until they got the second goal. Sean took us straight to the pool after the game and tried to regroup. There were a lot of injuries and players had taken knocks. On the Tuesday there was a really tough training session, but I didn't take part because I was injured. I was nearly glad I was injured, because it looked tough and Sean was pushing the lads all the way. He kept telling us that we could still go on and do something in the Championship.*

Against Louth, I have to say everybody, including most of the players, thought it was gone! It was great to get two goals in the last couple of minutes. For the first of the two, I had the ball and was running straight towards the Louth goal with Richie outside me on my left, and he was unmarked. So I just passed it over to him, but the angle he was left with was very tight. His finish was brilliant and gave the goalkeeper no chance. Goals aside, Richie played very well when he came in and he was working hard, lifting and encouraging people. Then Graham scored, and the referee blew the final whistle! I couldn't believe it, just could not believe what was after happening. I have never seen an atmosphere like it anywhere. The noise was phenomenal and in the dressing room everybody was just on a high. It was really hard having to come out six days after losing to Dublin and it was so tense and nervous going into the Louth game because our confidence had been knocked.

I thought we were doing well against Donegal, and thought we could win. At the very end Donal Curtis almost scored. The ball was lobbed in and he got a hand to it, but it landed the wrong side of the post, unfortunately. It was so close to being in the net – we could have been heroes again. In the dressing room afterwards Sean told us he was proud of the effort we had made, especially in the second half. He told us that he thought we had played some good football and just seemed to lack a bit of luck or a break of some sort. He has always said that there is a fine line between winning and losing. If you win you're great, but six inches the other side of the post you're not. His point was proven against Donegal. Graham Geraghty didn't announce his retirement in the dressing room to the other players. I suppose he didn't want everybody talking about him and his retirement, and he was probably right not to announce it to the team. But when I heard he was retiring it was a bit of a shock. Losing a player like Graham is a big disappointment, and in time I hope he reconsiders.

I think Sean will be around next year. I certainly hope he is and I don't see any reason why not. The nature of the defeat to Donegal showed that we still have football in us, and I know a lot of teams were delighted when we were knocked out of the Championship.

HANK TRAYNOR: *Sean is very much a players' man. He is always looking after the players and, to be fair, he has sorted a lot of the lads out with jobs. He has also used his influence to settle lads with cars and houses, and he has been really brilliant about things like that. These are the sort of matters that nobody hears about.*

I thought things were going well in the camp prior to the Leinster final, and I was looking forward to running out to face the Dubs again. They got two lucky goals and that was enough to beat us. I thought we were getting back into it, but when Ray Cosgrove got their second goal, it finished the game really. The ball just hung in the air and he ran in after it and slapped it to the net. At the time it looked dubious, but in hindsight these things happen in football. Colm O'Rourke had something similar against John O'Leary years ago.

We only had a week to prepare for the Louth game and Sean ran the legs off us in training. He was in ratty form. He was like a bitch, but that was what we needed. He was like that in order to get us hyped up and ready for Louth. It worked well because we were down after the Dublin game, but Sean got us wound up and focused, and ready for the great escape! I thought we were gone. I really believed we were beaten. We never stopped trying and I never stopped trying, but I remember looking up at the scoreboard and I knew the small board had been put up for the amount of injury time to be played – and I thought we're gone! I scored a point myself, but things just seemed to be slipping away from us. I remember Cormac Sullivan went to kick the ball out towards Darren Fay, and Darren waved his hands at him saying, 'No, no, don't kick it to me', because he was knackered! So I ran over and past Darren, and Cormac gave me a quick kick-out. I gave a long pass up to Trevor and he won possession and headed towards goal. Eventually the ball made its way to Nigel Crawford and he passed to Kealy, who fired home his second goal. Then for the third goal, Trevor managed to flick the ball to Ollie when it looked like it was about to go out of play. Ollie ran along the end line and squared the ball in along the box and it made its way to Graham, and he slotted it in the corner. The place went mad and Graham took his jersey off and started waving it about. I just remember jumping up and down on the field, waving my arms in the air, and shouting at the crowd! It was a great atmosphere in Navan that evening. Graham was actually at a wedding down the country that day. We all met up in Bellinter at five o'clock and he arrived in a helicopter at quarter-past five all dressed up in the wedding gear.

NIGEL NESTOR: *I never saw Navan as packed as it was the evening we played Louth, and the atmosphere was unbelievable. I don't think Pairc Tailteann will ever be as full again. And what a comeback! The result was great, but we knew we were lucky. We didn't play well and were lucky we woke up when we did, because we were gone. Some lads did think it was over, but I still felt we could do something because we had a lot of the ball. Actually, I thought it was a draw as the game went into injury time. I didn't know we were losing at the time, and I actually got booked over in the far corner of the field because I ran into a Louth player to slow the game down. I actually believed I was doing a good thing by slowing things down, but looking back at it now, it was absolutely stupid because I was wasting time, and we were losing by a point. I only found out from some of the guys afterwards that we were actually losing and within seconds of being dumped out of the Championship.*

I often get physio from Sean and he does a lot of twisting and turning, and putting things back into place, but you don't ask any questions. You have to trust him. You say nothing, and he gives you a bottle of juice and you drink it.

I have been under a lot of managers at club level and with Leinster, but I have to say Sean is the best players' manager of them all. That is his greatest strength. He is able to manage all sorts of personalities. You would have to put him in the same mould as Alex Ferguson at Man Utd.

I mean, he has been able to manage the likes of Beckham and temperamental guys like Eric Cantona and Roy Keane. He controlled all those players. Likewise in the Meath dressing room there is certainly a whole clutter of personalities present and Sean is able to control all of them. He will always take time to ask how your wife or girlfriend, kids, Mum or Dad are keeping? He meets so many people everyday that how he remembers their names, I honestly don't know, but he always seems to get away with it.

OLLIE MURPHY: He pushed us hard at training on the Tuesday and the Thursday to prepare us for the game on the Saturday in Navan. Louth should have beaten us but, at the end, I remember getting the ball and running along the end-line towards the goal. We were in injury time and it looked like we were gone. A point would not have won it for us and, anyway, I was never going to score from the angle I was at, so I saw Graham in the centre and tipped it across to him and he scored the goal. I honestly thought we were gone. At half-time in the dressing room against Donegal, Sean was optimistic. We were not that far behind and he really got us all going again and motivated for the second half. We went out and played a hell of a second 35 minutes, but it just wasn't to be. After the game Sean told us to hold our heads high. He told us we had done our best, and to return to our clubs and come back ready for next year. I would say that Sean will definitely stay on. I reckon he will be there for another year, or even ten years maybe.

MARK O'REILLY: One of the things about Sean is that he's so mysterious! He'd say anything to you, and you wouldn't be surprised. I remember Mocky Regan's wedding in Dunboyne. Sean is such a busy man and you'd wonder how he manages things, but he does. We were at the wedding and I was sitting beside John McDermott and a few of the lads in a row, when the priest mentions that he is short of ministers of the Eucharist to give out Holy Communion. You wouldn't believe it, but one of the first men up to fill in was Boylan! McDermott was sitting beside me and he just turned to me and said, 'Is there anything the f***** doesn't do?"

He's still knocking out the potions to the lads. We call it 'Sean's jungle juice'. It doesn't do us any harm anyway. Sean's a great guy and it's amazing how he keeps the interest in it. He gets the best out of all the lads – he's well up for a bit of a laugh too. He has some funny mannerisms, you see, and sometimes he'll ask you to do something in the strangest of ways. It's funny when you see new players coming into the team. Sometimes they're looking at each other wondering is this guy serious, or what! Sean's definitely a legend. I've heard one comment about him, comparing him to a Coca-Cola advertisement on television. It said that, 'If Sean Boylan could eat football he'd be very fat, if he could drink football he'd be an alcoholic, and if he could sleep football he'd never get out of bed!' That's the best description of him I've ever heard. It'll be a different county when he goes!